THE SOCIAL

HISTORY OF A WAR-BOOM COMMUNITY

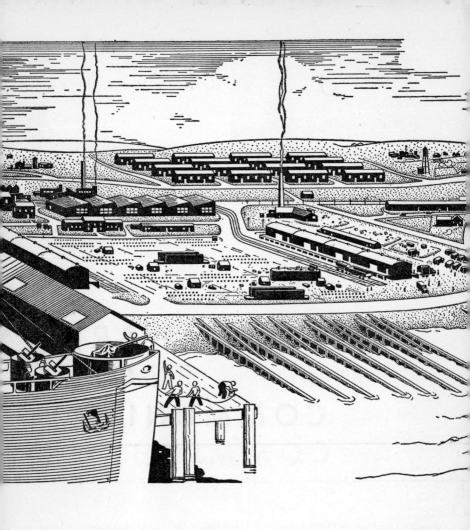

LONGMANS, GREEN AND CO.

THE SOCIAL
HISTORY OF A WAR-
BOOM
COMMUNITY

Committee on Human Development,
The University of Chicago

ROBERT J. HAVIGHURST

Institute for Child Study,
University of Maryland

H. GERTHON MORGAN

NEW YORK · LONDON · TORONTO · 1951

LONGMANS, GREEN AND CO., INC.
55 FIFTH AVENUE, NEW YORK 3

LONGMANS, GREEN AND CO. Ltd.
6 & 7 CLIFFORD STREET, LONDON W 1

LONGMANS, GREEN AND CO.
215 VICTORIA STREET, TORONTO 1

THE SOCIAL HISTORY OF A WAR-BOOM COMMUNITY

FIRST EDITION

Printed in the United States of America

CONTENTS

Part III: THE ADJUSTMENT OF INSTITUTIONS

Part IV: PERSPECTIVES

ILLUSTRATIONS

vii

PHOTOGRAPHS, between pages 44 and 45.

Landing ship group lays down a spectacular smoke screen
The Seneca shipyard and housing projects, from the air
Barrage balloons hover over a long line of LST's

TABLES

INTRODUCTION: WHY STUDY A WAR-BOOM COMMUNITY?

This book is an account of what happened to the people and the institutions of a small American town as it went through an industrial boom during World War II.

Seneca, Illinois, had a population of 1,235 in 1942; and a population of 6,600 two years later. The boom was due to the location of a shipyard on the bank of the Illinois River next to the village. One hundred and fifty-seven ocean-going LST (Landing Ship Tank) ships were built in Seneca and floated down the Illinois and Mississippi rivers to the sea. To care for the inrush of workers, public housing projects were built, business, churches, and schools expanded, and the whole institutional complex of the village was transformed. Six million dollars of government money was used to expand the facilities of the community. Another six million dollars was spent to equip a shipyard. Eighty-two million dollars was paid in wages to Seneca shipbuilders in a little less than three years.

The purposes of this survey were four:

1. To study the adaptation of social institutions to rapid social change. While social institutions were changing in all American villages before the war, due to the tension between traditional community procedures and technological or economic forces, this tension was greatly increased in Seneca by the national emergency.

2. To study the adaptation of people to new conditions of living. The residents of Seneca, oldtimers and newcomers, had to adjust their lives to changed living quarters, changed jobs, increases in income and cost of living, shortages in foods and other supplies, and new neighbors.

3. To study the influence of a crisis on the long-time history of a community. What was the effect of the boom on the life of the community? What residues did it leave? What permanent changes in community life resulted?

4. To make a record of one significant bit of American life during wartime. This book should provide on-the-spot data for a page of the "History of America in World War II," which will be written by a future generation of historians.

This study makes no special contribution to social theory, though the authors hope that it makes sound use of social theory. It is a case study.

Boom towns were a characteristic of World War II, as American technology mobilized to produce the materials of war. Two hundred counties increased in population by 20 per cent or more from 1940 to 1944. San Diego, California, and Hampton Roads, Virginia, doubled their populations. Charleston, South Carolina, and Mobile, Alabama, increased by two-thirds. The San Francisco Bay region and Portland, Oregon, expanded by two-fifths. All of these cities swelled up and suffered from a kind of civic indigestion, which the government did its best to alleviate by liberal doses of public works and expert advice from doctors of civic health.

Similar to and yet different from these large congested areas were the cases of Seneca and the many other towns and small cities that boomed on a miniature scale. The multiplication in size was even greater (it was five to one in Seneca), but there was more room to expand. In the three midwestern states of Illinois, Indiana, and Wisconsin there were a dozen booms in which a village became a small industrial city almost overnight.

How a Small Community Adjusts to a Boom

A boom town in wartime is different from a boom town in peacetime. Boom towns in peacetime know congestion and like it, because the remedy is set in motion by the boom itself. Private capital is attracted by the opportunity to invest in a rapidly growing town that expects to hold its growth permanently. Public bond issues are readily approved with the expectation of repaying the debt out of increased tax income. But the boom town in wartime cannot attract private capital. Neither are communities willing to take on, at their own expense, the expansion of school, water, sewer, and business facilities for a population that is bound to be temporary. It is one thing to build or to expand a factory for production; the cost of the expansion can be included in the charge made for the product. It is quite another thing to increase the capacity of the community to serve the needs of the new manpower drawn to the factory.

A stable community by its very nature resists a boomlike expansion. It is a place built by and for people who are sedentary in disposition and habit. A boom brings in people who are migratory and restless. Hence a wide variety of problems and conflicts may be expected when such a community is subjected to a temporary war boom.

A boom is a twofold process, consisting, first, of the arrival of new people who swarm in like bees; and, second, of the expansion and creation of institutions to meet the needs of the newcomers.

As soon as the people come they need houses, food, schools, and play space for their children; health and sanitation services; police and fire protection; and the other tangible and intangible things that enable people to live and work successfully. It is characteristic of a boom that these human needs exceed the community's capacity to meet them. The community has certain institutions and certain physical facilities, such as churches and business establishments and streets and houses, which must be expanded rapidly to meet the new demands placed upon them. This expansion may come about through the use of private capital and private initiative, as it usually does in a "natural" boom, which carries with it expectations of permanence. However, in a war boom there is more emergency and less expectation of permanence, and consequently private capital and initiative are supplemented by government capital and initiative.

In either kind of boom, "natural" or "artificial," the goal of expansion of institutions and facilities is the same—to preserve and create "community values" that enable people to remain and live and work with reasonable comfort and satisfaction. This was the goal in Seneca. The community had to expand and develop to the point where it met the needs of five times as many people as it originally housed—otherwise people would not stay, ships could not be built, and the war effort would be handicapped.

Success in reaching this goal would depend on several factors:

Leadership. The quality of a small number of individuals upon whom responsibility would fall for maintaining and leading the institutions of the expanding community.

Physical and economic facilities. The amount of money available to pay for rapid expansion of facilities; and the basic equipment of the community for accommodating more people with buildings, businesses, schools, and churches, with water supply and sewage disposal facilities, with roads, and with space for expansion.

Institutional experience. The previous experience of people in the community with social and economic institutions, on the basis of which expansion could proceed; their knowledge of the operation of business, industry, schools, recreation services, and so on.

Favorable community attitudes. The attitudes of the community in general toward newcomers; the degree of resistance to change; and attitudes toward public and private operation of community institutions.

If all these factors were present to a satisfactory extent, Seneca's adjustment to the boom would be optimum. Where one or more factors was not adequate, adjustment in this area would be unsatisfactory, and Seneca would fail in that respect to satisfy the requisites for successful community life.

Certain hypotheses can be stated in advance about the nature of the adjustment of a small rural community like Seneca to war-boom conditions. These are:

1. The local community will provide the nucleus and the initiative in expanding the non-material services—those that promote the moral and intellectual and spiritual aspects of community life.

2. Governmental and other outside agencies will take the lead in expanding the physical or material services of the community.

3. There will be misunderstanding and friction between the "old" and the "new" elements in the community, and between the forces of stability and progress.

The boom in Seneca will be described and analyzed in the light of these hypotheses, and the factors that make a community adjust well or poorly to rapid expansion.

How the Study Was Carried Out

The procedure followed in this study was simply that of recording the relevant changes as they took place. After the senior author had selected Seneca for study (because it was conveniently located), he visited two sources of information—the Chicago Regional Office of the Federal Public Housing Authority, and the Seneca Superintendent of Schools. With the assurance of cooperation from these sources, the study was undertaken. Assurance of cooperation was then obtained from the Chicago Bridge and Iron Company, which operated the shipyard, and the Chicago Regional Office of Community War Services (then the Office of Defense Health and Welfare Services). The study was begun in September, 1942, about a month after the boom started.

The information in the hands of the authors was to be shared with agencies interested in Seneca in return for access to further information through these agencies. This arrangement was readily accepted, and the authors encountered no serious difficulty in obtaining data from any major agency, public or private. Some of the information was confidential at the time it was given, and of course was not disclosed as long as it was necessary to keep it secret. Two progress reports were mimeographed (March, 1943, and December, 1943), and distributed freely to people who were interested in the study.

The services of several persons employed by the University of Chicago for this research were put at the disposal of agencies in Seneca as a means of gaining both good will and information. Miss Sallie Marks gave a good deal of time in the year 1942–43 to advising the Superintendent of Schools. Miss Helen Brecht worked as a nutritionist in Seneca for a part of the year 1943, forming study groups in the housing projects and assisting where she could while she made a study of food-buying and food-using practices in the community. The service aspect of the study was mainly limited to the first year, although advice was given to several agencies at later times, upon request.

The collecting of data in Seneca was done principally by two field workers. Dr. Minna C. Denton, specialist in home economics, spent about half the time between January, 1944, and July, 1945, in Seneca. She divided her time between a systematic study of food-buying habits (which is not an integral part of this study) and a general reporting of events in Seneca. Dr. Denton proved to be an excellent interviewer. She liked the people of Seneca and she was accepted as a participating member of the community. Her journal has provided most of the direct glimpses of life in Seneca that are recorded in this report.

The junior author, then a graduate student in the Department of Education of the University of Chicago, was responsible for the systematic collection of data on Seneca. He was given free access to information in the offices of the Chicago Bridge and Iron Company in Seneca, the housing projects in Seneca, the Superintendent of Schools, and the Chicago Office of Community War Services. He also spent a good deal of time studying children in the elementary school of

Seneca, getting material that he used in his Ph.D. dissertation.

An advisory committee of the University of Chicago faculty assisted in the planning of the research. Thanks are due especially to Professors Newton Edwards, Samuel Kincheloe, Lydia Roberts, Margaret Hessler Brooks, and W. Lloyd Warner for their assistance in the planning. The Reverend Walter K. Morley, Director of Social Service for the Protestant Episcopal Diocese of Chicago, and the Reverend Benson Fisher who worked briefly in Seneca under the auspices of this diocese consulted with the authors and shared information with them.

The study was financed by a grant from the Social Science Research Committee of the University of Chicago, and the authors are especially grateful to Professor Louis Wirth, then secretary of this committee, for his personal interest and his advice in connection with the project.

Of the many individuals who assisted the authors by securing information for them, a few should be singled out for special mention. Without their cordial assistance certain important phases of the study could not have been carried through. Thanks are due especially to Doris Graves and Gerald Hoben of Seneca; Edward Payne, Assistant Yard Manager, and Edward Alt, Personnel Director, of the Seneca Shipyard of the Chicago Bridge and Iron Company; Orton Keyes, General Housing Manager, and Ethel A. Kuhn, Project Services Adviser of the Federal Public Housing Authority Projects in Seneca; Eri Hulbert, Community Relations Adviser, Chicago Regional Office of the Federal Public Housing Authority; and Robert Hillman of the Chicago Office of Community War Services.

The authors appreciate the financial assistance given by the Chicago Bridge and Iron Company, through Mr. H. B. Horton, to aid in the final preparation of the manuscript.

A thorough job of editing the manuscript has been done

by Dr. Bernice Neugarten, Research Associate of the Committee on Human Development of the University of Chicago. She is responsible for making this report as coherent and readable as it is.

A NOTE ON METHOD

The primary data for this study are observations recorded on the spot by the authors and their field assistants, and records from the offices of public and private agencies operating in Seneca. The interviews are both primary and secondary data, primary in that they report what people actually said, and secondary when considering the facts about which the people were talking. Newspaper reports were used as little as possible, and every effort was made to get independent evidence on every fact for which a newspaper story was the initial source. While there was no local newspaper in Seneca, the papers of neighboring towns and the metropolitan press carried a number of feature articles about shipbuilding and about life in Seneca. Many of these articles were inaccurate. Whenever a newspaper report has been used, this fact is so stated in the chapters to follow. Interpretations and evaluations are entirely those of the senior author unless it is otherwise stated.

No facts have been altered, except the names of a few individuals. For obvious reasons, it has seemed wise to disguise the names of the people who are the principal characters in the more dramatic episodes of the story. They will recognize themselves, but their names will not be known to the reader who is not acquainted at first hand with Seneca.

PART I: **THE SETTING**

1.

Seneca before the Boom

One looks down on Seneca from the high rolling prairie that ends in a bluff dominating the flood plain of the Illinois River. The bluff descends sharply a hundred and fifty feet to the flat bottom land. Across the flat plain runs the north-south highway to a shining steel bridge over the river and then on up the bluff on the south bank of the river.

The east-west highway, U.S. 6, is the main traffic artery. It hugs the foot of the bluff and skirts Seneca on the north. All day and all night it carries a rapid stream of trucks, passenger cars, and buses. Parallel to it runs the railway.

The village lies on the main line of the Rock Isand Railway, seventy-five miles southwest of Chicago. Highway 6 connects it with Joliet to the east, and Ottawa, LaSalle, and Peoria to the west. The stores and houses of Seneca cluster about the north-south highway, just south of its intersection with Highway 6.

Seneca in 1940 was a quiet little town, hardly stirred by the swift-flowing life of highway and railroad. South of the railway station on Main Street was a block of old houses, and then two blocks of nondescript business buildings. The wooden structures lacked paint, and two of them were on the verge of caving in. Even the few two-story brick buildings were dingy. There was no bright red paint, shiny chrome, or neon lighting. The newest and most imposing building carried the inscription "Built 1910 A.B." [sic.]. Sidewalks were broken and full of cavities.

Crossing under Main Street in the "business district" was the old Illinois-Michigan canal bed, here a ditch of stagnant water partly filled with brick and machinery from what were once the canal locks. Farther south, Main Street crossed Rat Run, an open sewer of stinking water full of rubbish and discarded auto fenders and oil cans.

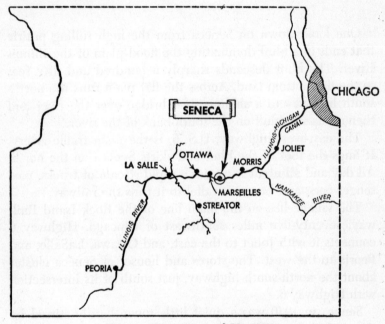

Fig. 1. Seneca and Vicinity.

Leaving Rat Run behind, Main Street improved as it passed several roomy white wooden houses set back in ample yards. Then it was a country road again, running between cornfields to the high bridge over the river.[1]

On the bridge there was usually no sound but the singing of birds. To the west, down the river, was a tall grain ele-

[1] See the map of Seneca, in Chapter 3, Figure 8.

vator with a barge riding quietly at its side. To the east and
about a mile away was the Hay Barge Company shipyard,
a small plant only a year or two old. To the southeast on the
river bluff was the smokestack of the Dupont Dynamite
Plant, since 1928 the principal industry of Seneca.

Back in the village the houses spread out for two or three
blocks on either side of Main Street. They were mainly
wooden constructions of one-and-a-half and two stories, with
here and there a newer two-story red brick or white-painted
colonial-style house built within the past twenty years. On
Lincoln Street between Main Street and the Lutheran church
were a few blocks of well-kept middle-sized wooden houses
and grassy lawns. This was called the "Street of Widows"
because so many elderly women had inherited these houses
from their husbands. Irreverent youngsters had christened
it "Gabby Street."

This was Seneca in 1940. Like a thousand rural towns in
the Midwest, it was down at the heels and had seen better
days. The life of the town flowed slowly. The busy stream of
traffic skirting the town on Highway 6 belonged to another
world. And as though from another world came the sudden
sound and the rush of air and the silver streak of the Rock
Island's streamlined Rocket trains as they flashed past Main
Street.

There was nothing in Seneca to foretell the fact that, by
one of the vagaries of World War II, it would suddenly be
transformed into an industrial boom town.

THE HISTORY OF SENECA

Seneca's history spanned less than a hundred years. Like
the rest of northern Illinois it was wilderness in 1830. Settlers
came overland from Pennsylvania and Ohio to take up land
in this backwoods area. The state at this time was populated

principally in the southern half, by people who came down the Ohio and up the Mississippi rivers. Chicago in 1833 was only a village of 1,200.

The opening of the Erie Canal and the development of transportation on the Great Lakes brought immigrants from the East, mainly from the New England states. These immigrants took up land in the northern part of Illinois. Chicago began to grow. The state appropriated money for the Michigan and Illinois Canal, to connect Chicago with the village of LaSalle at the head of navigation on the Illinois River. The first spadeful of dirt was dug by an Irish laborer in 1836, and twelve years later, in spite of severe financial difficulties, the canal was completed. Immediately the counties along the canal began to grow in population.

Seneca was laid out in 1857. The town was founded by Jeremiah Crotty, and for a time called by his name. A history of LaSalle County, published in 1886, gives an account of the life of Seneca's first citizen.[2]

Jeremiah Crotty was born in Cork, Ireland, and came to this country in 1827. After becoming disgusted with a Micawber-like life about New York city waiting for "something to turn up," he concluded to go out in the country and turn it up himself. His clear head and willing hands soon found enough to do, and after one year's residence in New York, eight in Pennsylvania, and three in Maryland, where he was married to Ellen Blake, he came West. He made his appearance at Lockport in 1838, at canal contract lettings. He had no recommendations such as the rules required, but he put in his bid and was made all sorts of fun of by the high-toned, ruffle-shirted gentlemen who came to carry off all the bids in triumph. He contented himself in his corduroy breeches and knit jacket, smoked a cob pipe and kept his mind to himself, and to the surprise of the aristocratic crowd won the contracts,

[2] *History of LaSalle County, Illinois* (Chicago: Inter-State Publishing Co., 1886), II, 359–61.

laid out before their bewildered eyes $6,000 in gold as his backer or recommendation and went away, leaving them in a state of ludicrous bewilderment. As an evidence of his solid sense, he took contracts that others had beggared themselves in and made money. He discovered that much of the canal way was through beds of soft, shaly slate or soapstone. Other contractors adopted the old slow drill and sledge hammer process to remove this material. He employed a gigantic plow of his own invention and with four yoke of oxen literally plowed up the solid rock, running night and day with two sets of teams and men, "beating the frost" and doing ten times the work with the same outlay that the others could. He had contracts for different sections of the canal between Aux Sable and Ottawa, and most of the Chicago, Rock Island and Pacific Railroad between Minonk and Ottawa. The harder and more expensive jobs he managed himself, and the others he sublet to others. He contracted on the canal until 1842, when work was suspended until 1844. He again went to work on the canal; was in Tennessee a short time and went to Elgin, where he took contracts on the Northwestern Railroad. He remained at Elgin until December 15, 1850, when he removed to Manlius Township and settled on land now comprised in the village of Seneca. He had entered this land in 1848 and had a house built on it in 1849. John Higgins and P. Burk did the carpenter work and R. Cosgrave the mason work. This was the first dwelling-house erected in what afterward became Seneca Village. In 1857 Mr. Crotty laid out a village on the bluff which took the name of its founder. Lots were sold for $1 each, and up to the year 1860 the village contained about fifteen dwelling-houses and two stores. The stores were kept by Crotty & Hickleing and Martin Seeley. The Chicago, Rock Island and Pacific Railroad had been built in 1852, and a station house erected in 1854. Mr. Crotty's son was the first station agent and was also the first Postmaster. Letters at that time averaged about three a week and the rest of the mail was in proportion. It was soon found that in the valley near the railroad would be a more convenient place for business houses, so in 1862 Mr. Crotty erected a store on the present site of the saloon owned by E. Waterman. Martin Seeley built and kept the second store, and the next one was built by J. Armour. It was occupied by Underhill & Vaughey. The first elevator was built by J. Crotty. The first death was that of Anastasia Crotty, who died in May, 1853. Henry Cuddigan was the first child born in the village and Thomas F. Wendle, Mr. Crotty's bookkeeper, was the first man to enter into matrimonial relations in the village. Such is a brief sketch of the early history of Seneca as related to the writer by J. J. Crotty, son of Jeremiah Crotty, who lived at Seneca, laid out and founded by him, about thirty years, and the postoffice was named "Crotty" by the Government. He died leaving a widow and three sons—William, Matthew and John J., and three grandchildren, sons of his daughter, Mary McGorrisk, deceased, who were his heirs. His estate was valued at about $100,000. Although a man of much eccentricity of character, he was universally respected and died mourned by all who knew him. He died July 28, 1879, at his home in Seneca, in his eighty-first year. Old age and a general breaking down of the system for about nine months previous to his death had confined him to his house, and for the greater portion of the time to his bed, so that his demise was not unexpected.

Northern Illinois was growing fast around the middle of the nineteenth century. Chicago, with 1,200 inhabitants in 1833, had 112,000 in 1860. Seneca was incorporated as a village in 1859, and grew rapidly for thirty years, when the population reached a level of about 1,200. After this there was a slow recession for forty years.

The newcomers to Seneca in the early days were chiefly New Yorkers and Irishmen. The New Yorkers were substantial citizens, well-educated for those days, mostly Whigs who later became Republicans. They were the aristocrats of the community, and they mingled with ill grace among the roistering Irishmen who, rich or poor, would boast about their whiskey-drinking prowess. Jeremiah Crotty himself listed among his achievements his contributions to churches and schools, which totalled over $2,000; and, at the same time, a claim to having consumed seventy-five barrels of whiskey in America.

The Irish were Democrats and Catholics. Some were enterprising construction bosses like Jeremiah Crotty, or grain merchants and canalboat owners. The majority were laborers who worked at digging canals and building railroads. They built a fine church; and the Catholic church has always been the largest in Seneca.

But in the end the Irish were outnumbered and outvoted by the easterners. The township, after giving a majority to Pierce in 1852, voted Republican regularly, beginning with Frémont in 1856. Not until Franklin D. Roosevelt ran for his second term as president did Seneca fall away from the Republican ranks, although the vote was always much closer than it was in the neighboring northern Illinois towns.

The settlers from the East came mainly from New York, Pennsylvania, and New England. Other immigrants came from England, Germany, Norway, Switzerland, and France.

Situated on the canal and the railroad, Seneca became a trading center. In the decade of 1860–70, a fleet of two to three hundred canalboats plied between LaSalle County and Chicago. On a typical day, fifteen boats would pass through Seneca, each with a load of a hundred and fifty to two hundred tons.

The canal made Seneca grow, just as it made Chicago the greatest grain port in America. Chicago depended on Seneca and a thousand other midwestern towns to ship corn and wheat—at first by canal and wagon road, and then by railroad and canal. Meanwhile, white-sailed schooners, bringing lumber down Lake Michigan to Chicago, made it the largest lumber port in the world. Canalboats just emptied of wheat were filled with lumber for the return journey, lumber to be used for barns and farmhouses.

How the canalboat figured in the lives of early Seneca

residents is made clear in the following account of the grandfather of one of present-day Seneca's leading businessmen:

Martin J. Hogan was born in New York City in 1848 and came
with his parents to northern Illinois, where he was educated in the
common schools.

In the spring of 1862 he first worked on the Illinois and Michigan Canal, where he was employed with his Uncle Martin, running a boat for the Illinois Stone Company between Lemont and
Chicago. From the spring of 1866 he was engaged as captain of a
boat by Edwin Walker of Lemont, Illinois, until the fall of 1873,
during which time he had saved enough money to purchase a half
interest in the grain boat "Thomas Ryburn," running between
Marseilles and Chicago, which he managed himself until January,
1878.[3]

At that time he went into the grain business, which he and his
son and grandson have since conducted in Seneca.

The period of Seneca's greatest prosperity was 1870 to
1890. The town had the biggest grain-shipping business in
the county. A newspaper, *The Seneca Record,* was started
in 1878. A "fine iron bridge" was built to cross the river in
1877. The school building, still used as an elementary school
in 1940, was built in 1884 and described at that time as "a
magnificent structure, erected at a cost of $10,000." The first
Catholic church was built in 1858. The Methodist church
was organized in 1865, and the Baptist church in 1864. This
was the heyday of the "Peru Accommodation Train" which
ran on Saturdays from Peru to Chicago. One could go from
Seneca to Chicago in the morning, see the sights and do one's
shopping, and get back in time for supper.

Seneca was a boom town in those two decades. By 1880
the town had factories making tiles, carriages, sashes and
doors, and windmills. There were three hotels and eight

[3] Michael Cyprian O'Byrne, *History of LaSalle County, Illinois* (Chicago:
Lewis Publishing Co., 1924), II, 41–42.

saloons. Within a five-year period, five young men set up grain, lumber, hardware, and furniture businesses, and later passed them on to their sons. These sons, as old men, were still doing business in the same locations in 1940.

When fire struck at the business district one day in 1879, and nineteen buildings were destroyed, there was capital enough and confidence enough to put new brick buildings in place of the burnt-down wooden ones. Most of these were still standing in 1940.

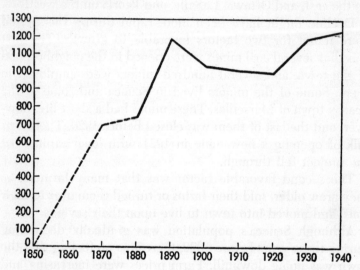

Fig. 2. Population Growth in Seneca to 1940.

Seneca's nineteenth-century boom had the optimism and exuberance of youth. There was no one to hold back on spending. The old men encouraged the young men, firm in the belief that their sons would prosper with the development of the West, just as they themselves had prospered.

With the 1890's the boom lost momentum, and Seneca, like other northern Illinois towns, leveled off. There followed fifty years of relative repose, during which young men grew old and their sons became the leaders of Seneca's life—sons who had never seen Seneca grow. Population decreased from 1,190 in 1890 to 994 in 1920. The canal gradually lost out in competition with the railroad. Seneca lost its few small manufacturing establishments and was left to make a living as a trading center for farmers. Contact with the outside world was through the railroad and the electric interurban, which ran on a frequent schedule to Morris and Joliet and Chicago on the east, and Ottawa, LaSalle, and Peoria on the west.

Decline might have been more rapid during this period were it not for two factors favorable to growth. The first was that several coal mines were opened in the neighborhood of the town, and several hundred miners were employed in them. Some of the miners lived in Seneca and some in the nearby town of Marseilles. These mines had a short life, however, and the last of them was closed before 1920. There was talk of opening a new mine in 1921 with local capital but the project fell through.

The second favorable factor was that many farmers, as they grew older, sold their farms or turned them over to their sons, and moved into town to live upon their savings.

Although Seneca's population was gradually decreasing during those years before 1920, there was no feeling that the town was going downhill. Farm prices were increasing and business was good. One of the grocers, who has been in business in Seneca for forty years, recalls the years from 1900 to 1915 as good years for business. Those were the days when roads were bad and farmers came to town very seldom, but when they did they bought in large quantities. The grocer says, "I remember selling five carloads of potatoes in four weeks' time, once. 'Twas nothing for a man to buy five hundred pounds of flour at a time. They'd go to the depot and load their wagons right out of the freight car. Mrs. Byrne,

she'd buy enough canton flannel every fall to last her six boys
for underclothing all winter, two or three bolts at a time, like
as not. Buying was altogether different then, to what it is
now. I used to buy tea at New Year's, green tea of course,
this has always been green tea territory, but you can't get it
any more. I bought twenty-four chests of eighty pounds
each,—and then *that* wasn't enough to last us through the
year."

To the older residents of Seneca those years in retrospect
seem like a golden age. Seneca was the center of life for a
flourishing farm area. Once a year the famous Fourth of July
celebration brought people from far and near. A maiden lady
who had lived all her fifty years in Seneca described the celebration: "Yes, thirty years or more ago, we used to *really*
celebrate the Fourth of July. The merchants all trimmed up
their floats—horses and wagons they were then—and they
worked hard to see which would have the best one. There
was the float with the Goddess of Liberty—they always chose
the same girl because she had such beautiful long golden
curls—and the rest of us girls to represent each state, with
haloes on; my, how hot it was, out in the sun on those floats,
the haloes hurt your head! Then there were the firemen,
projecting their ladders up into the air, showing how fast
they could run up them. They had the grandstand just back
of the lumber yard. There was always a speaker from away.
And refreshment booths, pink lemonade and popcorn. And
dancing!"

These celebrations were superseded by the carnivals that
Father Higgins organized to raise money for the debt on the
Catholic church. The carnival lasted a whole week. There
were raffles and dinners and out-of-town entertainers and
bands and dancing. Crowds filled the town. On one Fourth
of July there were said to be seven thousand visitors. Father
Higgins, who was a "folksy" man, was succeeded by Father

Preston, who didn't approve so much of carnivals, and the celebrations died out.

Seneca had the reputation in those days of being a tough town. It had many saloons, and drunkenness was said to be common. Methodist and Baptist ministers did not like the place. They blamed its reputation on the Irish element and on the coal miners. Young people from the surrounding towns thought it was a bold adventure to visit Seneca. A middle-class man from a neighboring city said, "You know, when I was a boy, if we went to Seneca, we had to be very careful to explain our reasons and to tell what we did."

Seneca might have gone on at the tempo of these years, except for the coming of the automobile and the hard road. A bond issue of sixty million dollars for the building of paved roads was approved by the voters of Illinois in 1918. This was only the beginning; and by 1930 Illinois was a network of concrete that enabled the farmer to get into his automobile and speed past the rural villages on his way to the city, regardless of weather and season.

One of the old residents says that the building of Highway 6 was the ruin of Seneca. This happened in 1922. About this time the electric interurban railroad was abandoned; the tracks were torn up and sold for junk; and the handsome station in Seneca was sold at a nominal price to a man who turned it into a store.

In spite of these changes, Seneca grew from 994 to 1,185 in the ten years from 1920 to 1930. Establishment of the Grasselli Powder Company southeast of town in 1928 had something to do with this growth. This plant was taken over by the Dupont Company in the same year, and has been in operation ever since. The Dupont Company employed 134 men in 1940, most of whom lived in Seneca. The deepening of the Illinois River to provide a channel for river barges on the Great Lakes-Gulf Waterway brought the building of the grain elevator on the river and made Seneca once more a grain-shipping center. And a number of farmers retired from their farms and moved into town.

The depression of the 1930's made no great change in Seneca. It is true that the bank failed, and business dropped off. Several business structures became permanently vacant and began to deteriorate. Nevertheless, Seneca did not lose population. About 1938 the John I. Hay Barge Plant was established, to make river barges in a shipyard located on the riverbank east of town. Though its work was intermittent, this plant employed some sixty men when in operation.

SENECA IN 1940

Seneca in 1940 was a small agricultural-industrial town, similar in many respects to other small towns of the Midwest. Its population was 1,235, exceeding by a small margin the previous peak that had been reached in 1890. About one hundred and fifty of its adult males were employed at the barge company and the powder plant; the others were retired farmers and owners of small businesses, with a handful of professional men. The tempo of life was slow. People lived in one-family dwellings, with yards for the children to play in. There was little in the way of formal recreation—not even a movie theater. Much of the social life of the town centered about the churches, of which there were four—a Catholic, a Methodist, a Lutheran, and a Holiness Methodist.

Children enjoyed the advantages and the disadvantages of small-town living: the open space of the countryside, the fishing in the river, and hunting. There was one elementary school, and one high school, both of which offered the traditional curriculum. Some of the adolescents finished school and went off to college; the majority stayed in Seneca and were gradually absorbed into the economic life of the community.

The people of the town, as has already been described, were relatively homogeneous; second, third, and fourth generations of American stock, with a large group of Irish Catholics, and a smaller group of Norwegian Lutherans. There were no Negroes, and there had never been more than one or two Jewish families. New population elements had not entered the Seneca area for a generation. Table 1 shows how towns and cities in this area had become stabilized

TABLE 1

POPULATION TRENDS IN THE SENECA AREA BEFORE THE BOOM

	1920	1930	1940
LaSalle County	92,925	97,695	97,801
Grundy County	18,580	18,678	18,398
Joliet	38,442	42,993	42,365
LaSalle	13,050	13,149	12,812
Ottawa	10,816	15,094	16,005
Streator	14,779	14,728	14,930
Morris	4,505	5,568	6,115
Marseilles	3,391	4,292	4,455
Seneca	994	1,185	1,235

THE SOCIAL STRUCTURE OF SENECA

Seneca had a social structure that had evolved slowly and that was now relatively stable. The town had its "old families," and its "solid citizens," its working class, and its chronic ne'er-do-wells. A system of relationships had developed between these various groups of people that was similar to the social class structure of the larger, urban communities, though the lines of difference were not so sharply drawn.

The "upper crust." There was fairly general agreement on the people who made up the "upper crust." When several people who had lived all their lives in Seneca were asked to name the town's "best families," they agreed completely on six families, and there was fair agreement on another three

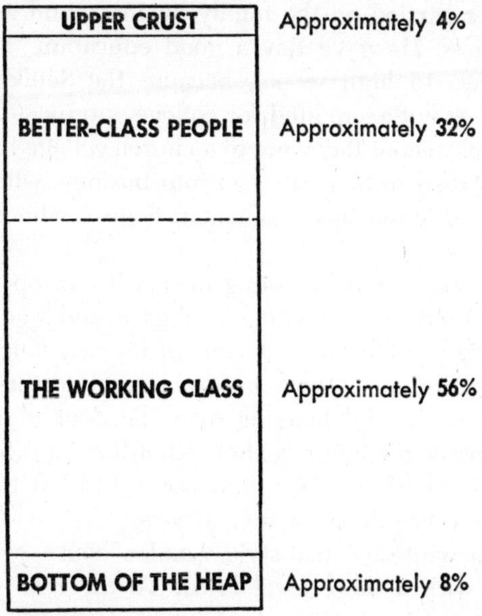

UPPER CRUST	Approximately 4%
BETTER-CLASS PEOPLE	Approximately 32%
THE WORKING CLASS	Approximately 56%
BOTTOM OF THE HEAP	Approximately 8%

Fig. 3. Social Structure of Seneca in 1940.

or four. The "upper crust" consisted mainly of "old families," together with families of two or three professional men who had formed close friendships and in one case had married into an "old family." Ray Nichols was a member of the "upper crust":

Ray Nichols was Seneca's leading citizen. He owned a lumber business and several farms. He was the leader of the Methodist Church. In all civic enterprises, such as a drive to raise money for the Red Cross, or a campaign to vote a bond issue for a new school building, Ray Nichols was either the leader or he was consulted in the selection of the leader.

The grandfather of Ray Nichols came to LaSalle County from New York State in 1856, and settled in Seneca shortly after his period of service in the Civil War. He went into the grain business and bought land, making a specialty of raising fine horses.

Ray's father carried on the family business, and added to it a lumber business. He gave Ray a good education. The boy was sent to Ottawa to high school, because the Seneca three-year high school was not accredited for college entrance. Upon graduation from high school Ray went to a church college for two years, and then returned to Seneca to go into business with his father. Ray was one of three businessmen in Seneca who had gone to college.

Ray was a strong, stocky young man, with an open face, eyes which looked on the world with a level gaze, and a good-humored laugh. As he grew older, he lost some of his easy laughter, but he did not lose his humor. One morning he came to the office of his lumber business to find hanging over the door a sign, not too carefully painted, reading, "Nichols Knot-hole and Splinter Emporium." He enjoyed this joke immensely, and left the sign right there over his office door for several years.

Ray built a white colonial-style wooden house, set back from Main Street with a large level lawn. To the rear was a small garage and barn. In the barn he kept his favorite saddle horse, which he could be seen riding in the late afternoon on any pleasant day. He married a schoolteacher, and together they raised a girl and a boy.

Although Ray came closer to living like a "gentleman" than anybody else in Seneca, he never "put on airs," and he was universally liked and trusted. He met everybody, high or low, with the same controlled but genuine friendliness. In time of crisis, Seneca people looked instinctively to Ray Nichols for leadership.

"Better-class people." Seneca had a substantial group of "better-class people"—perhaps a hundred families. Businessmen, professional men, several of the management staff of

the Dupont plant, some retired farmers, and numerous "old families" were in this group. These people were the leaders in the churches and in the social life of the town. They contributed most of the membership in the women's philanthropic sorority, Delta Theta Tau. Henry Harris is an example of Seneca's "better-class people":

The father of Henry Harris was one of Seneca's pioneers. As an infant, he had come with his parents from Pennsylvania in the 1840's, and he grew up in Grundy County. As a soldier in the Civil War, he fought in the battles of Pea Ridge, Chickamauga, and Mission Ridge. After his discharge as a second lieutenant he went into business in Seneca; and in 1881 started the hardware business which his son, Henry, carried on after him.

Henry Harris, Jr., went into his father's hardware business in 1895, at the age of sixteen. Business was good; they had just put up a new building and their stock was as modern as their store. In a few years Henry married a local girl, and they had two boys, one of whom grew up to go to college and become a college professor, while the younger boy went to the Pacific Coast and found a job in business.

The usual civic responsibilities of one of the town's leading businessmen came to Mr. Harris. He served for a time on the village council, and for twenty years he was secretary of the school board. Although business deteriorated slowly in Seneca, especially during the depression years, it always brought in a living, and Mr. and Mrs. Harris lived comfortably.

In 1940, Henry Harris was sixty-three years old, and a tired man, asking no more than to carry on for another ten years in his accustomed manner—to run his business on the basis of giving good value for money received; to go home at the end of the day to a well-cooked supper, to read his newspaper, and to retire early; to live out his conservative and "good" life.

The "working class." The dividing line between the "better-class people" and the "working class" in Seneca was the least visible of the social class lines. Many people who worked with their hands were in the "better-class" group. Still, the "working class" differed substantially from the group just above it in terms of income, education, and civic attitudes. The working-class people were a family-centered group. They did not think often in terms of community. The only organization they belonged to was the church, where they followed the lead of the people higher on the social scale. This was the largest group in Seneca, just as it is in similar communities. Johann Brinker was a member of this social class:

Johann Brinker had been Seneca's only shoemaker for forty years. Born in Holland, he and his wife came to America in 1892, and settled in Seneca in 1899. They had raised a family of seven children, but now lived alone in a little stucco house which had cost $4,000 to build in the middle twenties. The house had an enclosed front porch, a living room and dining room which opened together. It was well-lighted and comfortably furnished, with a well-jacketed coal stove for heat, and a white porcelain coal range for cooking.

The Brinkers lived comfortably on a small income from his shoe-repair business. They spent $100 a year for coal, $3 a month for electricity, $2 a month for telephone. For kindling, they bought two loads of corn cobs at $4 a load. Peaches, apples, grapes, and raspberries grew in the orchard behind the house; and they raised chickens and bees. Mrs. Brinker canned three hundred to four hundred jars of fruit and vegetables a year; baked all the bread and whatever cookies they used. They purchased pigs at suitable intervals from farmers, had them slaughtered, then canned the meat or cooked part of it and packed it under rendered lard.

Life was quiet and peaceful. Aside from his business, his bees, and his orchard, Mr. Brinker's main interest was keeping up with the lives of his twenty-three grandchildren and fourteen great-grandchildren. The Brinkers could afford to take life easy for the remainder of their days.

"The bottom of the heap." Seneca had very few people who could be singled out as shiftless, immoral, or dull-witted, and placed at the "bottom of the heap." There were two or three families whose daughters were reputed to be sexually promiscuous, and several other families who were always just being added to, or just being dropped from, the county relief roll. Perhaps twenty families in all could be identified with this class.

The Brooks family was at the "bottom of the heap." "Old Man Brooks" worked at odd jobs, on and off, when jobs were plentiful. But people didn't like to have him work on their grounds or in their houses, because he always seemed dirty, with his scraggly whiskers and his shabby clothes. Children were warned against him when he was seen rolling drunkenly homeward from his favorite saloon.

Nobody knew much about Mrs. Brooks, except that she took in washing, and would send one of her daughters to collect the dirty clothes and deliver the clean ones. The daughters were bold youngsters who went out to do household work in their early 'teens, and never got beyond the eighth grade in school. One of them had a baby whom Mrs. Brooks reared along with her own large brood.

They lived in a small house near Rat Run. Two or three of the children slept in the shed at the back of the house. A school-teacher went to see Mrs. Brooks about some trouble she was having with one of the children. When she came away she said, "I don't know where they put all those children. They must hang them on hooks!"

Whatever the community may have felt about them, the Brookses were fiercely loyal to themselves. They would fight any-one who criticized them. At school the Brooks children would instantly attack any child who was unwary enough to call them names.

The four social classes in Seneca have some resemblance to the lower four of Warner's six classes that he found in

Yankee City, a New England town; and to the lower four of five social classes that he found in Jonesville, another midwestern town.[4] In Warner's terminology, the Seneca groups would be designated as "upper middle," "lower middle," "upper lower," and "lower lower" classes. Seneca did not have a group equivalent to the upper class as found in a larger town or a great city.

The Boom Comes

This was Seneca when World War II began. Just another rural village in the Middle West. No future; but a good place to bring up a family.

Then came the war in Europe, and American participation. Seneca was picked up and made into an arsenal of war. Ten thousand people came to work in Seneca. The population multiplied fivefold. The community was pitched into a confusion of change.

What would become of Seneca?

[4] W. Lloyd Warner and Associates, *Democracy in Jonesville* (New York: Harper & Brothers, 1949).

W. Lloyd Warner and Paul S. Lunt, *The Social Life of a Modern Community* (New Haven: Yale University Press, 1941).

2.

The Prairie Shipyard

BUILDING THE LST

When the United States entered World War II, one of the urgent needs of the nation was for ships. New types of ships were needed for invasion purposes. The Navy designed a ship that was capable of carrying a cargo and troops ten thousand miles, discharging them on a beach, not at a dock, and retracting for additional service. This was the LST, the Landing Ship Tank. It was fitted with doors and a ramp in its bow to unload cargo on a beach, and it carried light guns for self-protection.

Since all coastal shipyards were working full time on other types of ships, new yards were necessary, and it was decided to build several of these yards on inland rivers with sufficient depth to float the relatively shallow craft down to the sea.

The United States Navy entered into an arrangement whereby it would pay for a shipyard to be constructed under specifications to be agreed upon with the Chicago Bridge and Iron Company. The company was then to build LST's under the supervision of naval officers.

The Chicago Bridge and Iron Company was a builder of steel structures such as oil and gas storage tanks, water tanks, blast furnaces, large diameter pipelines, and penstocks. Steel for these structures was fabricated at the company's plants in Chicago, Birmingham, and Greenville, Pennsylvania. The main office was in Chicago.

Although shipbuilding had not been a major activity, the company was thoroughly accustomed to the principal phase of the project as planned by the Navy, which was to fabricate large steel pieces at the plant and to weld them together at the site of construction. Accordingly, the Chicago Bridge and Iron Company created a Shipbuilding Division and sought a location for its shipyard.

Seneca was chosen as the site for the shipyard for a number of reasons. In the first place, the river shore at Seneca was right for a shipyard. At this point on the river, the geological formation known as the Saint Peter Sandstone lay only two or three feet below the surface of the flat bottom land on the north bank of the river. By stripping off the loose top soil, a level, solid floor of sandstone was exposed. This formed a stable support for the weight of ships and made unnecessary the expensive sinking of piles and the construction of extensive launching ways. The Illinois River was wide enough and deep enough (after some dredging) to permit the launching of an LST, and it was part of the Great Lakes-Gulf Waterway, which had a nine-foot channel up the Illinois and down the Mississippi to the Gulf of Mexico.

In the second place, a survey of labor supply showed that the area within thirty-five miles of Seneca had a large pool of manpower consisting of people who already had some mechanical skill or could be readily trained for shipbuilding jobs.

Other reasons for the choice of Seneca were its proximity to a main power line of the Northern Illinois Power Company, the presence of a railroad siding near the site of the yard, and the relative proximity of the company's main office, seventy-five miles away in Chicago.

The Chicago Bridge and Iron Company already owned about two hundred acres of river-bottom land on the outskirts of the village, adjacent to the barge-building yard of the John I. Hay Company, a subsidiary. It was decided to use this land.

The soil was scraped off the construction area and thirty berths for ships were made with low concrete supports. These were arranged in three rows extending north from the riverbank. There were fifteen berths in the center row, and the other fifteen were constructed eight on one side and seven on the other, staggered so that fifteen ships could be pulled onto the center tracks. The hulls were completed on the outer berths, and were then transferred to the center tracks where the remainder of the work inside the hulls was done. The ships were launched sideways from the launching ways at the end of the center berths.

Ships were moved from one berth to another on low cars running on narrow gauge tracks. The cars were equipped with hydraulic jacks to lift the hulls from their concrete berths. As many as thirty ships could be in process of construction at a given time.

Surrounding the construction area were shops, outfitting docks, offices, and parking space for workers' automobiles.

The shipbuilding process was an adaptation of the assembly method, which had been perfected for the manufacture of automobiles. It was called the "task system." The entire work of building the ship was broken down into 378 separate tasks comprising 1,146 operations. Each employee was trained to perform one job with one particular task crew. Upon completion of its task, a crew moved on to other ships to perform the same work. The task system can only be used in shipbuilding during wartime or some other emergency when there is a demand for a large number of ships of the same model.

The construction of a ship consisted of the erection, fitting, and welding of the hull, the installation of machinery as the hull progressed, and then the mechanical, steel cleaning, piping, sheet metal, electrical, pipe insulation, painting, and outfitting tasks. Construction of the first ship took six months, but the time was cut down until the last ships were being constructed in three months.[1]

The first government contract was awarded the CBI in March, 1942. Work on the shipyard was started the first of May, and the first keel was laid June 15, before the yard itself was completely equipped. The first ship was launched

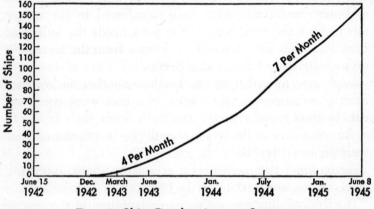

Fig. 4. Ship Production at Seneca.

December 13, 1942, shortly after the shipyard came into full operation. One ship was launched in December, one in January, two in February, three in March, and four a month from April, 1943, to April, 1944; then the schedule was stepped up to seven a month until June, 1945. The one hundred fifty-seventh and last LST was launched on June 8, 1945.

CONDITIONS OF WORK

On a hot summer day the shipbuilding area was a scene of noisy, dusty, sweaty action. The hulls loomed high but

[1] For more information on the LST, see Appendix A.

were dwarfed by electric light poles with floodlights for night work, and by enormous cranes that crawled about on caterpillar tracks. Air-driven chipping and buffing machines gave out a savage noise like the growling of a thousand angry dogs. Dust billowed out from the holds of the ships. Inside the hulls it was hot—130° F. when the sun beat down in the daytime. Welders' torches flashed with an eye-searing glare. Men generally wore welders' helmets; and women workers looked like men, with grimy overalls, sweaty faces, and men's headgear. So the people worked, each at his own job in his task crew, pausing occasionally to straighten his back and listen to the latest pieces of popular music played on phonograph records and broadcast from the loudspeakers —music interspersed with announcements from the office and brief exhortations to avoid accidents, buy war bonds, and eat the right kinds of food.

At night it was the same except that the hot sun's rays were replaced by the cooler floodlights. In the winter work went on just the same, but it was bitterly cold working with steel out in the open.

A fifty-four-hour week was the usual thing throughout the boom. It consisted of six nine-hour days. With pay at the rate of time and a half for all hours beyond forty, this meant that most workers were paid for sixty-one hours. The hours of beginning work on a shift were staggered somewhat, so that traffic in and about the yard was spread over a period of an hour or two.

Jim Malan, a typical worker, had the following kind of daily routine:

The alarm rang in his War Homes Apartment at 6:30. Jim groaned and rolled out of bed, then doused his face in cold water at the lavatory. His wife put on her wrapper and went into the living-room-kitchen to start breakfast. She cooked bacon and eggs and oatmeal, enough oatmeal for the children's breakfast as well.

Jim came in all dressed for work, sat down at the table and ate his breakfast in silence, while Mrs. Malan fixed his lunch. She made two sandwiches with lunch meat, filled a thermos bottle with hot coffee, and put a piece of pie into Jim's lunch box. Jim left at 7:10 for the ten-minute walk to the shipyard, just as his wife called the three children who slept in a double-deck bed and a cot in the second bedroom.

Automobiles and men and women on foot were streaming toward the shipyard gates as Jim arrived; while a smaller stream of people from the night shift crews marched in the opposite direction.

Jim punched the time clock and walked to the toolroom to check out his welding equipment. Then he joined his task crew to begin welding the hull of a new ship. He worked steadily until noon; then knocked off for a half-hour lunch period. Jim and several of his friends sat in the shade of a hull to eat and joke together. Just before time to start work again, the foreman appeared to ask who wanted to work the following Sunday. This meant double pay, and Jim volunteered. But he grumbled to a friend, "I want that extra twenty bucks; but my wife and kids won't like it. They want me to take them to a movie in Ottawa Sunday."

Work started again at 12:30 and continued until five o'clock. Toward the end of the afternoon Jim found excuses to walk outside the hull in which he was working, take off his welder's helmet, wipe the sweat off his face and neck, and feel the coolness of the air. One time he spoke to his foreman. "It's nothin' but work, work, work, from sunup to sundown, and Sundays, too. I think I'll join the Army and get a soft job with the Army Engineers. I hear they've got two men for every job!"

The foreman jeered at him. "You're chained to this job, brother, and you know it. You're essential! You couldn't get out of here even if you wrote to your congressman. Anyway, your old woman wouldn't let you go."

Five o'clock and Jim's crew gave over their places to the next shift; checked in their tools; filed through the narrow passageways past the time clocks with their staccato music; and spread out from the shipyard gates toward their homes. Jim got home at 5:15, washed up and put on clean work clothes, and sat down to supper with his family. "I got to work Sunday," he said. "Guess we'll have to wait a week for that movie in Ottawa."

"Ma," said twelve-year-old Sandy, "I wish we could move back home! We never have any fun with Pop any more!"

Jim felt comfortable and relaxed as he walked down the street after supper. His muscles ached slightly; but with a pleasant ache that he knew he could relieve by sitting in a chair at the tavern with a stein of beer in his hands. So he loafed for a couple of hours; walked across the street to the union office and paid his monthly dues; and then went home to bed.

Unionization. The shipyard was completely unionized, as far as its craft workers were concerned. They belonged to American Federation of Labor unions. Union offices were located in Seneca, and in Marseilles, five miles away.

Relations between labor and management were harmonious. In fact some workers with anti-union sentiments complained that CBI management was in league with the unions. Since about 80 per cent of the Seneca workers had never belonged to unions before, many of them were lukewarm, and some were actively hostile toward unionism, feeling that they had been forced to join the union.

Mr. and Mrs. Schmidt were hostile to the union. She had been working at the shipyard cafeteria, and her husband was a welder. When the cafeteria workers were unionized, she quit her job rather than join the union. Her husband refused to join the union, but stuck to his job. According to Mrs. Schmidt, he was transferred to another department and put on the night shift, which he detested. She said, "They tell him he will have to do the work that nobody else wants. It's not so much the paying of dues he objects to as it is the people in the union. He's a religious man. He hates cussing and drinking, and the union men are mostly cussers and drinkers. He had his own welding business downstate. We're thinking of going to Peoria where he can get a job with a small non-union firm."

The fieldworker asked Mrs. Schmidt about the attitude of CBI management toward the unions. "Oh, they're just in cahoots with each other," replied Mrs. Schmidt. "They have to be!"

The overwhelming majority of workers took up union membership willingly, but not with enthusiasm. Knowing this, the labor leaders did not attempt much of an educational campaign among their new members. They concentrated on building up a strong organization among their older members, and upon collecting dues. The latter posed something of a problem, for, according to the union leaders' estimates, no more than half of their members would stay in the same line of work after the war and thus want to keep up their union affiliation. The other half might be expected to be careless about paying dues. The CBI management was cooperative in this matter, although it did not collect dues for the union. The management allowed a representative of the Boilermakers' Local, the largest of the shipyard unions, to receive payments on the premises two days a week. They also agreed to insert notices of delinquent dues in the time-card racks along with the workers' time cards, if these notices were made out by the unions.

The men who became "mechanics" by the rapid upgrading system used by CBI were not recognized as such by their unions. They were kept in the "apprentice" class for the full union apprenticeship period. This was not unfair, for these men were trained to do a specific operation as one member of a task crew, and nothing else. For example, a man might be trained to make the electrical connections for one set of instruments. He would perform this operation in all the ships. Although he might be classified and paid by CBI as a "mechanic" electrician, he might know nothing about wiring a house, and he would not be recognized by his union

as anything more than an apprentice electrician. Lacking the
rounded experience of a journeyman worker, his was a "duration" job and he knew it. Only a few of the younger and
abler men expected to remain in the same kind of work after
the war.

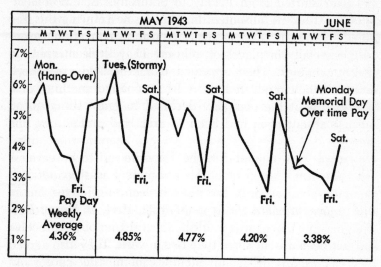

Fig. 5. Absenteeism—Daily Percentage Graph.

Absenteeism. Absenteeism was a considerable problem at
Seneca, as in war industries generally. The management
maintained a continual propaganda against it during the first
year, through its news organ, *Our Prairie Shipyard,* and
through charts displayed in the yard. Figure 5 gives the
record of absenteeism for the month of May, 1943, as it was
published in *Our Prairie Shipyard.* The average was about
4.5 per cent per day. Lowest day for absenteeism was always
Friday (payday) and highest days were Saturday and Monday. The influence of overtime pay for Monday, May 31
(Memorial Day), is shown by a decrease of absences. The

special launching program on Saturday, June 5, was probably responsible for cutting down the usual Saturday absences on that particular day. Illness was estimated to be responsible for about one-fifth of the absences during this period.

Since pay day had such a good effect upon attendance, it was later shifted from Friday to Saturday, as a means of reducing weekend absenteeism. Noticeable results were obtained—noticeable also to Seneca businessmen. Their business, especially in places of amusement, fell off sharply on Friday evenings. They appealed to the village council of Seneca, which requested the CBI to change payday back to Friday. But the company declined to grant the request because absenteeism had been so greatly decreased by the change.

A word was coined for the opposite of absenteeism—"presenteeism." Much favorable publicity was given to people with good records for presenteeism. For example, in *Our Prairie Shipyard* for September 22, 1944, an Honor Roll of eighty-five names was published, consisting of people who had not been absent since they began work in 1942.

Morale-building. The maintenence of morale among the workers was a matter of continual attention by the management. The major procedures used for this purpose were:

Our Prairie Shipyard—a newspaper published twice a month
Launching ceremonies
Ceremonies surrounding the Award of the Army-Navy "E"
The LST Invasion Exposition
High wages and the bonus
Recreation [2]
Exhortations to stay on the job, by letter and word of mouth.

Our Prairie Shipyard, published by the Public Relations Department, came out approximately twice a month until the

[2] The recreation program is described in Chapter 9, "Recreation."

middle of 1944, when it was reduced to once a month. For the first few months it was a small twelve-page lithoprinted booklet, with few illustrations. But beginning in March, 1943, it appeared in a new and larger format, with sixteen to twenty-four pages in 8½ x 11 inch size. Photographs were used liberally, and the effect was definitely interesting. A rough analysis of the topics emphasized in various periods follows:

Period I. September, 1942, to June, 1943
Absenteeism
  "Don't Slow Up the Ship" "Stay on the Job"
  "AWOL on the Production Line May Cost a Life in the Firing Line"
Sabotage
  Several stories of workers being convicted of sabotage in other war production plants
  Warning against hiding of tools aboard ship so as to save checking them in and out of the tool house
Sports
Safety
War Bonds
Production Suggestions
  Rewards for good ideas on production short cuts
Patriotism
  "We're Doing Our Part To Help Win the War"
  "What Can We Do To Win the War?"
  "Speed Our Ships"
  Photographs of members of workers' families who were in the services.

Period II. June, 1943, to January, 1944
Sports—Increased emphasis
Safety—Increased emphasis
War Bonds
Absenteeism—Decreased emphasis
  Pictures of employees with perfect attendance records

Personal Items—Personal news about employees, such as births, marriages, etc. Many photographs, including pictures of family members in service

Reports of Launchings—Photographs.

Period III. January, 1944, to June, 1945

Sports

Safety

War Bonds

LST's in Service—Pictures of ships in service and letters from crewmen on these ships. Descriptions of life on board an LST. Information about the construction and equipment of an LST

Former employees now in military service—Pictures

Absenteeism—Emphasis on "presenteeism." Pictures and lists of employees with perfect attendance records

Personal items—Personal news, photographs of family members in service, and photographs of children of employees

CBI peacetime products—Photographs and stories

Thefts from the shipyard—Accounts of thieving from the shipyard and warnings that the FBI was watching for thieves.

One feature of *Our Prairie Shipyard* was the poetry contributed by employees of the yard. Much of it was sorry doggerel, but occasionally there appeared something of more than passing interest. The following poem drew favorable comment:

Seneca Ship Yard

S hips that are born in the heart of a prairie,

E ngendered in haste and in fury begotten,

N ameless and young. . . . They are ready to ferry

E ngines of wrath to the never forgotten

C ountries that languish in serfdom and carry

A yoke placed by hands that are bloody and rotten.

S hips that are born of brain and of toil

H undreds of miles from the shores of the sea. . . .

I nstruments lethal. . . . Made ready to foil

P lunder and rape of all men who are free.

Y onder. . . . Above . . . They who perished are watching,
A wed by a sight in a corn growing dell;
R ows of new ships. . . . Our nation is marching
D ooming the blood-thirsty butchers to Hell.

Solomon Katz
Badge #1408

Launching ceremonies were probably the most influential
of the morale-builders. Coming once or twice a week, they
were frequent enough to serve as a tangible measure of production that could be kept continually before the eyes of the
workers. With music, visitors, and speeches by celebrities,
they reminded the workers continually that what they were
doing was of importance to the welfare of the nation.

The ceremonies varied greatly in the amount of fanfare
that was devoted to them. The launching on July 4, 1944,
was a special occasion, with two thousand workers allowed
to invite family members, and with a speech by Captain
Dowd, U.S.N., former supervisor of shipbuilding for the Chicago District. The Ottawa *Republican Times* of July 5 said:

The employees of the Chicago Bridge and Iron Company shipyard at Seneca spent July 4th on the job. At noon all of the employees were dismissed for a short period to witness the launching
of LST 628. Two thousand employees who had not previously had
a member of their family to a launching were issued passes. Harm
Galley and his Shipbuilders Orchestra, made up entirely of shipyard employees, furnished the music. Merle J. Trees, executive
vice-president of the Chicago Bridge and Iron Company, presided at the ceremony, being introduced by Walter B. Colby,
public relations director.

The principal speaker on the program was Capt. Wallace R.
Dowd, U.S.N., former supervisor of shipbuilding, and now located
at the Bureau of Ships, Washington, D. C.

Capt. Dowd said: "During the past month all of us have read
of two very important happenings in different parts of the world.
East, our men have landed in Normandy. West, the marines and

army have landed on a very important island of Japan, Saipan. In the eastern operation a great number of LST's were used. In the western operation also a considerable number were used.

"Unless those LST's had been available in both landings the results would have been questionable. Undoubtedly all of you have seen the pictures of two LST's on the beach. High and dry into the beach are their noses, stay there when the tide is right, and if the tide drops let the ship hang there until the tide comes up again to float it off.

"In both operations there were very, very few LST's lost, and very, very few damaged. Why is that? In the first place, there were few lost because of the people operating them, because of the people who were supporting the air protection. Because of the battleships, cruisers, and destroyers giving the artilleries big gun bombardment in the places where those vessels were to land. The same is true at Saipan. The fact that there were very few lost is an attribute to the way these vessels were built. The LST can and will stand considerable punishment.

"It is vitally necessary that all of us recognize, as you have recognized, the necessity for giving our all here in building these vessels in order that those people and those men and women, in some instances, who are fighting this war in advanced areas may have the best possible tools with which to win this war. I assure you that from what we can see, from what we read in the papers, the people out there are doing a grand job. All of you here are doing a good job.

"Early in April I had the temerity to stand in front of you and challenge you and dare you to produce nine LST's during the month of May, and seven during the month of April. I am going to confess now that I knew that you could do it, you didn't think you could do it. I knew you could if you put your heart into it: and you did.

"It is grand to be back here. I feel that I am coming home. Two years ago on the 15th of June the first keel was laid at Seneca. It was a grand ship. Your reputation is world wide. Everyone realizes that the best LST's came from Seneca. I want to thank you all for the privilege to come back here and talk to you.

Looking back two years ago to a cornfield and seeing today a great shipyard as this one is really a treat to me and I am sure it is to everyone else."

Commander Paul S. Goen, U.S.N. (retired), supervisor of shipbuilding, complimented the employees on the work they were doing in a place that a little more than two years ago was once a cornfield. George T. Horton, president of the Chicago Bridge and Iron Company, mentioned how much this yard was indebted to the Navy, especially the Bureau of Ships. He paid tribute to the nerve, courage, and foresight of naval officers who did much toward the success of the Seneca shipbuilding program and expressed appreciation to the employees for their loyalty.

Mr. Trees then introduced the sponsor, Mrs. J. P. Abernathy of Ottawa. A short time ago when it was decided to hold a public launching on July 4th, each department nominated a sponsor to christen a ship on July 4th. The Navy selected Mrs. Abernathy who has one son, Pfc. D. P. Abernathy, 21, who has been overseas for twenty-three months with the United States Marine Corps, and now is hospitalized in the Hawaiian Islands from wounds received at Tarawa. He received a citation from Admiral Nimitz and also the Purple Heart and the Silver Star. Another son, Pfc. John [Abernathy], 23, has been in the service two years and is now in New Guinea. Just before Mrs. Abernathy crashed the bottle of champagne against the bow of LST 628 she said:

"I am so happy to be chosen as sponsor for LST 628. May God watch over her whatever her destination may be. I christen thee LST 628."

In a few seconds the ship hit the water and shortly after the yard was cleared of visitors and the Seneca shipbuilders resumed their work speeding additional ships toward the launching ways.

A human interest note to the ceremony was the presence of Ensign George Waldo, who will be the combat skipper of LST 628. He had with him his bride of less than twenty-four hours. They were married in Chicago on Monday evening.

A great variety of women were invited to sponsor the ships. They were wives and daughters of top management and of yard workers; women employees; wives and daughters of navy officers; and they included the twelve-year-old daughter of an officer in charge of ferrying LST's down the river to New Orleans. On Labor Day, the daughter of the secretary-treasurer of the Boilermakers' Union was the sponsor. Perhaps the most popular launching of all was that of the 100th ship, on September 28, 1944, when Cesar Romero, movie actor, was the guest of honor. Quoting from the Ottawa *Republican Times* of September 29:

Cesar Romero, movie actor, who is a boatswin's mate 2-C in the United States Coast Guard, participated in ceremonies yesterday afternoon that marked the launching of the 100th LST constructed at the Seneca shipyard of the Chicago Bridge and Iron Company.

All of the 8,000 employees of the day shift were dismissed for a half-hour to witness the launching program, which was recorded and rebroadcast at midnight to the 2,000 night shift workers.

The program was opened by Walter B. Colby, public relations director. D. A. Leach, yard manager, presided. The invocation was given by the Rev. Robert Snider, pastor of the Streator Church of the Nazarene, who is employed as a timekeeper at the shipyard, in addition to carrying on his ministerial duties.

Lt. Melvin Lanphar introduced Romero and Boatswain's Mate 1-C Thomas L. Coakley of the Seabees, who is a veteran of the invasions of Sicily, Salerno, and Normandy. Coakley told of his own personal experiences and of the important part played by LST's in the invasion operations.

Lt. Drake introduced Mrs. E. L. Johnson, wife of Commander E. L. Johnson, U.S.N.R, supervisory cost inspector of the Ninth Naval District, who sponsored the ship. Lt. Drake is the officer in charge of contracts and payments for the supervisor of shipbuilding, Chicago, and served as a second lieutenant during World War I.

Lt. Ruben H. O'Neal, combat skipper of LST 647, along with his officers, witnessed the launching.

The award of the Army-Navy "E" pennant on June 12, 1943, was an impressive occasion. The Navy had awarded "E's" to ships and crews for some years, in recognition of excellence; and with the coming of war the same awards were extended to war plants. The requirements for the award of the Army-Navy "E" were: the quality and quantity of production must be excellent; there should be no work stoppages, and fair labor standards must be maintained; effective and efficient management must be demonstrated; there must be an efficient record on accidents, health, sanitation, and plant protection; a low rate of absenteeism must be shown. One of the obstacles to earlier receipt of the award at Seneca was absenteeism. This was considerably reduced in the month just before the award.

The ceremony was held in connection with a launching, and work was stopped at the yard for an hour.

Present for the occasion were Admiral C. L. Brand of the Navy, Major Howard C. Meadows of the Army, and President George T. Horton of the CBI Company. The invocation was offered by the Reverend Clyde McGee, pastor of the Bethany Union Church, Beverly Hills, Chicago. The ship was sponsored by Miss Katherine Trees, daughter of Merle J. Trees, executive vice-president of the Company. To give Miss Trees a few pointers on how to break the champagne bottle on the ship's bow, Mrs. Harriet Williamson was called to the stand in her welder's clothes. Mrs. Williamson had sponsored the first ship to be launched.

The acceptance speech for the award was made on behalf of the Company by President Horton, and on behalf of the employees by Joe Madura, Safety Director, who accepted the "E" pins to be worn by the workers. The "E" pennant was raised on the flagpole. The band played and the crowd sang "America."

Four stars were later added to the "E" pennant as four renewals of the award were made.

In addition to launchings and the "E" awards, there were

other morale-builders: high wages, a year-end bonus, and the LST Invasion Exposition to be described below. Another morale-builder was of a different kind, and was called out by the leakage of manpower away from Seneca after midsummer of 1944. Many workers were sensing the end of work at Seneca and were anxious to get back into jobs with better peacetime prospects. Alarmed at the numbers of workers who were quitting, Donald A. Leach, yard manager, sent a letter to all employees on the last Saturday in July entitled "Wanted —No Deserters." As published in the Ottawa *Republican Times* of July 31, the letter said, in part:

Conflicting statements made in the press and by radio have many of our employees disturbed about the future of this work. We still have seventy-four ships to deliver to the Navy for use in mopping up the Pacific. This program will go on until the middle of 1945.

Quoting from a letter just received, from Ralph A. Bard, undersecretary of the Navy:

"Our battle of production will end only with the defeat of Japan. This means that for the next year the Navy must rely upon the civilian employees of its own naval establishment and upon the workers in the private plants and shipyards of Navy suppliers throughout the country to keep our Pacific operations going at top speed; as we approach nearer and nearer Japan, the tempo will increase and the necessity for more and more supplies available at the proper place and time will become more and more vital to our success. The Navy depends on you—we know you will not fail."

Our sons will fight the enemy in the Pacific. They will not quit until he is defeated. We must have LST's to supply these boys with all the necessities for making successful invasions. They must be supplied long after the war ends to hold what we take. Don't let down your sons in the armed forces. Stay on the job at Seneca until the last ship is built. This means employment for you until the middle of next year.

Don't be a deserter.

Waste of manpower? There was talk in and about Seneca of wastage of manpower at the shipyard, just as there was talk of this kind in the neighborhood of most war industries. No comparative judgment can be made, since data are lacking on the amount of loafing and the amount of superfluous labor at Seneca as well as other plants. That there was a good deal of loafing on the job is certain, though the stories that were current in Seneca were probably greatly exaggerated. Whether there was also a certain amount of hoarding of excess labor by the Company is not certain. Probably all war plants that, like the Seneca shipyard, were operating on a cost-plus fee basis with the government employed more workers than they absolutely needed. This insured them against undersupply of workers if Selective Service should suddenly increase its demands; and it also helped them meet the demand for speedier production. The extra workers cost them nothing, since the cost was paid by the government.

In this respect, the war-production companies were probably no worse than the military services, which notoriously hoarded manpower in excess of their immediate needs. While there is no basis for judgment of the CBI record on the use of manpower, it may be fair to point out that industrial executives who had been used to judging themselves and their colleagues in terms of their efficiency of production—the smallest possible cost in labor and materials—would probably tend to carry on these habits for a time, at least. This factor probably operated at CBI, as elsewhere, to counteract the temptation to hire superfluous workers.

No doubt a certain amount of idleness would be inevitable in a production operation characterized by the task system. For a time, at least, the schedule would inevitably leave some task crews with little to do for a few hours while their predecessors were finishing a job. The wrinkles in any production process are erased slowly, and any unexpected change of one sort or another, such as a shortage of some material, can play havoc with the schedule. Anyone who has worked in a mass production plant knows that delays of this sort occur in the best-managed factories—but the people of a rural and semi-industrial area are less familiar with such situations, and would be quick to criticize.

In similar fashion, work on the night shift was reputed to be easier than work on the day shift, allowing opportunities for a nap. The following conversation, for example, might give rise to unpleasant stories. It took place between two young men workers on the night shift, as they were riding to work on a bus. Bill was telling Jim how sleepy he was.

"Well, anyway, it's a short week—and a good one for pay. I'm taking in about $90 this week, what with overtime for Thanksgiving. Paid my union dues today for the month, $3.50. Trouble with making all this money is, a man don't get no chance to spend it. Two, three beers, that's about all. You've got to sleep. I didn't this morning though. I got up early and went to the fire. I didn't sleep much of any today. God, but I'm sleepy. Hope they haven't laid out much work for tonight. Guess not, being Monday. Saturday night they'll be crowding us hard, but Thursday I slept two, three hours. Finally the guard called me. He said, 'It's half-past two. Thought you'd want to be called by this time!'" (Jim spoke up about his dislike of his job, and how his stomach bothered him when he worked at night.) Bill replied, "Well, now, a night job's got it all over a daytime job when you come to that. You get out of all that racket, it's quiet at night, and it ain't so hot in summer neither, and it pays better than a daytime job."

The stories that went around finally aroused the Putnam County Taxpayers Association in Granville, a town to the north of Seneca. Hearing that manpower was being wasted at the shipyard, this association prepared to write to the Senate Investigating Committee, headed by Senator Truman in Washington, requesting an investigation. In this plan they were at first encouraged by a reporter for the *Chicago Tribune* who came to Granville to confer with them. The story from that point on is told in the following news report, which appeared in the *Putnam County Record* for March 23, 1944:

Last week the *Record* stated that the Putnam County Taxpayers Association was interesting itself in reports of waste of manpower in the Seneca shipyards and that a letter was sent to the Truman Committee requesting an investigation. It was also stated that a *Chicago Tribune* reporter had been in conference with the association directors and had obtained material for a story on the situation.

The letter mentioned was written but when the reporter reached his office in Chicago he telephoned the association president, Joel W. Hopkins, requesting that the letter be held until he could return to Granville and meet with the directors of the association.

In conference Friday afternoon, George Hartman of the *Tribune* revealed that after leaving Granville Wednesday night he spent the next day with the plant officials at Seneca to have both sides of the story and when he returned to Chicago, Navy officials were waiting to discuss the subject with him. His conclusion was that no story should be published.

An invitation extended by the officials of the Chicago Bridge and Iron Co., operators of the shipyard for the Navy, was accepted by the directors of the taxpayers' association to visit the plant Tuesday and discuss the matter with them.

Accompanying Hopkins Tuesday morning were H. E. Hutton, Magnolia; Chas. B. Robinson, Joel H. Whitaker, the *Record* publisher, Granville; and a LaSalle *Post-Tribune* reporter, who met the Chicago reporter and Lyle Barton, tax investigator, of Galesburg, in Seneca. C. O. Read of Senachwine Township and Thos. W. Dore of Hennepin were unable to accompany the other three directors.

The reasons for the interest shown by the taxpayers were explained to the company officials and Navy representative by Mr.

Hopkins. It was agreed that a trip through the yards should be made before any discussion was held and for the next six hours the visitors were shown the works.

It has been remarked that the visitors would be shown just what the management would want them to see, but take it from this reporter that was not the case. If there was any part of the plant that wasn't wide open for inspection it wasn't the officials' nor the Navy's fault. The warehouses, machine shops, boats in all phases of construction, including those in the river almost ready for sailing, were everything but given to the Putnam County men for souvenirs.

Late in the afternoon the discussion took place in Vice-President Pillsbury's office and the taxpayers expressed their conviction that there is a waste of manpower and taxpayers' money in the shipyard. The management agreed. Commander Goen agreed and they explained the causes; some of the circumstances were beyond their control. However, it was also explained that by May 1 the shipyard will be so much more efficiently operated that the local group is invited to return and check again at that time.

Chairman Hopkins was quoted in the Ottawa *Republican Times* of March 22, 1944, as follows, concerning what his group had seen and heard:

"There were times when we turned corners and men leaped to their feet as if they had been resting," Hopkins said. "We found men sleeping, but I understand they had gone to sleep on their lunch hour. In most cases where we found men idle we were told they were waiting on the crews working ahead of them—waiting for one crew to finish the job so the next crew could get to work. Can't that lag be eliminated?"

"I think you'll understand that lag better when you realize that there are 300 tasks to be performed in building each ship," Pillsbury explained. "Each task is performed by one or more small crews that normally work on one ship and then move to the next. The advantage of this system is that inexperienced workers learn

Landing ship group lays down a spectacular smoke screen in Cadet-Midshipman training operations.

Official U. S. Navy Photograph

The Seneca shipyard

Aerial Photo Service

projects, from the air.

to do their specific tasks skilfully with a minimum of training. Tasks can be upset by delayed material and equipment and by changes in design found necessary through battle experience. When one task is upset it delays others."

"Well, we don't want the plant to get a bad name, and we feel something should be done to inspire the workers to greater effort. If they are lax they definitely delay winning the war," said Hopkins, and Robinson suggested incentive payments to induce greater effort.

Hines said the incentive system already was in use to some extent, but that to make it function completely would require a good deal of research and planning.

"Well, couldn't you cut down the size of some of the crews and have fewer men do more work?" asked Whitaker, and Goen said that step had been ordered by the Navy two weeks ago.

"We've put each crew in the position of making it cry for more help," added Hines. "Some crews have all they can handle at all times, but we're forcing each to get along with as few men as possible. We are trying to have the men and women do today in four days what they formerly did in six."

Goen explained there had been an upturn in idleness in the yard last summer when sufficient material could not be obtained.

"But now we are getting sufficient supplies in all categories and we are turning out boats faster than ever," Pillsbury interjected. "If we get the additional 2,700 more workers, we can easily turn out a boat every four days. And that's what the Navy wants."

One fact of considerable significance is that there was a steady reduction in the number of hours' labor required for construction of each ship, thus indicating an increasing efficiency of the production process. This is shown in Figure 6. The first ship required 875,000 man-hours of labor. Of this total, 550,000 man-hours were required in direct labor on the ship, and another 325,000 man-hours were needed for other labor incidental to the operation of the shipyard. Eventually the total man-hour cost was brought down to 270,000, and the direct man-hour cost to 170,000—less than a third of the original man-hour cost.

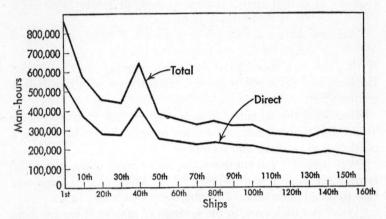

Fig. 6. Direct and Total Man-hour Cost of Ships at Seneca.

RECRUITING MANPOWER

One reason for locating the shipyard in Seneca was the presence of a substantial number of workers within the commuting radius of thirty-five miles. It was expected that the bulk of the workers would live in the cities and villages in this area, with a relatively small proportion migrating into Seneca and living there.

The village of Seneca could supply relatively few workers, since the two local industries—the John I. Hay Company and the Seneca works of the Dupont Company—would undoubtedly carry on and even expand their operations.[3] But in the nearby cities of Ottawa, LaSalle, Peru, Marseilles, and Spring Valley, there were 2,750 men registered on the active files of the U. S. Employment Service as available for work. Other

[3] The Hay Barge Plant took a barge-building contract from the government and stepped up its employment from 60 to 260 people. The Dupont Dynamite Plant increased employment from 150 to 240 during the boom.

small cities within commuting distance were Streator, Morris, and Pontiac. It seemed reasonable to suppose that five thousand workers could be obtained, some four thousand to come from the area around Seneca and the other thousand to migrate into Seneca from greater distances. The figure of five thousand itself was generally thought to be an overestimate of the need for workers in the shipyard. Privately, government officials and others who were in a position to make an informed guess said that the number of employees might go to thirty-five hundred.

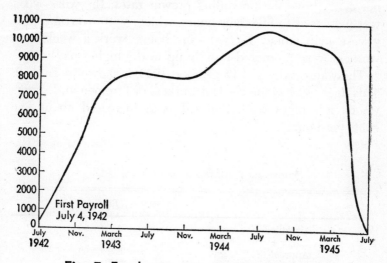

Fig. 7. Employment in Seneca Shipyard.

But everybody was underestimating. Eight months after shipbuilding began the employment total reached nine thousand. The number fluctuated about this figure for a year, and then rose to a maximum of 10,600 in the summer of 1944. With this labor force, the yard launched a ship every four days during a peak production period of fourteen months.

The recruiting of a large labor force was a new problem to

the Chicago Bridge and Iron Company. This company before the war employed about five thousand people in all its plants. This number expanded to 23,000 at the wartime peak in 1944, with over 10,000 in Seneca. In all of the Seneca shipyard, including management and clerical staff, there were only 265 people who had worked for CBI before the war. Consequently, the recruiting and training of manpower were major tasks for the Company.

Wage rates. To recruit workers for the shipyard, a high wage scale was established. Hourly rates were set about 50 per cent above the prevailing prewar rates; the work week was increased to fifty-four hours, which, with overtime pay, gave a man money for sixty-one hours' work a week; and workers were promoted rapidly up to the higher pay rates.

The wage scale as of December, 1943, is shown in Table 2. This does not include clerical workers or foremen and supervisors. For night work the scale was increased about five cents per hour.

TABLE 2

SHIPYARD WAGE SCALE, DECEMBER, 1943

Level	Rate per hour
Unskilled	$ .83
Laborer	.88
Apprentice	.93
Helper	1.00
Craftsman (mechanic)	1.20

The shipyard kept going twenty-four hours a day, including holidays and sometimes Sundays. For work on Sundays and holidays the pay rate was twice the regular rate. When there was a special drive for production, as in May, 1944, most employees worked seventy hours a week, including Sunday, thus getting paid for eighty-five to one hundred hours.

There was also an incentive pay plan in certain departments, which permitted a man to earn even higher wages by faster work.

Other recruiting methods. In addition to paying attractive wages, the CBI did several other things to recruit workers. They advertised extensively in all the newspapers of the surrounding territory. They sent representatives to two places in the South where oil refineries were being closed down. They sent a representative to southern Illinois to recruit miners at the beginning of the seasonal shutdown period. In all these cases they carried on their recruiting under the supervision of the War Manpower Commission. They also paid the travel expenses of incoming workers.

A device used partly for recruiting new workers and partly for building the morale of old workers was the LST Invasion Exposition. Sponsored by the U. S. Navy and the CBI Company, this exhibition was shown in Ottawa, LaSalle, Streator, Morris, Marseilles, and Seneca in April and May, 1944. It included a band, and was usually featured by a parade made up of patriotic organizations. At the Exposition there were exhibits connected with the building of an LST; and there was always a War Manpower Commission booth to show the necessity for more workers at the shipyard.

In October, 1944, a fully equipped LST was drawn up to the river shore at Ottawa and opened to some twenty-five thousand visitors. This ship, a veteran of the Normandy invasion, made a tour up and down the Ohio and Mississippi rivers.

A great deal of the training of workers was done in the shipyard and on the job. But the craft of welding (approximately one worker in eight was a welder) required special training. Courses in welding were instituted in the high schools of Ottawa, LaSalle, and Streator, the government paying the cost. From these classes the trainees went into a

Welding School at the shipyard, also subsidized by the government.

Most new workers went directly into a training program in the shipyard where they started as "apprentices" in a crew where they could learn from the more experienced hands.[4] Apprentices who showed aptitude were soon advanced to the level of "helper," where they did more advanced work. If they continued to improve their work, they became "mechanics," a general title for welders, fitters, electricians, scalers, shorers, and so on. In the early days, when the labor force was expanding most rapidly, a man with average ability could move from apprentice to helper to mechanic in three to six months. Later on when employment reached its peak and turnover was not high, advancement was much slower.

As shown in Figure 7, the number of workers employed by the CBI Company at the shipyard hovered about the 8,500 mark during most of 1943, and then was forced up to a peak of 10,600 in June of 1944. It then fell somewhat until autumn, and remained fairly constant around 9,500 until March, 1945, when demobilization began at the shipyard. The increase in 1944 was caused by the urgent need for LST's, which were being given a high priority by the Navy. The schedule of production was increased at this time from one ship a week to one every four days. This schedule was maintained for the following year, despite the fact that the working force decreased by nearly a thousand. The high rate of production was maintained in spite of the decrease of manpower partly because of increased efficiency, and partly because the work that was started during the period of maximum employment resulted in ships that were launched after employment had fallen off.

Women were employed in the yard as well as in the office.

[4] For job classifications of shipyard workers, see Table 22 in Appendix A.

The presence of women workers was dramatized by the choice of a woman welder to launch the first ship. A course to train women as welders was conducted experimentally in the Ottawa High School, and it succeeded well enough to be repeated. However, very few women were promoted to the status of "mechanic." They were usually assigned as helpers to men.

There were eighty-two women employed as yard workers in April, 1943; this number increased to the point where there were over a thousand in August, 1944. The proportion of women to men in yard work eventually reached about one to eight. (The number of women employed as office workers increased from 228 to 409 in the same period.)

In addition to the employees of the Chicago Bridge and Iron Company, there were three small groups of people working in the shipyard. The U. S. Coast Guard kept a force of men in Seneca during the early part of the boom to guard the shipyard, and, when necessary, to preserve order, direct traffic, and otherwise keep things moving. The United States Navy had a small body of military and civilian personnel at work inspecting ships and preparing reports. The cafeteria, which served an average of six thousand meals a day, was operated on a concession by an outside catering firm with its own group of workers.

Labor turnover. Labor turnover was considerable, especially during the early part of the boom. At that time employees were being drafted into military service in considerable numbers [5] and there was also some turnover due to the fact that new workers were trying out the shipyard and being tried out in turn. All in all, some twenty-seven thousand people were hired, to maintain a labor force that averaged about nine thousand. Compared with other war industries, this may

[5] By March, 1943, the number of former Seneca employees in military service was 350.

not have been a high rate of turnover. The stories that were current about turnover at West Coast shipyards would indicate that their labor force was less stable. For example, a story went the rounds about the Portland, Oregon, situation. It said that three men had to be hired for every job—one was just quitting, another was on the job, and a third was being hired to take the second man's place.

Whether or not labor turnover in Seneca was better or worse than elsewhere, it posed a serious problem. There was need of an agency to supervise the process and to take steps to keep the labor supply adequate. Consequently, there was created a Manning and Replacement Board, which was a joint project of the CBI Company, the War Manpower Commission, and the Selective Service System. This board compiled information on the effect of Selective Service on the manpower problem in the shipyard. The board regulated the numbers being taken by the military draft so that the production of ships would not be curtailed.

Another factor that decreased turnover was the employment stabilization plan introduced by the War Manpower Commission in the Seneca area in October, 1943. This was an order prohibiting a man who quit a job in "essential" industry from being rehired by another company within sixty days, unless he had been given a release by his previous employer or by the Manpower Commission.

A third factor tending to hold workers on the job was the annual bonus, paid at Christmas to employees who had been working for the company for at least six months. This bonus amounted to approximately 5 per cent of the annual wage, and ran from $150 to $250 for most people. The effect of the bonus was probably shown in the fact that the fall in employment from 10,600 in June, 1944, to about 9,800 in October was arrested at that time, and employment held approximately constant until after the bonus was paid.

The Men Who Built the Ships

The great majority of the workers came from Illinois. In June, 1943, when 8,500 people were employed, 89 per cent came from Illinois and no other state furnished as many as 2 per cent.[6] While there were more out-of-state people among those hired in the later period, this could hardly have reduced the proportion coming from Illinois by more than a few per cent.

TABLE 3

FORMER OCCUPATIONS OF SHIPYARD WORKERS

(Working force of June, 1943)

Former Occupation	Per Cent of Working Force
Professional workers; e.g., engineers, teachers, physicians, nurses	4
Skilled workmen whose skills could be used directly in the shipyard	23
Skilled and semi-skilled workmen who would have to adapt themselves to shipyard work; e.g., machine operators, cement workers, glassworkers	14
General construction workers	11
Clerical workers; e.g., stenographers, clerks, bookkeepers	13
Service workers; e.g., storekeepers, waitresses, service-station operators	7
Farmers	4
Security workers; e.g., guards, firemen	4
Unskilled workers	17
Miscellaneous	3

The occupations of the shipyard workers before they came to Seneca are shown in Table 3. One-fourth of the workers when they came had well-developed skills that they could immediately employ on their jobs in the shipyard. For exam-

[6] These data on the characteristics of workers are based upon a tabulation of every fifth card in the files of the personnel office at the shipyard, made on June 22, 1943.

ple, about three hundred and fifty experienced welders and about two hundred and fifty electricians who had been trained before the war were on the payroll in June, 1943. About three-quarters of the workers had to be trained for their jobs at the shipyard.

The mean age of the workers, in June, 1943, was 37, and the range was 16 to 74. Thirty-one per cent were under 30. The average age of the working force increased as time went on, because more and more of the younger men were taken into military service. Eighty per cent of the employees were married, and the average number of children per family was 1.6.

In terms of education, shipyard workers varied to the extent that is typical of the American population: 47 per cent of those on the payroll in June, 1943, had not gone beyond the eighth grade in school; 24 per cent had some high school work; 21 per cent had graduated from high school but not gone farther; 8 per cent had gone to college; and 1 per cent had pursued graduate work beyond the college level.

Those who did not already live within commuting distance of Seneca found places to live within this area. The residence of workers in June, 1943, is shown in Table 4.

Ottawa had more shipyard workers than Seneca. Every city and village within thirty-five miles had its vacant houses filled with Seneca workers. Large old houses were remodeled into apartments. Trailer parks appeared in all the nearby towns and individual trailers were located in back yards.

Most workers came to the shipyard by automobile. In late 1943, some sixty-eight hundred people came to work every day by automobile, and several hundred more by bus. The parking lots at the shipyard accommodated twenty-five hundred automobiles. In a car-occupancy study for a typical twenty-four-hour period there were 1,977 vehicles with an average of 3.41 persons and a total occupancy of 6,730.

TABLE 4

RESIDENCE OF SHIPYARD WORKERS (JUNE, 1943)

City	Number
Ottawa	1,900
Seneca	1,500
Marseilles	700
Streator	660
LaSalle	630
Morris	400
Peru	340
Spring Valley	230
Pontiac	170
Oglesby	150
Others	1,800
Total	8,480

The company maintained a Transportation Department, which, among other functions, arranged ride-sharing clubs and issued gasoline coupons and tire certificates. The issuance of rationing coupons was made possible by a plant area rationing board set up by the Office of Price Administration. This board issued rationing certificates just sufficient to provide automobile transportation to and from work.

THE JOB IS FINISHED

And so the LST's came out of the heart of the continent. Iron ore from Minnesota, coal from Kentucky, limestone from Indiana; all cooked up in a South Chicago blast furnace, boiled into steel in the open hearth, stamped and beaten and rolled into plates in the rolling mill; then shaped and welded into ship parts in Chicago; loaded onto freight cars and hauled on the Rock Island Railroad to Seneca; fastened together by corn-belt men and women and launched into the Illinois River.

Once a week or oftener, a new blue-gray LST, without name except for the number painted on her bow, had left the dock at Seneca and started silently downstream. She slipped by Starved Rock, which stands lofty and somber over the river. In a few hours she had sighted the bridges and factories of busy Peoria and Pekin, and moved into the quiet lower reaches of the Illinois, past the sleepy river towns of Havana and Beardstown and on to the Mississippi. Then she picked up speed and drove past the river cities, St. Louis, Cairo, Memphis, Vicksburg, Natchez, Baton Rouge, and New Orleans. Then out over the western or eastern oceans, to the South Sea Islands, Okinawa, Sicily, or the beaches of Normandy.

One March day in 1945, the last hull was laid. As each task crew finished its job, the men were laid off. Officials of the U. S. Employment Service set up an office in the shipyard to interview the men as they left, to direct them to other war industry centers, and to give them a notice of release that would permit them to take war jobs elsewhere.

The last launching was on June 8. The last big crowd filled the parking area with their automobiles and surrounded the launching ways with dust and color. Standing high on the ways above, surrounded by empty berths and idle machinery, the last LST seemed larger than those that had gone before. Mrs. Al Kline, wife of the superintendent of electrical maintenance, broke a bottle of domestic champagne against the ship's bow, and for the 157th and last time, there was a flash of silver foam, and the story of the shipyard was officially over. The fighting in Europe was finished. In the Pacific, the Japanese were on the run. This ship might never see battle.

Two weeks later, on Friday, June 22, this ship left the outfitting dock and started down the river. Some women and children of Seneca rose at 4:30 A.M., walked in the dawn to the bridge high over the river, and dropped flowers on the ship as she glided beneath them.

There were two hundred families left in the government housing projects on that day, and most of them were soon to go. A wild cottontail rabbit came from the cornfield beyond and took up residence under the steps of a shipyard building.

The job was finished.

PART II: THE ADJUSTMENT OF PEOPLE

3.

A Place To Live

If men were to build ships in Seneca, they would have to have houses for their families. They would not stay long on the job if their children were clamorous and their wives were dissatisfied. Thus the provision of tolerable housing conditions had high priority over other matters.

All the existing housing facilities were filled to overflowing in an area thirty-five miles surrounding Seneca. All vacant dwellings were filled up in the neighboring cities of Ottawa, LaSalle, Streator, Marseilles, Morris, Peru, Spring Valley, and Oglesby. Trailers appeared in back yards and in vacant lots in Seneca. Single houses were remodeled into multiple dwellings, and spare rooms were rented in all the surrounding towns. But after all available living space was occupied, still more was needed.

The need for new housing could not be met by private business. The practical certainty that shipbuilding in Seneca would be stopped after the war, together with wartime prices and restrictions on building materials, made the investment of private capital in new housing a hazardous if not impossible matter, and the only alternative was public housing.

The Federal Public Housing Authority was called on to supply the need. The FPHA built, in total, 1,467 family units and a dormitory for 300 men.[1] Made entirely of wood, these dwellings were expected to last ten to fifteen years. The aver-

[1] The FPHA also built housing projects in Ottawa, the county seat, for Seneca shipyard workers.

age cost was between three and four thousand dollars per family unit, and the units ranged in size from one room with kitchenette to a four-room dwelling. It was expensive housing, considering what the government received for its money; but speed, not cost, was the primary concern. The dormitory and the first family units in War Homes were housing war workers within sixty days of the beginning of construction. Construction workers were encouraged to do as much overtime work with overtime pay as they could. Anybody could hire on as a carpenter if he could drive a nail straight.

The first public housing in Seneca was a fleet of trailers of the Farm Security Administration. Although intended as temporary dwellings for construction workers, the trailers were kept in use, 225 of them, throughout the boom.

Late in June, 1942, the Federal Public Housing Authority completed its dormitories for 300 men. This was followed quickly by the War Homes apartments, whose 475 units were completed and filled during the summer and fall of 1942. Victory Court, consisting of 485 family units, was completed in the spring of 1943. A Trailer Park of 125 trailers was established near Victory Court in the summer of 1944, and Riverview Homes, with 380 family units, was opened in August, 1944.

In addition to the public housing projects, several private trailer camps grew up on the outskirts of Seneca; and seventy-five private trailers were located in back yards and vacant lots. Non-government trailers reached a peak number of about 190 early in 1943.

Many private homes provided space for roomers and a few were converted into rooming houses. The number of people cared for in this way was not very large and probably never exceeded 350.

Very few private homes in Seneca were remodeled into

apartments. This was probably due to the governmental control of rents, combined with the scarcity of labor in Seneca. Roomers were not crowded several into a room as they were in some other war industry centers. There were no "cothouses" in Seneca, with six or eight men sleeping in a room with two-deck and three-deck beds. The FPHA dormitories probably set a standard that Seneca residents with rooms to rent were constrained to equal.

Table 5 summarizes data on the dwelling units in Seneca.

TABLE 5

How People Were Housed
Autumn, 1944

Type of Housing	No. of Units
Public Housing	
Victory Court	485
War Homes	475
Riverview Homes	380
Government trailer parks	350
Dormitory rooms for single men	300
Private Housing	
Private homes	350
Trailers distributed individually	75
Kiner's Trailer Camp	43
Hollywood Trailers and Cottages	30
Thorson's Trailer Camp	12
Hay Trailer Park	30
Rooms for rent in private homes	350

THE PUBLIC HOUSING PROJECTS

The procedure in establishing public housing in Seneca was as follows: The Chicago Bridge and Iron Company and the United States Navy asked the War Manpower Commission for a certain number of workers in Seneca. The Manpower Commission called in the National Housing Agency to study ways and means of housing the new workers. The func-

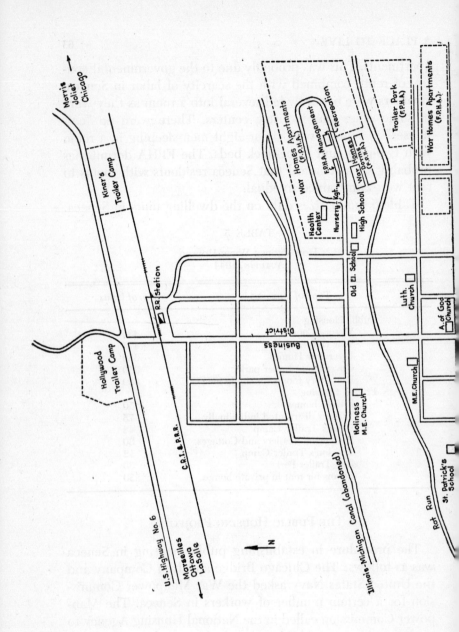

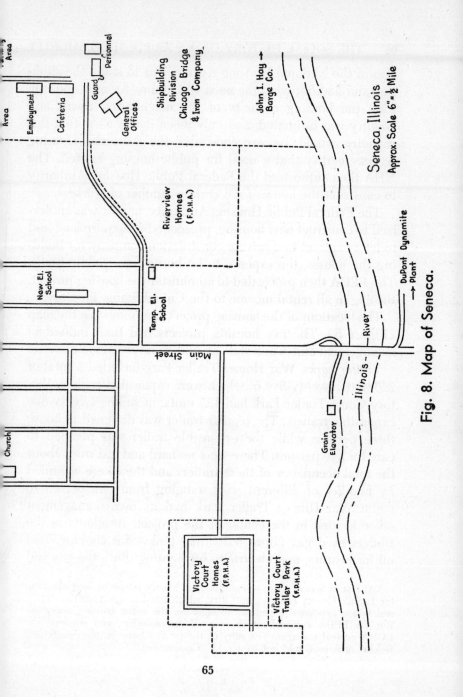

Fig. 8. Map of Seneca.

Seneca, Illinois
Approx. Scale 6" = ½ Mile

John I. Hay
Barge Co.

DuPont Dynamite
Plant

Shipbuilding
Division
Chicago Bridge
& Iron Company

Riverview Homes
(F.P.H.A.)

New El.
School

Temp. El.
School

Main Street

Grain
Elevator

River

Illinois

Church

Victory Court
Homes
(F.P.H.A.)

Victory Court
Trailer Park
(F.P.H.A.)

Area

Employment

Cafeteria

Guard

Personnel

General
Offices

65

tion of the National Housing Agency was to study the situation and find out what the need was, if any, for new housing. First the housing capacity of the neighboring towns and country was estimated, and only when it was clear that this capacity would be exceeded did the National Housing Agency certify that a need for public housing existed. The NHA then authorized the Federal Public Housing Authority to construct the houses for a certain number of workers.

The Federal Public Housing Authority, once it was authorized to construct new housing, proceeded to acquire land and to let a contract to a private construction company for building the houses, the expense to be borne from public funds. The FPHA then proceeded to administer the housing project, turning in all rental income to the United States Treasury.[2]

The locations of the housing projects are shown on the map (Figure 8). The five housing projects had their individual management offices and staff, all under one executive director.

Trailer parks. War Homes Trailer Park included a total of 225 units, twenty-five of which were expansible trailers. Victory Court Trailer Park had 125 units, including twenty-five expansible trailers. The regular trailer was designed to house three persons while the expansible trailer was planned to care for five persons. There were no hard and fast rules about the total occupancy of these trailers and they were occupied by families of different sizes, ranging from one person to eight. War Homes Trailer Park had its own management office located in the center of the project. Residents in the trailers used gas (from individual tanks) for cooking, fuel oil for heating, and electricity for lighting. Both the gas and

---

[2] At first in Seneca there was still another agency in the housing situation, the LaSalle County Housing Authority, which acted as agent for the FPHA, and which appointed a general manager for the entire housing operation. But the FPHA eventually took over all responsibility, and removed the LCHA general manager. The story of the conflict between the county and federal agencies is told in Chapter 13, "Government."

fuel oil were bought by the worker, but the electricity, bulbs, and fuses were furnished by FPHA. Toilet facilities for the War Homes trailer residents consisted of twelve community centers. Two large trailers were set up for laundry purposes.

Though not always filled to capacity, the trailer parks had many long-term residents who preferred the privacy of a separate establishment to the thinly-partitioned apartments of the housing projects.

Dormitories: There were four dormitory buildings, housing a total of 300 men. Each resident had a private room, which was furnished with bed, bedding and linen, chair, chest of drawers, mirror, floor lamp, and closet space with a shelf. Each dormitory room had two half windows. There were central lounge rooms and central bathrooms in each dormitory building. Heat was provided from central hot-air heating units, and each individual room had a heat control device. The hot-air ducts were used as a cooling system in the summer. Maid service was provided. Only single men and men who were living away from their families lived in the dormitories.

War Homes: Seneca War Homes consisted of twenty-two separate buildings containing a total of 475 apartments. Each building had a central hot-air heating plant with each apartment equipped with heat control units. Each building was provided with a central lounge. However, these lounges were not used as much as was anticipated, and most of them were later converted into apartment units. The apartments were one and two rooms in size and were furnished. A single central administration office served the entire War Homes area, including the dormitories.

On the evening of her first day at the project, a woman described her War Homes apartment as follows:

The movable furnishings of the apartment were listed on a sheet of paper and are as follows: one chest with four drawers, one large table, two chairs, one floor lamp with shade, one mirror, one two-burner hot plate, one asbestos pad 24x24 inches, one large icebox, one sink stopper, one lavatory stopper, one medicine cabinet, two soap dishes, one shower curtain, one towel bar, one toilet-paper holder, five clothes hooks, two window shades, one clothes rod, two light bulbs, one wastebasket, one ash tray, two maple beds, two mattresses, two bed pads, two pillows, one ash tray. We have two curtain rods that are not listed.

Since we have now tried the furniture we can speak with authority regarding its comfort. The two chairs are dining-room chairs with arms. The bed springs are like cot springs and the bed has two extra legs in the center to keep it from swaying. The mattresses are cotton, the bed pads have shrunk so they lack a foot of covering the mattresses each way. The beds are hard and unyielding.

The electric plate is two-burner and dirty. It must have received very hard use. The former occupant of this apartment told me that she took her own plates with her. I cleaned the icebox today. It is lined with wood, and has wooden shelves. Since we have an apartment which was really planned for a two-room, we have a larger box than the other one-room apartments have. The icebox walls are about an inch thick and sound hollow when tapped. We can't get ice until tomorrow so I don't know its capacity. The icebox is placed in the farthest corner from the door so the iceman has to cross the complete length of the apartment. The cabinet contains four open shelves over the sink and stove; one drawer, two closed shelves and three open shelves, below. Former tenants built two shelves over the icebox. The sink is a deep one and the working surface on the side is already warped and cracked. The floors are stained, but look as if they have been stained over dirt. Neither cupboard nor floor was sanded before finishing. The floor boards are already spreading and quarter-inch cracks before the sink are common.

The clothes closet is merely an alcove with a shelf, clothes poles, and hooks. The entire front is open to the living room. We plan a curtain for it. The only feature that shows any intelligent planning is the kitchen cabinet. I swept the porch after it stopped raining. Porch floor is laid with one-half inch spaces between the boards. It looked as if water drained under the porch. One wonders about the mosquitoes this summer with such a good breeding place close at hand. Despite the chilly weather the apartment is warm. The furnace is on and we have plenty of hot water. Our first night is a quiet one; both neighbors went to bed early. Now the stillness is almost unbelievable.

Victory Court: Victory Court was a project of houses rather than apartments. The long flat-topped buildings were composed of joined units, each with its own coal heating stove and gas cooking stove. Units varied in size from no bedroom to two bedrooms. They were rented either furnished or unfurnished. Since Victory Court was some distance from the shipyard and the village, bus service was provided to carry workers to the plant and children to the schools. There was a central administration office with a recreation room and a nursery school.

Riverview Homes: Riverview Homes was built last and best of the housing projects. Its buildings were smaller and less barracklike than those in the other projects. There were two or three units to a building, with one, two, or three bedrooms per unit. Instead of standing in long, flat-topped rows, the Riverview Homes faced in all four directions, and looked somewhat like a bungalow suburb of a city. They had sloping roofs, with varicolored composition covering. Paved roads and cement sidewalks replaced the mud and gravel roads and wooden sidewalks of the other projects. Heating and cooking arrangements were similar to those of Victory Court. Riverview's 380 units were never fully occupied, for the end of the boom was in sight when the project was finished.

The rentals in the housing projects were modest, in line with those prevailing in public housing projects in other parts of the country. The single men in the dormitories paid $20.00 a month; unfurnished apartments ranged from $24.50

to $30.50, depending upon the number of rooms; and furnished units ranged from $26.50 to $41.25.[3]

TABLE 6

TURNOVER OF RESIDENTS IN HOUSING PROJECTS,
AUGUST, 1944

Project	No. of Families in Residence	No. of Families Who Had Moved Out of Housing Projects	Total No. of Families
War Homes (dormitories and apartments)	773[*]	1,563	2,336
Trailer Park	192	595	787
Victory Court (apartments and trailers)	598	494	1,092
Riverview Homes	9	—	9
Totals	1,572	2,652	4,224

* Includes the single men residing in dormitories.

Transiency. Table 6 gives information on turnover in the housing projects up to August, 1944. When a family left the housing projects, its record card was removed to an inactive file. If, however, the family moved from one housing project to another, its record card was simply moved from one active file to another. The turnover was greatest in Trailer Park, with three families gone for each family in residence there. War Homes also had a large turnover, though a great deal of this was probably due to turnover among the single men in the dormitories. Victory Court, which was opened later than

[3] For more detailed information regarding distribution of living quarters, capacity and occupancy, and rentals in the government housing projects, see Appendix A, Tables 23, 24, 25, and Figure 17.

the other two projects, had the least turnover, although even here almost as many people had left the project as were residing there, and the average length of residence there was about nine months, while the project had been open eighteen months.

Life in the Housing Projects

The course of events did not run altogether smoothly for residents of the housing projects, especially in the first year. There was constant friction between local, federal, and CBI housing agencies, and there was rapid turnover of housing management personnel. Tenants took up their problems with housing management, with CBI personnel, and frequently with both. At first there was little confidence in management officials, and there was much confusion and irritation over questions of authority.

The first year. In addition, there were the usual difficulties of getting a new project started under emergency conditions. Most of the tenants were quite unused to the communal type of housing; they were accustomed to dealing with an individual landlord rather than with a business office; they were not used to living in furnished quarters, and most of the women lacked their accustomed type of cooking facilities. Complaints came thick and fast.

The weather added to the frustration of tenants and to the confusion of management. Fall and winter were wet at first, then cold. Without paved streets or sidewalks, the approaches to the dwellings were stretches of mud and ice. The central heating plants in War Homes failed during the first cold spell. Water pipes froze. Stoves had to be secured for every dwelling unit while the central heating plants were being reconstructed. Tenants blamed the management for all these inconveniences.

As an indication of tenants' attitudes, the following letter appeared in the June 25, 1943, issue of *Ship and Home,* a newspaper printed in Victory Court. The letter was occasioned by the feud then going on between local and federal housing agencies over the removal of Fred Bretz, the General Housing Manager; but the letter illustrates the more general types of complaints current among housing project residents:

With the cancellation of lease of the Seneca War Homes held by the LaSalle County Housing Authority at noon June 19th, by the Federal Public Housing Authority, the last semblance of democratic procedure vanished in so far as the tenants are concerned. Get ready neighbors. The day is near at hand when you must salute the totalitarian regime which now reigns at Victory Court.

We must gird ourselves to not again, even in private, mention the need of suitable cooking facilities. Scrub and rub ye women who sacrifice to "Speed Our Ships." Burn your buttox on that red hot baby of a stove especially designed for you by the great inventors and over-all planners of "F.P.H.A.—the supreme." Don't dare complain about the height of that perfectly appointed combination (sink). Get a box and reach in and wash the clothing your husband so carelessly soiled building tank landing ships to be used at Guadalcanal, Italy, France and the Low Countries.

Don't you dare tell a tenant your kitchen temperature is 120 degrees Fahrenheit. Your kitchen is cool. F.P.H.A. designed that pig pen hades affair and they cannot be wrong. If the walls of your toilet room fall away and the cracks become as windows and your modesty forces you to refrain from answering nature's call, hide away in the timber nearby and remember never let a criticism of the construction of these ideal little apartments pass your lips.

Many of the difficulties that arose stemmed from the fact that the housing projects were essentially an urban graft on rural stock. The projects consisted of apartments, row houses, and multiple-family dwellings—all city-type housing. Most of the people had lived in single-family dwellings, with at least four or five rooms and a yard. They were uprooted from their familiar surroundings and placed not only in cramped quarters but in new surroundings. If their neighbors were not agreeable, they were unable to move. Thus their adjustments were partly to new neighbors and strange living quarters, as well as to a landlord who did business through government regulations and red tape. The legal and fiscal requirements of the management, which were common to all federally operated projects, seemed alien and even frightening to the tenants.

There was, for example, the matter of leases; the management required every tenant to sign a lease. This was a new experience to most of the tenants, for leases are seldom used in the smaller cities, and almost never in the case of low-rent homes. The experience of signing a lease is unpleasant even to hardened city dwellers who have to do it every year. It seemed to many tenants that they were signing away all their rights.

The lease-signing situation in Seneca could hardly have been planned to arouse more concern than it did. Leases were not distributed for signing until the spring of 1943, after a hard winter in which the heating system had failed, the managers had been changed twice, and until after spring thaws had made a muddy mess out of the approaches to War Homes. Many workers were about ready to quit their jobs and go somewhere else where living conditions might be better.

The lease itself was mild, as leases go. It did not bind the tenant to pay rent for more than two weeks after he had declared his intention of leaving. It granted the housing management the right to enter the premises to make repairs.

The affair of the lease came to a head in War Homes at the regular monthly meeting of the Tenants' Council on April 1,

1943. Reports were read on health, maintenance, recreation, religion, and victory gardens. The meeting went on in a perfunctory way, but there was tension in the air. Attendance was unusually large.

Finally someone from the floor asked about the lease. At this the chairman turned the meeting over to the manager of War Homes, Mr. Delaney, who, despite much heckling from the audience, managed to read the lease aloud. When he had finished reading, most of the discussion was devoted to the clauses permitting management to enter the premises at any time to make repairs; and requiring the tenants to give fifteen days' notice before moving out. The reasons for objecting were that possessions had been stolen, and that the shipyards could discharge a man without notice, and yet he would be held for fifteen days' rent.

Mr. Delaney replied that they never entered to make repairs without first finding out when the tenants would be at home; and the fifteen-day notice was amended by local management to two or three days. In the discussion, someone said that Mr. Delaney was the third manager, and the first to ask whether tenants would be at home before allowing workmen to enter. Therefore they had no assurance these policies would continue. An executive from the shipyard said that he hadn't even read his lease before signing it, and pointed to the CBI record of fair dealing and the importance of aiding the war effort. This failed to pacify the dissenters. Finally it was agreed to hold another meeting, with Mr. Bretz, the General Manager, present.

A few nights later the meeting was continued, with Mr. Bretz and the lawyer for the local housing authority present. Mr. Bretz began by reading the lease. He was continually interrupted by people with grievances. One man had his icebox raided by the man who came to fix the stove; another family was awakened by a workman coming to make repairs;

another lost some carpenter's tools. Someone wanted to know why they had to state their income on the housing blank.

Any attempt by Bretz to explain a point was answered by variations of the statement, "You're the third manager and there will soon be another one for us to deal with."

The affair of the leases finally died down and people signed them. It was certainly not entirely due to this distrust of leases by people not accustomed to them, for in Victory Court there were a series of tenants' meetings parallel to those at War Homes, and the subject of the lease was never mentioned. However, Victory Court had got off to a better start, had some strong local leadership, and changed managers only once.

There were other evidences that the bulk of the tenants felt hostile to the ideas of "planning" and "collective living," which they associated with urban housing projects. They were suspicious of the efforts of the Federal Public Housing Authority to promote community organization in the housing projects. They didn't want "social workers nosing into our lives." It is true that unfortunate staff selections helped to foster this kind of mistrust during the first few months. For example, a middle-aged social worker was placed on the staff who had hardly been outside of a large city. When first seen in Seneca by the authors, she was still trying to discover what direction Seneca was from Chicago. She was responsible for the assignment of quarters to new residents. It was about a year before a really able and diplomatic person was put in charge of the human relations aspect of housing management in Seneca.

Furthermore, the LaSalle County Housing Authority (the local housing agency) in its relations with FPHA exemplified the rift between provincial small-town America and cosmopolitan metropolitan America. A member of the LCHA gave evidence of this in his description of the first meeting between LCHA and representatives from FPHA. The FPHA brought an architect to Seneca to lay out the first housing project. As described by the LCHA member,

He was from New York. His name was Horowitz, or something like that. He met with us one evening. I can still see him standing there with his pipe in one hand and a dreamy look in his eyes. He said, "I've had a dream about Seneca. This is going to be a paradise on earth!" He dreamed it up on the sleeper on the way here, I guess.

Then the LCHA and other local people wagged their heads and said, "I told you so," when the first cold spell caused the heating units to fail. The local "experts" guessed that the architect was used to spending his winters in Florida and didn't understand the midwestern climate.

There were always rumors of Jews being at the bottom of the housing troubles. Often it was "Chicago Jews" or "New York Jews." On the staff of the housing project there were never more than two or three Jews; and only two important positions, that of "Management Aide," and that of manager of Victory Court, were held by Jews.

At the time of the conflict over Bretz' dismissal there was a great deal of anti-Jewish talk. At that time there was but one Jew on the staff of the housing projects, Miss Anne Loeb.

Anne Loeb was the "Management Aide" for the housing projects, and later she became Manager of the Riverview Housing Project. In her work as Management Aide she had special responsibility for the "human element" in the administration of the housing project. She promoted the development of clubs, recreational projects, child-care services, and helped to establish laundry, food services, canning centers, and other services that were needed by people brought for the first time into a small and crowded community.

Anne was a tall, straight young woman about thirty years old, college trained to be a teacher but never satisfied with the everyday type of teaching job. She burned to be of service somewhere. Although she presented a rather cool and starched surface to the world, underneath was a passionate drive to do something about the human problems which she discerned so clearly. She was a student always, and quick to observe the trouble spots in her neighborhood.

Since the ordinary work of teaching did not satisfy her, she took up the teaching of children with special difficulties in learning. When the war came, she went into government service and was assigned to Seneca. Immediately she began to read everything she could get on the subject of public housing. This was characteristic of her. She wanted to *understand* her job.

Anne Loeb was caught in the cross-fire of charges and counter-charges at the time of the conflict between FPHA and LCHA. Having been appointed by FPHA, she was naturally suspected by the LCHA group. Furthermore, being a Jew, she could be used in the complaints against "Jewish Management." The complaints against her were so bitter that she was on the point of being withdrawn from Seneca by the FHPA. But Florence Nichols, one of old Seneca's leading residents, hearing about the matter and feeling that Miss Loeb was being unfairly treated, went to see several influential people in Seneca and induced them to put in a good word for her. Florence said to the people she knew, "We're treating her just like Hitler would want us to treat the Jews." Anne was allowed to stay in Seneca, and eventually she won general approval from tenants and from administrators.

Anne Loeb had qualities which were needed in the administration of boom-town institutions. She was willing to work whatever hours were necessary. She was not upset by emergencies. In fact she rather expected the unexpected, and was stimulated by it. Her mind was quick and flexible, and adapted readily to new situations.

When Riverview Homes opened and she was made Manager, she had the prospect of a relatively easy time. Riverview Homes were the best-equipped and best-built of the housing projects. By then, life was going smoothly for housing residents, and people were almost content.

Things settle down. The conflict between local and federal housing agencies was finally settled when the federal agency, FPHA, took over the management of the projects and replaced the local man, Bretz, with an outsider, Herbert Brim, a tested and successful housing administrator. This move resulted in the gradual lessening of tenants' difficulties—a process due in large measure to the personal attributes of the new General Housing Manager.

Herbert Brim was Executive Director of the Seneca Housing Projects during the last two years of the boom. Before coming to Seneca he directed a public housing project in Indiana, and before that he was on the staff of the Farm Security Administration. In his young manhood he had been a community recreation director. From this work he went into the real estate business, and, with the coming of the depression and the New Deal, he entered the government service. Thus he had about a decade of government employment before he arrived in Seneca.

Herbert Brim came to Seneca when the housing projects were in a bad state. The three successive managers during the preceding nine months had been unable to satisfy either tenants, the FPHA officials, or the CBI officials.

The first effect of Brim's personality was to stabilize the situation. He seemed cool and competent. People decided to give him a chance. Though he never made close friends, due to his rather distant and cold manner, he quickly won the respect and trust of people. They believed that he wanted to do the right thing, and they soon found that he knew how to administer a housing project.

Thus he set things in order very shortly; and he gradually developed a smooth-working organization, where everybody knew his own responsibilities. Complaints gradually died down. Life began to go smoothly in the housing projects.

Another man might have quarreled with the heads of recreation, the schools, or with CBI management, particularly since the Housing Administration had been the scapegoat for all feelings of frustration and hostility in the community. But Brim kept his mouth closed and his eyes on his business, and avoided trouble. He did not try to make Seneca's housing projects "the best in the country." He seemed content to keep things running smoothly.

After a first year of confusion and frustration in housing, it was good to have things go smoothly. People lived more equably and even began to enjoy life in the housing project; yet none of them thought to thank Herbert Brim for it. He was competent but they had a right to expect competence. He knew how to administer a housing project but a good administrator doesn't make friends or become a popular hero, however important his job. He was merely one of the necessities for good adjustment in Seneca.

Creating community life. In addition to problems of management, and problems arising from what might be called rural-urban differences in attitudes, there were problems of adjustment between neighbor and neighbor.

War Homes had the most varied pattern of life of all the housing projects, because it had the most varied group of people. Almost all of the shipyard management people who lived in Seneca were in War Homes, with unskilled laborers living next door. Trailer Park residents, who used the War Homes recreation and nursery school facilities, were considered by many War Homes residents as "poor relations." And three hundred unmarried men or men without their families lived in the dormitories in the heart of the War Homes project.

The efforts of FPHA to promote a community feeling in the various housing projects met with indifferent success in War Homes. While a Tenants' Council was formed soon after the dwellings were occupied, the Council never functioned efficiently. A newsletter to keep tenants informed about their common interests and problems was undertaken, but was discontinued after the first issue.

The fact that the Tenants' Council was not successful in

War Homes (whereas the Council in Victory Court was generally considered a success) was probably both a cause and a result of the lack of community feeling or action in War Homes. The residents seem never to have thought of themselves as making up a single social group.

Mrs. Dawson was in the drugstore buying a copy of *Newsweek* when she spoke to the field worker: "I get so tired of knitting and reading," she said. "I tried for a while to be friendly with my neighbors, but I've just given it up. I've never known people who lived like that before. They beat their dog, and they beat their children, and they drink and gamble. They're just not my kind of people!"

Mrs. England told of her troubles with her next door neighbors on both sides, who drank and quarreled. About two o'clock one morning the quarreling and furniture throwing became so intense that Mrs. England's nerves gave way; she became hysterical; and her husband called a doctor. All of a sudden the room next door quieted.

Mr. England complained next day to the housing management, and was told that he would have to prefer charges against his neighbors. Then he asked some of his other neighbors if they would bear witness to the charges he specified. At first, they all agreed; but when it came to actually signing his paper of complaints, they declined. The affair was settled by management finding another apartment for the Englands.

A young married woman with no children, but with a little dog named Trixie, her husband a foreman, said, "I like it here just fine. Excuse the bare windows and furniture. All my curtains and spreads are in the wash. A woman right here in War Homes does my wash. She does it just fine."

It was the fact of such wide disparities in economic, social, and moral behavior that tended to prevent War Homes from being a successful community. With a few exceptions, the people even refused to think of themselves as members of a smaller community—such as one of the twenty-two blocks in War Homes. A few small social cliques were formed, each consisting of two to five families.

One exception to this general pattern was the formation of a social unit in the 200 block of War Homes, which became known as "Gold Coast Row." This block, closest to town and the most desirably located of the War Homes units, was set aside informally for CBI executives, who exerted pressure on FPHA when necessary to keep the block for executives only. This was contrary to FPHA policy, which would have assigned people to housing units in the order they came in, and in accord with the sizes of their families. Since the rents were the same in all parts of a project, there was no way by which people who thought of themselves as superior in status could get off by themselves, except by informally allocating certain space to themselves and keeping others out.

A friendly critic said to an FPHA representative, "There is just one thing in which I do not agree with you people in FPHA concerning housing. I think you should give some consideration to social status in location of people on the housing projects." What he meant was that, with no differentials in rents, and with people living in the same kind of housing regardless of income and social status, it would naturally be difficult for community feeling to spring up. One of the top local executives might live next door to an apprentice fitter. And really next door, with only a thin partition separating their living rooms, and a rail dividing their porch space. People with all kinds of social backgrounds were thus thrown into close contiguity. This gave people an excellent opportunity to discover that, after all, some kinds of people were good neighbors, regardless of their education or income, and other people were bad neighbors. Many people did discover this, and no doubt became more democratic in their social attitudes as a result of the experience. But in this kind of situation there was bound to be a great deal of standoffishness at first, while people eyed their neighbors, sniffed the odors of their cooking, listened to the language of their children, waited to hear the noise of domestic quarrels through the partitions, and watched to see how the garbage was disposed of.

One of the housing officials himself spoke of "the mistaken philosophy of housing planners that the personal and social life of the tenants in any housing project can be regulated by planning design. My experience has shown that neighbors will associate with each other intimately only as long as they do not find other residents of the community whom they prefer to accept as intimate friends. The longer a housing project operates, the more evident become groups or cliques who associate with each other because of similar common interests, habits, and standards."

The variation in social backgrounds of people in War Homes explains why they did not form many intimate social groups along neighborhood lines. Another thing that hindered the development of a true community was the incompetence of the housing management during the early and formative months, which resulted in the discouragement of the leaders in the Tenants' Council. Another factor working to prevent the development of civic activities was the tendency to think of War Homes as no more than a temporary dormitory. Since it was temporary, and since life was not too difficult, it was hardly worth while to make the effort necessary to get a civic organization functioning.

Victory Court was a marked contrast to War Homes in the development of community organization. An effective Tenants' Council sprang into existence early and continued to function throughout the life of the project; a Victory Court newspaper ran successfully during the first year; and a Con-

sumers' Cooperative was established.[4] The Victory Court
Tenants' Council started out with a number of committees—
Laundry Space, Recreation, Victory Gardens, Cooperative
Store, Health, Newspaper, Youth Council—and immediately
began to solve problems related to play space for children,
coal stoves' smoking, noise, garbage disposal, laundry space,
furniture, and recreation.

The fact that community organization worked fairly well
at Victory Court was probably due to the following facts:

1. The Tenants' Council was immediately successful in
clearing up some of the difficulties that plagued Victory
Court residents, such as inadequate cooking facilities, lack
of laundry equipment, and poor roads. Complaints and suggestions received immediate attention from housing management. This successful start gave the Council prestige with the
residents, and it was able to conduct more constructive
projects later on.

2. The management of Victory Court was better. The manager and his staff were able to work with the Tenants' Council and to steer the Council's activity into useful social and
recreational channels.

3. Victory Court residents were more largely families with
children, who had to spend more time at home and thus had
a stake in improving the social life of the local community.
The fact that Victory Court was a mile from town also worked
to keep people at home.

4. Victory Court residents had a smaller range of incomes
and social status than War Homes. Thus they were able to
participate more fully as a community of people with common interests.

5. The natural leaders in Victory Court could operate un-
hampered by the presence of people above them in social

[4] The Consumers' Cooperative is described in more detail in Chapter 8,
"Business."

status. None of the top twenty CBI and Navy executives lived in Victory Court. The absence of this top group left a group of skilled workers, foremen, and minor executives at the top in Victory Court; men who were able to assume and to exert leadership. Robert Maxwell was one of these people:

One of the pioneer families to enter Victory Court in the bleak and muddy March of 1943 was the Maxwell family. Robert Maxwell got a job as electrician at the shipyard, made a home for his wife and four children (the oldest was eight years old), and then immediately began to build a community.

Robert Maxwell liked people. He attended meetings, large and small, never failing to accept an invitation. He was "for" everything. He scattered his energies. Inside of six months he was President of Victory Court Tenants' Council, Business and Advertising Manager of *Ship and Home* (the Victory Court newspaper), Member of the Victory Court Recreation Committee, and Chairman of the Cooperative Store Committee. In addition, he operated the motion picture projector for a regular Sunday evening showing of pictures in the community hall.

Maxwell was an exception among working-class people in his liking for organization. He was thrown repeatedly into positions of leadership simply because others would not accept such responsibility. He was one of a small group of "little men" in Victory Court who assumed leadership in the absence of people of higher socio-economic status, such as those who lived on Gold Coast Row at War Homes.

While many of his neighbors were slightly suspicious of him because of his passion for organization, Maxwell became a well-liked figure. This is illustrated in the following anecdote:

In the winter of 1944-45, Robert cut his finger while at work. Infection set in, and he was seriously ill for some weeks. As Christmas approached his wife was busy nursing him, and feeling tired and worn out herself. She had no energy to prepare a Christmas celebration for her children. A few nights before Christmas there was a knock on the door, and the children were delighted to see a group of neighbors with a fully-decorated Christmas tree and a basket of gifts which they deposited in the Maxwells' living-room.

People of Maxwell's status in War Homes were over-shadowed by the executives, and, in their presence, could not function successfully as leaders. Yet the upper-middle-class group in War Homes—the CBI and Navy Executives—were too busy with a social life of their own and with their jobs to accept leadership responsibility.

Riverview Homes got off to the best start of all the housing projects. Dwellings were better designed; roads and side-walks were better; the project opened during warm, dry weather; management was good. In addition, some of the community leaders of Victory Court moved to Riverview Homes for larger quarters. However, the lifetime of River-view Homes was too short to permit complete and effective community organization.

This description of life in the housing projects has perhaps emphasized too much the lack of community organization and has slighted the very good situation in which most of the residents found themselves. Many families lived in clean houses with up-to-date equipment for the first time. While many of them must have missed the privacy of a single-family house with its play space for children, yet they all lived around a parklike space that was safe for children, well supervised and well equipped with game facilities. For the younger children the play and child-care facilities were far better than anything that could be found in the ordinary middle-class neighborhood of a city.

Facilities for group recreation for adults were also excellent. Each of the housing projects had a large social hall, and the men's recreation hall at War Homes was completed in the fall of 1943. Whenever a group of people could get to-gether around a common interest, there was plenty of oppor-tunity to enjoy social life.

Life in the housing projects had the potentiality of being very satisfactory. The physical necessities for a happy social life were adequately supplied. One has only to think of the alternatives for these war workers—living cooped up in a trailer in someone's back yard; renting a few rooms in a crowded, dirty tenement in a lower-class section of a neighboring town; renting part of a farmer's house—to realize that, with all their inadequacies, the housing projects still supplied a pretty good way of life.

LIFE IN THE PRIVATE TRAILERS

The two hundred workers who brought their own homes with them to Seneca presented a different situation. The private trailer, whether tied to a post in somebody's back yard or anchored with a fleet of others in a vacant lot, signified a way of life that was different from that in the housing projects— and different also from that in the government trailer parks that were attached to the housing projects. The family with their own house on wheels were resourceful wanderers, able to come and stay or come and go, not subject to the limitations that kept ordinary people close to home base.

In Seneca the trailer people were representative of the middle economic group of the population, foremen and skilled and semi-skilled workers. People less skillful and less provident could hardly pay for and keep up a trailer. The trailer people included some who had worked for CBI before, building oil and water tanks at other plants, and who thus had grown accustomed to a nomadic existence. These people found it easier and more pleasant to bring their houses with them than to hunt for temporary lodgings in each new town, lugging heavy baggage up the stairs of blowzy rooming houses. Living in a trailer "is like taking home along with you," they said.

The trailer dwellers of Seneca were some of them young and some of them middle-aged; some with children and some without. They and their kind in a thousand war industry centers worked a change in the age structure of America's trailer population—a population that had been before the war mainly elderly couples, retired from business, and out to see the country.

Their trailers were mostly of the factory-built type, some of them with conveniences to match an efficiency apartment in the city. With the latest in fluorescent lighting, electric cooking, refrigeration, and innerspring mattresses, they offered comforts that the housing projects of Seneca could not supply. Even the older factory-built models were no less well equipped than the average unit in the housing projects. Only a few of the trailers in Seneca were of the casual, homemade variety.

At Kiner's Trailer Camp in a shady place at the edge of town there were usually at least forty trailers. Here something of a community developed. The men organized two softball teams, and built horseshoe pits.

The other camps were smaller, closer to town, and had less community life. People in the trailers located singly or in twos merged into the working class of old Seneca; they seemed to have no special group characteristics and never appeared as a separate group in any reports or observations.

4.

Newcomers and Oldtimers

The population of Seneca grew rapidly beginning in the summer of 1942, and reached 5,000 within a year. Then growth continued more slowly for another year and a half, ending with a maximum of 6,600 in December, 1944. Table 7

TABLE 7

SENECA POPULATION ESTIMATES, 1942–45

Housing Areas	June 1942	March 1943	Aug. 1943	Dec. 1943	Aug. 1944	Dec. 1944	May 1945	Sept. 1945
Private:								
Houses........	1200	1400	1450	1500	1550	1550	1300	1200
Trailers........	......	500	550	550	550	500	225	10
Public:								
War Homes...	......	1180	1260	1260	1250	1330	750	160
Dormitories...	......	300	260	295	295	300	140	0
Trailer Park...	......	620	650	600	690	440	170	0
Victory Court..	......	270	990	1500	1575	1410	580	0
Victory Court Trailer Park.	......	......	......	......	260	10	0	0
Riverview Homes......	......	......	......	......	300	1050	670	0
Total.........	1200	4270	5160	5705	6470	6590	3835	1370

and Figure 9 show the population estimates at various dates. These estimates are based upon FPHA records of occupancy in the public housing projects; upon a questionnaire distributed in May, 1945, to residents in private houses in

Seneca; and upon several counts of the number of private trailers in Seneca. The estimates have been checked against the school census that was taken every August.

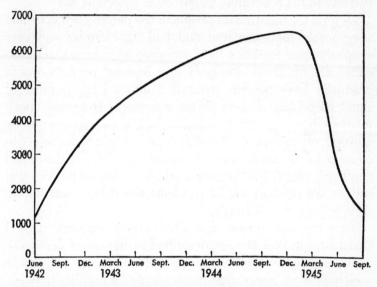

Fig. 9. Population Change in Seneca during the Boom.

SOCIAL CHARACTERISTICS OF THE NEWCOMERS

While many of the old-timers of Seneca spoke of the newcomers as "all those Southerners"—in some cases, as "that poor white trash from the South"—the fact was that the large majority of newcomers were Midwesterners. A study of the residents of the housing projects (who constituted four-fifths of all the newcomers) showed that about 70 per cent came from Illinois. Sixty-five per cent of the families came from distances of less than two hundred miles. Only about 15 per cent of the newcomers came from the southern states. (See Tables 26, 27, and 28 in Appendix A.)

The typical newcomer was a man from a small town in the Middle West, aged thirty-seven, who had worked at a variety of semi-skilled occupations, who was married and had one or two children. (See Tables 29 and 30 in Appendix A.)

Despite the fact that all people in the housing projects paid very nearly the same rent and had very similar and very simple housing facilities, there were considerable social differences among them. Probably the housing projects would gradually have become structured into a large number of small friendship clusters if free movement from one apartment or housing unit to another had been encouraged by housing management. But the management definitely discouraged this practice, which would have been a costly and confusing affair. Furthermore, when a housing project was full, as War Homes was almost from the start, it was impossible to move at all freely.

Thus the newcomers—with a few exceptions such as Gold Coast Row in War Homes, described earlier—were democratically jumbled in the housing projects. They did not choose their neighbors. Social class factors made for hostility between neighbors in some cases; for friendship between neighbors in other cases.

A lady from Chicago whose husband was a foreman said that she had tried to be friendly with her neighbors in War Homes, but "I'd not care if I never saw any of them again." She complained of their dirtiness. Many of them never lived with modern improvements before, she said. Their dogs were not housebroken and they ran over her porch. The people were cruel to animals and children. The little dog next door was beaten with a knotted rope by its owner when he was drunk. This lady had a good deal of free time and she had looked for work. Possessing no special skill, she found nothing available except cleaning work, and of course, she said, she could not think of doing such a menial kind of job.

In contrast there was the Hayes family. Mr. Hayes was an electrician. They brought furniture from their home in northern Illinois and made their two-room apartment quite comfortable. Finding their next-door neighbors very congenial, they opened the connecting door between their bedroom and that of their neighbors so that their two children and the two neighbor children might have four rooms in which to range.

A neighborhood clique of three families was formed in one of the blocks of War Homes. The men were skilled workers, rather individualistic and anti-union. All three families came from Illinois. One of the women said,

We ladies right in this neighborhood that are congenial, we have a little club. We often have our luncheon together. Or we play pinochle or bridge; or sew. Oh, it's been a wonderful experience here. I've learned so much about folks. Well, there's a little woman next door from Oklahoma. One of us ladies knocked; she called "Come in!"—and there she was, sitting in the sink undressed, ready to take her bath! She said she thought it was "just one of my friends" when she said to come in. It does seem to me there's more folks of that kind that are from the South. Mrs. R. and I tried to teach her, we could see she'd never had a chance to learn, but we couldn't get anywhere with her.

Was there any evidence of social structure on a broader scale among the newcomers? Was there a hierarchy with those at the top having the greatest social prestige; those at the bottom being thought of as worthless; and those in the middle recognizing the existence of people above and below them on the social scale? The evidence indicates that there was such a hierarchy, but the structure was not a rigidly stratified one.

A social class is defined as a group of people who participate intimately with one another, or would be willing to do so. They entertain one another and take their recreation together. They belong to the same clubs, churches, and other associations. They intermarry.

While there were social classes present among the newcomers, class lines were not so clearly marked as in older and more stable communities. Existence was too temporary in Seneca, too busy, and too much confused by boom-town conditions to permit the development of a stable set of social classes. Nevertheless, four social levels were easily discernible.

The "upper crust." The "upper crust" consisted of twenty-five or thirty families whose men were at the top of the shipyard hierarchy. Most of the men were college-educated, as were their wives. Several naval officers were in this group. Besides those who lived in the Gold Coast Row of War Homes, several bought or rented houses in Seneca or Ottawa. Their social life centered around the frequent launchings, when they entertained visitors from Chicago. The Boat Club in Ottawa was often the scene of their parties. The presence of naval officers set the tone for the social life of this group. To attain this level a man must have high status in the shipyard and his wife must have leisure and social skills. Harry Burnside was in this group.

Harry Burnside was as high in the shipyard hierarchy as any person living with his family in Seneca. He had a staff of twenty white-collar workers under him. Driving about in a large, late-model automobile, he was quite the "man about town." Not only did his function in the shipyard require him to make personal contacts in the neighboring towns; he also got around socially, becoming well known in golfing circles, and hunting and fishing clubs.

As a boy in Chicago, Harry attended both private and public schools, and two years of college, where he started on a business course. He quit college to go into a promising business job, and his business career was moderately successful. He was earning a salary of $6,000 a year at the beginning of the war. He married a girl whom he had known for several years in Chicago, and they had two children, a girl and a boy. Since the two children were old enough to look after themselves during the day, Mrs. Burnside had more time than she needed to keep up her small War Homes apartment in Gold Coast Row. She made friends early with the "upper crust" of Old Seneca, and took an active part in their social life.

The boy had attended a private school in Chicago, but took readily to the Seneca schools, where he was popular with teachers and children alike. He was good-looking, a good dancer, and was always in evidence at community dances and other social affairs.

A lady whose husband was a Navy inspector at the shipyard unwittingly explained why they had not made a place for themselves in the upper-crust group. She said,

When we first came, I thought I'd like to work, and I got a job as a welder. They gave me a good berth, they treated me swell, and I liked the work. But my husband didn't like the idea of my working—you lose caste with the Navy families if a woman works—and I didn't like the class of women I met there. So I quit. No, I don't like the class of people employed there; don't care to know them.

This woman then became a leader in Girl Scout work, and she and her husband both were active in such civic affairs as they could find in Seneca. But they remained just below the "upper crust."

"Better-class people." The better-class people consisted of about two hundred families whose men had white-collar positions or were foremen or, in a few cases, skilled workers. These people found their own social cliques, such as the clique of three families whose ladies had a "little club" and tried to teach better manners to their young neighbor woman from Oklahoma.

From this group came most of the leadership in the Tenant Councils of the housing projects. They believed in civic activity. Many of them were active in the Seneca Methodist and Lutheran churches. These were the people whose names appeared again and again on committees, and who were leaders of the many activities that sprang up in the housing projects.

One lady in this class, whose husband was a sub-foreman, complained about her living quarters in Victory Court, because they had such unpleasant neighbors. The neighbors used profane and obscene language and her little boy was beginning to pick it up. So she went to the management and asked to be moved. The person in the office told her that "everybody wants to move," and it could not be arranged. The lady said that if she couldn't get better neighbors she was going back home to Iowa. She said, "My boy is more important than the money we are making."

One of the "better-class" women spoke about a neighbor who was spending money too freely.

This woman always and regularly cashes the war bonds they buy just as soon as she can, and spends the money. Winter before last she bought a fur coat. Last winter she bought another and grander one. Well, a lot of us got to talking, and we said to her, "Why don't you save some of your money for a rainy day, that's bound to come some time?" She said, "Oh, the government'll take care of us then; we went on relief before and it took care of us when we needed it!" We said, "You mean *we* took care of you!" She was right mad, and she said, "No, the government did it before and it'll do it again. You're just fools not to spend your money and get the good of it!" We couldn't make any impression on her. Some folks are that way.

Mr. and Mrs. Wayne Morgan were representative "better-class" people.

Mr. and Mrs. Wayne Morgan were the ideal Texans. Open-faced and open-handed, enthusiastic and energetic, they could always be counted on for help in any good cause. Although Baptists and thus "entitled" to take a vacation from church since there was no Baptist church in Seneca, they became active in the Methodist church. Mr. Morgan helped to reorganize the Sunday School, where he taught a class of boys. He was a striking figure, tall and red-haired, standing between two pews toward the rear of the church auditorium and explaining the life of Christ to the group of high school boys clustered about him.

Mrs. Morgan was the secretary of the War Homes Tenants' Council, and vice president of the Women's Society in the church. In her middle thirties, she was becoming resigned to the fact that she was not to have children. Her free time she gave to every worthy project. She helped to get the first nursery school started, and she assisted with the War Homes Recreation program. With two years of college education, she had been active in Bible School work in Texas. This she did not carry on so actively in Seneca, although she helped in the Vacation Bible School of the Methodist church one summer.

Mr. Morgan had worked at a number of jobs in the oil industry, and at Seneca he became a foreman in the sheet metal department. He used his Seneca savings to add to those of earlier years as capital to start a business of his own. He and Mrs. Morgan went back to Texas after the boom, to invest their money in an automobile accessory business.

The working class. The "working-class" people made up the great bulk of the newcomers, from skilled worker down to laborer. These were hard-working people, respectable but not always as thrifty and sober as the "better-class" group would have had them. They belonged to no associations except churches and labor unions. They took no active part in the organization of Tenants' Councils. They made up the audience, the followers. They were the patrons of the weekly bingo parties in the housing projects.

Mr. and Mrs. Moore, of Arkansas, belonged in this group. He was a fitter in the shipyard. They liked their home in Victory Court and Mr. Moore spent his spare time building furniture for it. Among other things he built a bookcase for an encyclopedia they bought for $300. While the books were never read, Mrs. Moore said, "I always did want a set of encyclopedias—it's things like that that show you're not just trash or nobodies."

Another woman of this group, in Victory Court, complained about the neighbor children. She went over to the laundry to do some washing and took her two small children with her. She did not lock her door and when she came back she discovered eight children from the neighborhood running wild in her kitchen. They had overturned the fern, they had opened the icebox, taken out some sausages, chewed them and thrown them on the floor, they had torn the ration books and spilled some sugar, and scattered the children's toys all over the room. When she got them out she said she sat down and bawled. She said the people around there were a hard lot. Some of the little boys threatened each other with knives.

Mrs. Orville came from a farm home in Missouri where she had plowed the fields with mules before she was married. She and her husband worked in a factory in Missouri. She liked Seneca because it was cleaner than the factory town they had come from. When Mrs. Orville first came to Seneca she got a job driving a truck for the post office at fifty cents an hour. It was hard work, and she was dissatisfied with the low pay. "The woman welders at the shipyard get a dollar twenty cents an hour for sitting on their rear ends, so I decided there was not enough in this for me." She said, "Yes, I went to the Assembly of God Sunday School once. I ain't been to church yet, but that's my church."

Curtis Magee, Hammond Carpenter, and Hermann Plank were all members of the working class:

Curtis Magee was a foreman in the warehouse at the shipyard. Born in Scotland, he finished grammar school and then came to

America, where he settled in Chicago and worked in the freight department of several railroad companies. Finding advancement slow, he moved to Seneca at the beginning of the boom and started as an ordinary worker in the warehouse. His conscientious work won him quick advancement.

In Chicago, Curtis had met and married the daughter of one of the foremen in the freight house. They had three children, the oldest being about ten years old when they moved to Seneca. Both Mr. and Mrs. Magee were quite religious, Mr. Magee having become active in a fundamentalist denomination while they lived in Chicago.

They carried on their religious activities in Seneca, commencing with a Sunday School class in War Homes. Other people of like minds congregated around them, and the entire group eventually joined with the Holiness Methodist people in Seneca to build their new church.

The oldest child was a boy, Curtis Junior. His teacher described him and his family in the following statement:

"A very fine home. I have never met his parents, but I know they must be very fine. I have heard a number of people make comments about them. Curtis is very dependable and intelligent. Quite delicate and slow-spoken. Uses good English. Deliberate and ambitious."

Curtis Junior was unusually neat and clean, for a boy. He had a paper route in the War Homes area, and bought war bonds with his money.

Eunice, three years younger than Curtis, was one of the best-liked children in her room at school. She was accepted alike by oldtimer children and newcomers. Toward the end of the time in Seneca she became old enough to sing in the choir at the church, which she enjoyed a great deal. Her teacher described the family in this way:

"This is one family that seems to be very nice in every way. The mother came here to see us about excusing the children from school one day. An aunt was visiting them just for one day, and Mrs. Magee came in advance to see if it would be all right to keep the children out of school for a few minutes in the morning while they were seeing their aunt off. The mother is a very lovely person."

Of the way she spent her after-school time, Eunice wrote:

"I take care of my baby brother after school, and sometimes I go to the store. I wash the dishes and clean house. I work in the cafeteria in school at noontime. I go to the store for my neighbors. I take care of children on Friday and Saturday nights. I go to the recreation hall sometimes, when I don't have to take care of my brother. I ride my bicycle."

The Magees were at the top of the "working class" group. Their friends and associates were in this group, though the Magees themselves had some characteristics of the "better-class people."

Hammond Carpenter was a ranchman by trade. Leaving high school in Texas at the age of seventeen, he worked for the next thirteen years on ranches and farms in Texas and Oklahoma. Then for a few months in 1938 he tried a job in California, but soon gave it up and returned to Oklahoma where he worked on a cattle ranch for $68 a month and a house and garden. The lure of war wages brought him to Seneca from Oklahoma, where he soon worked up to $1.20 an hour as a "fitter." Now for the first time he was making real money. But neither Mr. Carpenter nor any of his family really liked it in Seneca. The only thing they liked was the Assembly of God Church, where the family sang as a quartet, while their son Sam played the guitar for them. Mrs. Carpenter worked at the shipyard as a welder's helper. She had completed the eighth grade in a Texas town and had one year beyond this in high school.

Hermann Plank spent all of his life on Iowa farms until he was about forty. At the age of thirty-five, he married a young widow with two young children and they farmed as tenants on a 160-acre farm. They had two children of their own. When the war started, Hermann took a welding course in Des Moines and then ventured with his family to Wisconsin to try war work.

When things did not turn out to their satisfaction, they moved to Ottawa in late 1942, and on to Seneca as soon as housing became available. Mr. Plank worked up to a pay rate of $1.20 an hour. They saved all the money they could, hoping to get enough for an automobile and a down payment on a farm back in Iowa. They were regular attendants at the Seneca Lutheran church.

Jerry Steel was among the working class at the Seneca shipyard, but his case was somewhat different. He had been in somewhat "better circumstances before," as he put it, and he was eager to identify himself once more with the "better class of people" after the war.

Mr. Jeremiah V. Steel was raised in Peoria, Illinois, where he graduated from high school. After a variety of white-collar jobs as a youth, he tried collecting insurance and selling automobiles, making a fair living until the automobile business went into eclipse with the beginning of the war. He then went to work as a truck driver at a war plant at $1.00 an hour, until he came to Seneca in 1943, when he started as an apprentice painter and soon worked up to the pay level of $1.20 an hour. He was forty when he moved to Seneca, and had two children.

Mrs. Steel dropped out of high school at sixteen and went to work for the telephone company, where she had been working for five years when she was married. In Seneca she got a job at the switchboard of the shipyard. Life was not as pleasant for her in Seneca as it had been in Peoria, where she had a companionable younger sister, and where Mr. Steel had much free time for travel. The family had made many automobile trips that combined business for Mr. Steel and sight-seeing for the rest of them. Mrs. Steel hoped that with the money they saved in Seneca they could get a good start in the automobile business after the war. This would be Jerry's last chance to make good in business, for he was already middle-aged. Mrs. Steel was afraid he would not succeed.

Of the two girls, the younger was in the Catholic parochial school, while Sally was in the eighth grade of the public school.

Sally wrote, concerning her move to Seneca, "When I knew we were going to move to Seneca, I thought it was the most cruel thing that ever happened to me, but after we got here and settled, I started liking it."

"The bottom of the heap." There were relatively few families among the newcomers who were reputed to be so shiftless and immoral that they "lived like animals" and were at the "bottom of the heap." Perhaps a total of a hundred and fifty families could be put into this category.

In one of these families, living in Victory Court, the woman and her husband both worked on the night shift. They had four children, aged nine, seven, five, and four. The wife got the children up and off to school in the morning, the two smaller ones being sent to nursery school for the day. She went to the store after breakfast to buy groceries, then came home in the middle of the morning and slept until suppertime. When the fieldworker walked home with this woman from the grocery store, she saw the remains of a meal on the table, the icebox pan running over on the floor, and children's clothes strewn around the room. The mother said that the children ate whenever they were hungry. They usually all had one meal together about eight o'clock in the evening.

A woman in War Homes was arrested on complaint of her neighbors for flogging her thirteen-year-old son. The sheriff found the boy's back and arms covered with welts and he charged her with cruelty to a minor. The boy's mother admitted having beaten him with the cord from a vacuum cleaner when he failed to come home from a movie when she expected him. This woman and her husband became notorious for their drinking and fighting.

These people at the bottom of the heap lived wherever the accident of their arrival placed them, and might be found next door to people of the "better class." Consequently their

way of living was always under observation by people above
them on the social scale. They could not go unnoticed, as
they might have done in the ordinary community where they
would live "down on the river flats" or "over by the town
dump."

Tom Andrews was one of this group.

When asked about Tom Andrews, the visiting nurse, who knew
the family well, would say, "Oh, he's one of the Andrews tribe.
They come and go, but there's always at least a score of them
there." In 1943 Andrews, the head of the family, moved to Seneca,
liked it, and sent back for his children and grandchildren. His son
Tom came up from southern Illinois with his wife and six or seven
children. Neither the school authorities nor the visiting nurse was
sure just how many children there were. This may have been due
to the fact that Tom's brother and sister and their families were in
adjacent trailers, with their children all so mixed together that an
outsider could never unscramble them. Or it may have been due
to the fact that one or another of the older children was usually
back in their southern Illinois "home town" staying with other
relatives.

Tom's record of residence was one of wandering from one farm
community to another in southern Illinois and Kentucky, accom-
panied by or going along with his brothers and sisters. His work
as a laborer on the night shift in the shipyard was his first venture
into industrial work. Mrs. Andrews had done farm work, too,
when she was not bearing children. In Seneca she worked on the
day shift at the shipyard.

The school superintendent, the visiting nurse, and the owner of
the trailer park all sought the mother's cooperation in connection
with problems involving the children, but all said that they had
failed. "This is one more problem family," said the nurse. Though
nominally "Baptist," none of the family was seen at church in
Seneca.

Flora, the oldest child, was an irregular attendant in the seventh
grade of school. She had a physical defect which caused her
trouble in walking. To her fell the responsibility for the care of

the children in the afternoons before the mother returned home from work.

Susan, the second child, was nine years old. She was a thin, frail, and unkempt child. Her straight bobbed hair was too long and never cut evenly. Her school attendance was so irregular that the teacher did not keep a record on her and did not bother to fill out a report card for her. She came to school about a month after the other children in the family, and the teacher put her at a table alone at the back of the classroom. "The Andrews kids have a reputation," she said. Susan seldom played with other children. At lunch and before and after school she stood around with her sister Flora. In writing about herself Susan often referred to "stomach trouble," "pills," and "vomiting."

Susan was rough in her play with some of the younger children in the trailer park. The mother of one of these children led other tenants to the owner and asked to have the Andrews family removed from the park. The owner was going to do this, but the Andrews decided to send Susan away instead. So she was sent back to the home town in southern Illinois to live with an uncle.

RELATIONS BETWEEN OLDTIMERS AND NEWCOMERS

"We were all like one big family before the boom," said an elderly lady who had lived comfortably in Seneca all her life. Oldtimers in Seneca tended to forget their own social differences and to feel as though they all belonged together when they faced the horde of strangers moving in upon them.

In spite of the formal fiction that "the latch string was out" to the newcomers, there never developed an easy set of relationships between the two groups. Aside from the churches, none of the Old Seneca organizations took newcomers in freely. For example, the business and professional women's sorority admitted only one newcomer, the public health nurse. Very few oldtimers ever set foot in a dwelling unit of the housing projects, although a considerable number did attend social events in the Social Halls of War Homes and Victory Court.

The newcomers felt that they were denied the welcome they deserved. Not only were they denied easy social intercourse with the oldtimers; they were also underrated. One of the "better-class' newcomers said,

"Seneca folks look down on us! Oh yes, they do. I got a washer-woman promised; she lived up there back of Sand's store somewhere. It was all arranged, what day I'd send her the clothes, how much she charged, when I could get them and everything. Finally I remarked how hard it is to get overalls clean when men work so close to dirty machinery. She said, 'Oh, I ain't going to work for none of them shipyard riff-raff,' and that was the end of it. So I found a woman who lives in War Homes to do it. She does use too much bleach; my pillow cases are all wearing out.

"But Seneca people needn't be so snooty; there were only four bathtubs in Seneca before the shipyard came. And look at all the new things they've got since we came. Two new churches, two new school houses, a lot of extra teachers and police, good sidewalks, and a sewer system."

Another woman, in the working-class group of the newcomers, expressed the same resentment. After saying that she had been made to feel she was not wanted in the Lutheran church, she added,

"I took my little boy into the Sweet Shop to buy a paper and git him an ice-cream cone. The clerk, she said to him, 'Whaddye want? Well, you don't get no stool if all you want's an ice-cream cone; git right down!' Then she turned to another woman and said, 'That damned shipyard trash!' Right in front of my child, too. I went out of there without no ice-cream cone nor paper neither."

It was wounded pride rather than the need for social intercourse with oldtimers that rankled with the newcomers. To a very considerable degree the newcomers formed communities of their own with social centers in the War Homes and Victory Court administration and recreation buildings. They did not feel very badly the lack of informal social contacts with people in Old Seneca. Their own communities were as large as Old Seneca. The main thing they had in common with the oldtimers was the use of the business facilities of Old Seneca.

Social relationships between the oldtimers and the newcomers were channelled largely through the churches and, for children, through the schools. Within a small group of people the churches served to bring new residents into close association with oldtimers. Feeling the potential importance of this type of church work, one of the ministers deliberately planned to mix the old and the new by forming his membership into four social groups, each one containing five old and twenty new families. Each week the oldtimers were to entertain the newcomers with a covered dish supper at the church. But his plan did not take hold.

Only a small proportion of newcomers went into Old Seneca churches. One of the two new churches consisted entirely of newcomers. The other, about evenly divided between old and new families, did promote close associations for its members; but this church always remained small in size.[1]

While the over-all picture is one of minimal interaction between oldtimers and newcomers, the extent of interaction varied somewhat from one social class to another. The social structure that grew up in the housing projects, with its four social levels, was roughly parallel to the social structure of Old Seneca, as the latter has been described in Chapter 1. While the newcomers of any social level lived very differently from the oldtimers of the same social class, still they shared most of the same value patterns and attitudes. The "upper

---

[1] See Chapter 7, "Religion," for a more detailed account of how Seneca churches adapted to boom-time conditions.

crust" among the newcomers could be equated in most respects with the "upper crust" of Old Seneca; the "better class" of newcomers with the "better class" of Old Seneca; and so on.

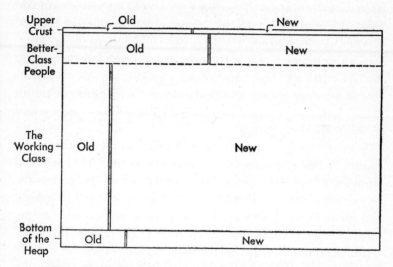

Fig. 10. Social Structure of Boom-time Seneca.

In Figure 10 is diagrammed the social structure of Old Seneca, and that of the newcomers. The social classes of Old Seneca should be thought of as existing side by side with those of the newcomer group, and not as merged with the new and larger groups.

One substantial difference between the two structures stands out. That is the relatively greater proportion of the "working class" in the wartime community. This group makes up three-quarters of the boom-time population, but only a little more than half of the Old Seneca population. If the community had stabilized itself under the boom-town conditions it would have been socially quite different from Old

Seneca. It would have been more like a working-class suburb of a big city.

Such social participation as did develop between oldtimers and newcomers was confined largely to people at the top of each social hierarchy. The upper group of Old Seneca quickly formed friendships with the "upper crust" of the newcomers. Houses in which to entertain gave the Old Seneca group a certain attractiveness; while the new group provided "launching parties" with an abundance of navy gold braid. When one of the newcomer group married into an Old Seneca "upper crust" family the event symbolized the social equality and unity of the two groups.

Some of Seneca's upper group tended to regard the upper group of the newcomers as "nouveau riche." This resulted from the avid interest in parties and dances on the part of the newcomers, combined with relative lack of interest in philanthropy and civic betterment. One member of Seneca's "upper crust" spoke of Gold Coast Row in War Homes as "just filled with social climbers." This same person said that the launching parties and the navy gold braid had "gone to the heads" of some of the young matrons in the newcomer group. However, this kind of disapproval was probably due in part to a difference in ages between the two groups, for the newcomers were mostly young people, while the Old Seneca group had a considerable proportion of elderly people.

Social relations between the "better-class people" of Old Seneca and the "better-class people" in the housing projects were limited almost entirely to the churches, where a small proportion of the newcomers of this group took active part and were accepted cordially by the oldtimers. This was especially noticeable in the Methodist church, where a majority of the Sunday school teachers and other leaders were "better-class" newcomers.

Relations between the working-class people of Old Seneca

and the newcomers were practically non-existent. A few of them met in the churches. Otherwise, there was no chance for them to meet and mingle. Their geographical separation prevented them from associating as neighbors.

POLITICAL ATTITUDES

As in social affairs, so also in political affairs there was relative isolation between newcomers and oldtimers, even though there was no marked cleavage in attitudes toward national and international issues.

Newcomers in Seneca were not elected to office in the local government, although some newcomers were included in the expanded police and fire departments. While newcomers had the right to vote in the local elections, few of them did so, and there was little interest in local political matters. For example, the primary election of April, 1944, drew out only two hundred voters in Seneca, almost all of whom were old residents.

TABLE 8

RESULTS OF 1940 AND 1944 ELECTIONS IN SENECA

| Date | President | | Governor | |
	Republican	Democrat	Republican	Democrat
1940	283	255		
1944	775	1014	801	936

In the national election of November, 1944, however, the interest of newcomers paralleled that of oldtimers, and the total vote cast was 1,828. Compared with the total Seneca vote of 538 in the election of November, 1940, and taking into account the fact that a number of newcomers voted as absentees in their old home towns, the number of votes in 1944 would indicate about the same degree of political interest among newcomers as among oldtimers.

A comparison of the votes in the 1940 and 1944 elections is given in Table 8.

While the data shown in Table 8 are not separated into votes by oldtimers and newcomers, it would appear that a relatively higher proportion of newcomers voted Democratic. The largest Democratic majority was given in the precinct containing Victory Court, Riverview Homes, and Trailer Park.

As the boom wore on, newcomers began to figure more prominently in local governmental affairs. For example, the Seneca Recreation Commission, when it was reorganized in the autumn of 1944, contained several newcomers, whereas the earlier Recreation Committee consisted entirely of old-timers.[2]

Summary

Relations between the old and new residents were kept to a minimum. This was largely because the newcomer was thought of, and thought of himself, as a man who comes today and goes tomorrow. It hardly seemed worth the effort to build up a social relationship with strange people for such a short time. The life of the newcomer to Seneca was characterized by:

the feeling that he was there for a temporary stay;
no sentimental attachments to the village or its institutions;
unusual discomforts due to crowded housing conditions;
freedom from the conventions of life in Seneca;
minimal participation in local institutions;
minimal social interaction with oldtimers.

[2] See Chapter 9, "Recreation."

The separation between oldtimers and newcomers, together with the fact that the newcomers outnumbered the oldtimers four to one, might have been expected to lead to serious social disorganization in Seneca. Crime, civic indifference, and hostility between the groups would be predicted. Yet none of these things occurred with enough intensity to create a serious problem. Instead, the village maintained its stability.

What were the factors that operated toward integration and stability? Was it the fact that the newcomers, by and large, resembled the residents of Old Seneca in so many ways? The fact that they, too, were Midwesterners, coming from small towns and farms, with many of the same moral and social values, and with many of the same attitudes toward community and government? Or was it the fact that Old Seneca had a set of social institutions that were flexible enough to accommodate the newcomers and to maintain community organization? The fact that schools, churches, business, and recreational facilities expanded quickly enough to meet the needs of the new population? The chapters that follow will, perhaps, throw light on these questions.

5.

Life in Wartime

The experience of wartime adjustment for the people in boom communities like Seneca—both oldtimers and newcomers—was probably more interesting, and also perhaps more difficult, than it was for any other group of people in America, with the exception of men and women in the armed services. The people fitted themselves into the nooks and crannies of wartime living. What things did they like? What things did they complain about? How did they change their style of living? Did they save money, or did their high wages induce higher spending?

Pleasant Experiences

For the vast majority of people, old and young, newcomers and oldtimers, life in wartime was an exhilarating experience. This was the predominant impression gained from interviews with a hundred or more people in the closing months of the boom. Three things appear to have combined to give the experience its pleasant flavor: (1) high income, (2) the feeling of playing a significant part in a victorious war, and (3) the association with many new people.

The favorable influence of high income is obvious. The excitement of taking part in the process of winning the war is perhaps not so easily understood when viewed from a post-war position, but it was real and strong while it lasted. In the schools, the children learned that their fathers were making

110

history. In the churches, these feelings were reflected in the sermons. And every week, sometimes twice a week, there was a launching, which gave a militant beat to the march of life in Seneca through the war years. On these days the whole town responded to the music and the fanfare that centered about the launching platform at the river's edge. Practically everybody in town witnessed a launching at one time or another early in the boom, and he could revive for himself the excitement and the pleasurable tension of the event on each succeeding occasion. He had a morale-building factor that was not present in other types of war industries, where the product was issued in a continuous and unexciting stream.

While, as has been described in the preceding chapter, there was no real integration of newcomers with the life of the community, there was pleasure in associating with new people—even if it was on a superficial level. This pleasure seems to have been felt especially by persons whose lives had been stable and secure but rather limited in variety of personal relationships. Speaking in social-class terms, it was the lower-middle-class people who seemed to enjoy this aspect of boom-town life especially.

An elderly lady from War Homes, who had lived all her adult life in a nine-room house in a small Illinois town, said,

"Oh, it's been a wonderful experience here! There are families from everywhere in the United States here. Why, right in this row are people from six states. I've learned so much about folks."

A young woman who had recently married one of the minor management officials and was doing her first house-keeping in War Homes, said,

"This is just living in tenements, of course. I'd like to write a book about the life here! Well, for one thing, how we women get along together, work together, play together, do all our living exclusively together. That's not usual in tenements, you know. Yes,

I've enjoyed it in a certain way. From what my friends tell me, I rather dread having to keep house in Chicago."

A middle-aged woman from Chicago whose husband held a clerical position in the office, said,

"I wouldn't take a thousand dollars for my experience here. I learned to know the world in Seneca! I suppose that sounds queer to you, coming from a Chicago woman, but I'd seen mostly my own kind of people in Chicago. I didn't know much about the other half and how they lived. I knew there were taverns, but I'd never had them under my nose before."

A similar sentiment was widespread among the middle-status people in Old Seneca. This was shown in their responses to a questionnaire that was circulated by members of the high school Social Problems class in May, 1945. One question read:

"There have been many pleasant things about living in a war-boom town. Would you say in just a few words what your most pleasant experience has been as a result of living here?"

Sixty per cent of the responses mentioned the meeting of new people and the making of new friends as the most pleasant experience. Another 10 per cent mentioned related matters, such as more "life" in the town.

Other topics mentioned by the oldtimers were: "new community facilities and improvements"; "better business and better incomes"; "patriotic and interesting work."

Unpleasant Experiences

The unpleasant experiences that people attributed directly to the fact of their living in a boom town—rather than to the more general fact of living in a period of wartime hardship—were three: crowding, gambling, and drinking.

People were crowded within small dwelling units, which in

turn were crowded together. Practically everybody in Seneca —oldtimers as well as newcomers—had to live in less space than he had been accustomed to before the war. Furthermore, practically everybody had a large number of extremely close neighbors. This was particularly true in the housing projects, where the partitions between living quarters were not soundproof, and where people could usually hear what was going on next door.

Mrs. Roberts of Victory Court lived with her husband and a five-year-old daughter in a two-room apartment. She was expecting another baby soon.

"It will be so good to have a yard and trees and privacy once more," she said. "This is no place to bring up a family."

The interviewer heard a child whimpering. "There's your little one calling," she said.

"No," said Mrs. Roberts, "that's next door, though it does sound as if it is in this house. You can hear so plainly, the next-door neighbors and even the ones next to them. And you can see their light at night through the cracks."

Mr. and Mrs. Sorenson, a young engineer and his wife living in War Homes, complained that they did not dare let their year-old baby cry, for fear he would disturb the neighbors. Normally, they would have let him "cry it out" at times when he was being unreasonable; but under the circumstances, they picked him up whenever he made the slightest disturbance; and the result, they feared, was that they were spoiling him.

It was often said, with some seriousness, that in the housing project you could hear your neighbor whenever he brushed his teeth. This made it very difficult to live impersonally, and to ignore the next-door neighbors.

For example, Mrs. Cramplen, whose husband was a foreman, reported her embarrassment and disgust at the situation next door to her. She had as neighbors on one side, Grandpa, who worked nights, and his daughter-in-law and her girl friend. The daughter-in-law's husband was away in the Army. The two women worked days, came home after supper, slept until midnight, then went out and picked up two men, brought them home and made love from one o'clock until two forty-five, and then hustled them out fifteen minutes before 3 A.M., when Grandpa came home from work.

This lack of privacy in the housing projects gave a certain advantage to living in a trailer; and many people preferred to remain in trailers even though more spacious quarters, with plumbing, were available to them in the housing projects. Another advantage of living in a trailer was stressed by a young woman who had traveled about from job to job with her husband for several years. They owned a trailer that they took with them when they moved. Their residence in Seneca was the most permanent they had ever had during their married life. She complained of the difficulties of living in temporary quarters. If they tried to live in furnished apartments they would have to carry their belongings in suitcases up at least two flights of stairs, into dark, dirty rooms that somebody else had left. She said,

"You mind other folks' dirt so much more than your own. You don't know exactly what theirs is and you have dark suspicions. Of course, their furnishings and dishes are old and ugly. Then you've driven for a day or two from the last place you've worked, and you've spent two or three days looking for an apartment and then you must unpack and press."

The other principal sources of unpleasant experiences—drinking and gambling—were mentioned by people of the more "respectable" sort, whose previous experience had not brought them into close association with people who drank regularly, or who gambled. Many were the stories told about drunken quarrels in apartments next door, children neglected by parents who frequented taverns at night, men gambling away their pay checks, and women playing away their grocery money in the slot machines. These feelings undoubtedly were restricted to a rather small portion of the newcomers; and to a minority, but a larger portion, of the oldtimers.

In the questionnaire distributed to residents of Old Seneca by the high school students there was the question: "What has been your most unpleasant experience as a result of living in a war-boom town?"

One-fourth of the responses mentioned liquor and taverns; 10 per cent mentioned gambling and immorality; one-fourth mentioned crowded streets, heavy traffic, and crowded living conditions; and 20 per cent mentioned food shortages and high prices.

What Did People Do with Their Money?

Practically everybody in Seneca doubled his prewar income during the boom period. A man who had been making $40 a week as an electrician could earn about $80 a week at the shipyard. Clerks in the stores had their wages doubled, and the businessmen at least doubled their profits. Boys and girls who had never worked before could earn at least fifty cents an hour.

What might be called the "basic wage" was about double that of prewar days. In addition, there were fabulous stories of the workers' earnings at the shipyard at certain periods of high pressure—times when a man could work as much overtime as he pleased, getting 50 per cent extra for ordinary overtime, and double pay for Sundays. During the early part of the boom, when the housing projects were being rushed to completion, the same situation prevailed for construction workers.

Not all wages were pushed up so high. The women working in shipyard clerical positions complained about their
"low" pay of $35 to $40 a week. One of them, when standing
in line at the Currency Exchange, showed her check for
$37.50 to a welder whom she knew. "Why, Anna," he said,
"your check wouldn't even pay my income tax," and he
showed her his check for $179.

When working at hourly rates, it seems hardly possible a
man could earn more than $130 to $140 a week, even with
Sunday and much overtime work. However, some of the more
highly skilled workers worked at piece rates, and may have
made up to $200 a week, as was claimed in a number of state-
ments.

Where did the money go? Did it go into high spending and
high living, or into savings?

Undoubtedly money was spent freely. Seneca workers
lived better, as far as food went, than they had before the
war. They wanted steak instead of sowbelly. They wanted
the best they could get, and they were willing to pay for it.
The grocer who never stocked tomatoes in January because
"people won't pay the price for hothouse tomatoes" soon had
tomatoes and strawberries and every other delicacy out of
season; and he found ready buyers. A Slovakian woman who
fired a boiler at the shipyard complained at the department
store because they had no men's shirts costing more than
$1.89. She wanted something better for her son. A woman
whose husband was a skilled worker said that she felt old-
fashioned when they went out with the young couples living
on either side of them, who thought nothing of spending $5
to $6 a couple for dinner, and of having four or five drinks,
and who called her a "slow poke" when she nursed her one
drink along.

Mrs. Thompson, whose husband was an electrician,
achieved an old ambition. They had eloped to be married,

and had kept their marriage secret for two years. By the time they were ready to announce it, they needed so many things that she did not get a wedding ring. But, with money from Seneca wages, they went to Chicago and bought a ring with diamonds in it.

The boom raised the cost of living to the highest level Seneca had ever seen. Nearly everybody, newcomers and old-timers alike, had to spend more money for the everyday necessities of life, and there was a great deal of complaining, especially on the part of the residents of Old Seneca. Some of the oldtimers blamed it all on the presence of the new-comers. "With all that easy money being made out at the shipyard, those people can't spend it fast enough. Makes prices go up for everybody, and makes it tough for the rest of us!" This was a typical statement, often heard from the old, retired farmers living in Seneca, who had been accustomed to living comfortably in prewar years on a relatively small out-lay of cash. Other oldtimers, taking a more realistic point of view, said, "Look how prices have gone up all over the coun-try! Inflation—that's the danger. The government better watch out!"

The high cost of food was the most widespread complaint. While prices were advancing in other types of commodities as well, many families could keep their expenses down by "making do" with their old furniture, equipment, clothing, and so on. But everybody felt the rub when it came to food. The few people who did not complain of high food prices were those who had come to Seneca from other war produc-tion areas where boom conditions prevailed. Most people guessed that food costs had doubled since 1940. (The United States Bureau of Labor Statistics' estimate for increase in the cost of food between August, 1939, and April, 1944, was, however, 44 per cent.)

Rentals were perhaps the only cost-of-living item that did

not increase in Seneca to any marked degree. An old house on Main Street, without plumbing, rented for $6 a month before the boom. It was later reconstructed and the rent was raised to $8. Before the war, $25 was a good rental for any store on Main Street, and there was little increase during the boom. Rentals in the housing projects were from $20 to $40 per month.[1]

Saving. The best estimates were that one-third to one-half of the shipyard workers were saving a substantial portion of their earnings.

Examples of saving were frequently mentioned to the interviewer:

"Yes, some shipyard workers have saved. Two or three that I know have bought small farms near Chicago; one bought a Wisconsin farm. One man is starting a chicken-growing business, and building a home in South Ottawa."

"Yes, I think people save here. The couple that lived next to us in Riverview had laid up three hundred war bonds, $25 bonds you know. That's $7500 if they keep them ten years."

"Yes, some have saved money. We don't seem to have saved much; I can't quite see where it's all gone to."

"It's so hard to save here, things are so high. Of course everybody buys war bonds. Maybe some do cash theirs regularly. But we haven't cashed any of ours. Some save more than bonds. There's a man from Kentucky; I guess they're used to living pretty cheap down there. The clerk at the store says he most generally buys about thirty cents' worth of lunch meat and a loaf of bread to last him over the weekend. He said he wishes the war would last just two years more; if it lasts even one year more he won't have to work no more."

Reverend Mr. Stark, of the Assembly of God Church, said: "All our people have saved. I know that Lambert, one of our best workers, a crack welder, has saved $5,000. The Texas and Oklahoma folks are our best savers; many of them have saved and

[1] See Table 25 in Appendix A.

bought little ranches back there that they're going back to. But I'd say only about a third of the whole shipyard saves, not half."

A War Homes resident said: "Well, I don't know about most saving their money. I used to work in a grocery. Lots of folks came in and wanted credit, with both of them working and earning good money. We put every bit we can save into war bonds. We want our own home. But so many folks gamble. Well, I know one trailer family has a notice to vacate in two weeks, and they won't have money enough to move back home, even with the two weeks' pay they get at the end."

"Do half the people save? There was one man got his release Tuesday, and had to wait till Saturday for his last check before he could get out of town. Perhaps 50 per cent who save something might be right."

Savings took two principal forms. Everybody bought war bonds, and most people left their money in this form. A good number, however, put their money into land and houses. It was a conservative kind of saving. No one spoke of putting money into common stocks.

The CBI followed the general practice of urging workers to put 10 per cent of their wages into war bonds. The money was deducted from the worker's pay, and his bonds were mailed to him as they were paid for. Ninety-eight per cent of the employees had such payroll deductions, though many people cashed their bonds as soon as possible. Reports from the CBI for two separate periods indicate that deductions for bond purchases averaged approximately 10 per cent of the payroll, and that additional bonds were sold at the times of the various War Loan Bond drives. A total of $9,000,000 of war bonds was purchased, as compared with a total of $82,400,000 in wages paid at the shipyard.

Giving to charity. In spite of increased income, Seneca people did not give much to the national campaigns for Red Cross, United Service Organizations, and other charitable war purposes. In the autumn of 1943 the National War Fund drive, headed by Old Seneca residents, set a goal of $6,600; but raised a total of $4,600. The usual gift from businessmen in Seneca was twenty-five dollars; and the usual gift from individual Senecans was one or two dollars. At the housing projects committees were formed to canvass everybody. Committee members were rebuffed frequently, and often turned away with a contribution of twenty-five cents. Seneca War Homes contributed $300, or less than a dollar per family.

The editor of the Victory Court paper, *Ship and Home*, wrote an editorial complaining that too many people were giving only twenty-five cents to the War Fund, while they could easily find money for beer; and noting that those who had been on relief a few years back now had a chance to show their gratitude. In the next issue of *Ship and Home* appeared the following letter together with a rejoinder in the editorial column:

From time to time the editor of *Ship and Home* receives expressions from the people. They are always appreciated, and when signed by the writer are placed in a column regularly reserved for that purpose.

A few days after the last issue of *Ship and Home* the following unsigned letter was received. Because it was unsigned, it could not be printed as an expression of the people. However, we wish to print it, with a few items of comment, in the editorial section. The letter read as follows:

"Dear *Ship and Home*—Have just finished reading your wonderful editorial on Victory Court. I'm sure they will get a big contribution next time they call at my door. It's things like that that really make one feel like giving.

"My husband gave a quarter, perhaps he is the 'gentleman' referred to. But if each one here gave a quarter, that would be 500 quarters, and that shouldn't be sneezed at. And as for not paying income taxes before the war, just how many did? Did you?

"And what has being on relief a few years ago got to do with building ships now? I'm sure we would all have been glad to have a steady job in the shipyard during those lean years. And do you see the Victory Court lined up at the tavern door waiting to get their 2½ quarts of beer? You seem to know just how much a dollar will buy.

"You never thought to count up how much it costs to just live now-a-days, and feed and clothe a family of six. Count it up, with pencil and paper. Count taxes of all kinds, bonds, insurance, rent, groceries, fuel, gas, school-books, and everything it takes to live and also doctor bills and medicine and dental care, and then a few contributions! We never give a ten-dollar bill, as you seem to expect, but always give something. They get my husband at the shipyard and then me at home, and we are not $100.00 a week people either.

"And if the time does come, when I must ask for help, I will feel entitled to it just as much as I ever did, because after all that's what we're fighting for. So that the people here at home will have care when he needs it. After all, that's part of being an American. Building character and health for the underprivileged.

"I am not a social parasite or a stinkamaroo. I think we all remember the hard times we have been through and are trying to save a little for the future. And really, we do know there's a war on.

"Really now, did you go without cigarettes yourself, in order to give an extra dollar? Or did you give just what you could conveniently spare?

"Of course, this will never appear in *Ship and Home*, but at least you know how a lot of us feel.

"An Angry Mother"

As previously mentioned, your editor wishes only a few words of comment.

1. God help the existence of worthwhile organizations if we collect only 500 quarters. It would take a heap of sneezing to explain that away to the boys.

2. Yes, we see the Victory Courters lined up to get their 2½ quarts of beer. In fact they line up quite frequently. The result is just quarters from many of them for the National War Fund Drive.

3. Your husband was not contacted at the shipyard for a contribution to National War Fund.

4. Contributions we can conveniently spare will not win this war. We must contribute till it hurts and hurts plenty. However, if your quarter was a hurting sacrifice, we congratulate you on your contribution and assure you it was appreciated.

Of the $4,600 which was raised, $2,765 was allocated to local agencies such as the Boy Scouts, the Library, and the Commercial Club, while the remainder went to services for military men and their families.

In 1944 the same goal was set, and approximately the same amount raised as in the previous year, something in excess of $4,000. The agencies to be benefited in Seneca from the 1944 fund were: Library, Boy Scouts, Girl Scouts, Mothers' Club of the Nursery School, the Seneca Recreation Commission, and the Commercial Club.

Similar difficulties were met in the annual Red Cross drives in the spring of 1943 and 1944. To these campaigns the CBI contributed most of the amount raised. CBI gave $2,400 in 1943 and $3,200 in 1944. Only a few hundred dollars were raised from individual gifts. In the spring of 1946, after the boom was over, the total Seneca contribution to the Red Cross was $1,300, of which $400 came from the Dupont Company.

The giving habits of shipyard workers were typical of those of working-class people generally. Except where the church was concerned—and a number of them gave liberally to their churches—these people did not give money readily for charitable purposes.

FOOD-BUYING HABITS

In the spring of 1944, home economists made a special study of food-buying habits of a sample of 175 families among the newcomers in Seneca.[2] Since members of a family differ in the amount of food eaten, according to age, sex, and type of work engaged in, food costs were figured per consumption unit rather than per person. For instance, women and adolescents figured as one consumption unit; an adult man at moderately hard work figured as 1.4 units; and children figured as less than one unit, ranging according to age.

There were wide differences among families, some families spending as little as $2 to $3 per week per consumption unit, others spending from $8 to $9. When compared to the amounts they were spending for food before coming to Seneca, the overwhelming majority reported greatly increased expenditures. The average expenditure for food per consumption unit per week was $5.35, whereas it had been $3.65 before arrival in Seneca—an average increase of 46 per cent.

Table 9 below shows the number of families who fell in each "food cost zone" before and after arrival in Seneca. "Be-

TABLE 9

FOOD EXPENDITURES BEFORE AND AFTER ARRIVAL IN SENECA

Amount spent per week per Consumption Unit	Before Arrival	After Arrival
$0.50 to $0.99	2.3%	0.0%
1.00 to 1.99	12.3	0.0
2.00 to 2.99	20.4	4.9
3.00 to 3.99	33.1	12.4
4.00 to 4.99	10.8	21.6
5.00 to 5.99	10.8	34.6
6.00 to 6.99	3.8	11.1
7.00 to 7.99	6.2	11.7
8.00 to 8.99	0.0	3.6

[2] Lydia Roberts, Minna Denton, Margaret Brookes, Helen Brecht and Dorothy Greey, "Food Buying Habits in a War Boom Town." Unpublished manuscript, University of Chicago, Department of Home Economics, 1946. See Appendix B for more details of this study.

fore Arrival," the $3 to $4 zone was the most frequent; "After Arrival," the $5 to $6 zone is the most frequent.

Food records for some of the heavy spenders ($8 and $9 per consumption unit per week) showed the following:

Family No. 10. Navy inspector, has traveled a good deal for the Navy. Daughter six years old. Claim expenditure of $25 per week, claim probably justified. Next-door neighbor, No. 9, a country-bred woman, wonders frankly, "Why, their grocery bills are nearly twice as much as mine, and I have two children, she has one; and her daughter gets her lunch at the nursery school, too. How could they spend so much?" It is easy to see why No. 9 spent less, for she used home-canned fruit and vegetables extensively; also they managed to get frozen meat from their home locker rather regularly. Also, No. 9 used one pound of dried beans and about two cans of canned beans weekly. No. 10 never used beans. No. 9 used more cereals and potatoes. No. 10 used oranges or tomato juice (commercial) for breakfast daily, where No. 9 used one dozen oranges weekly, and home-canned fruit. No. 10 used cream where No. 9 used top milk. No. 10 appears to have used more meat, though not more eggs.

Family No. 104 is the family of a mechanic, a body-and-fender specialist who had become a laborer. The wife estimated her former food costs in Chicago in 1942 as $15 per week, her 1944 spring food costs as $20 to $30 a week. Her daughter is a lusty child, two years old. They use 4 quarts of milk daily (all drink milk) and 2 bottles of cream weekly. They used to use less bottled milk and cream; bought canned milk then, which now they do not use. They buy 1¼ pounds of butter and 3 pounds of shortening weekly; formerly they bought 2 pounds of margarine and one pound of shortening. They buy a dozen oranges and four grapefruit weekly. They buy fresh asparagus, broccoli, peas, green beans. They use 3 dozen eggs weekly, bacon at breakfast, meat for dinner and for her husband's lunch, chicken almost every Sunday. She has trouble making her red stamps "do." They eat potatoes twice daily.

Typical food records for low-cost families ($2 to $3 per consumption unit per week) are given below:

Family No. 40 is a spray painter's family. Formerly he was a paper-mill worker in an Illinois village near Joliet. There they spent half as much for food as here; but prices were lower, and they had their own chickens and eggs, and bought milk from a neighbor at 10 cents per quart. The family has a son three years old, a daughter two years old, and "grandpop," who rooms in the men's dormitory, eats his meals with them.

She bought only one quart of milk daily for her family plus one tall can of milk weekly for coffee and a carton (12 oz.) of cottage cheese daily. She buys 2 or 3 dozen eggs weekly, but as the two men each have 2 eggs for breakfast daily, that leaves practically none for the rest of the family. She uses 2 loaves of bread daily, and 2 pounds of butter weekly, no oleo at present. She makes brown sugar syrup instead of buying syrups. They use oatmeal almost daily, potatoes once daily. "At home" she had her own chickens and eggs, and bought milk at 10 cents per quart (instead of 13 to 15 cents as in Seneca). She reported using meat daily and in her husband's lunch, bacon for breakfast—but had no trouble in making her red stamps last. No, she never bought chicken.

Family No. 82 is a pipe-fitter's family, one of the families that regularly travel for CBI. "We've got used to this now, we like traveling." They had been in Seneca since August, 1942. They came directly from a small town near Des Moines, Iowa. There is a daughter ten years old, who is a feeding problem, eats little except bread and butter. None of them are "big eaters." She thought their weekly bill was "from $10 up." Ten dollars per week would give them $2.94 per consumption unit. They use 1 or 2 quarts of milk daily, but one quart of this is consumed by the husband for his lunch. They use ½ pint cream daily, ½ pound butter weekly, ½ pint shortening or more weekly, cottage cheese 2 or 3 times weekly (12 oz. cartons), 1 dozen eggs weekly (or fewer) for baking only, 2 pounds of dried beans weekly, bake hot breads a great deal, eat lots of sugar on cereal, had to cut down on coffee lately because it takes so much sugar, have potatoes 4 times weekly, substituting macaroni or rice on other days, have meat once daily (and for husband's lunch) if they can get to the Marseilles market 4 miles away (they won't buy meat in Seneca), use no fish or chickens here, though they had both regularly in Iowa, seem to buy few vegetables here, though they canned 300 to 400 jars in 1942 in Iowa. They "manage pretty well" with their red stamps, though they used to have trouble at first, ate a little less meat then, too. But they have trouble with blue stamps; they were used to so much canned fruit, and now a can of peaches or pineapple is 43 points!

When newcomers were grouped according to whether they had come from rural, town, or metropolitan areas, the study showed that, as was to be expected, the rural families had been spending much less money for food than the metropolitan families. They had been accustomed to producing themselves much of the food they consumed. Upon moving to Seneca, these families had to increase their food costs very considerably—on the average, two to four times. At the same time, they continued to spend less money for food than other groups, indicating the persistence of a more frugal type of food-spending habit among persons of rural backgrounds.

When family diets were studied for nutritional adequacy, it appeared that 37 per cent of the families were eating satisfactory diets, 32 per cent were marginal, and 31 per cent were unsatisfactory. Rural families were averaging less adequate diets than metropolitan families. As compared to their prewar eating habits, it appeared that war workers had, by and large, improved their diets, although there was great variation on this score. Some families, although they were spending much more money than formerly, were eating less well than before, judged from a nutritional point of view. Still the majority—some 60 per cent—were obtaining more satisfactory diets.

Executives and skilled workers were eating better-balanced diets than unskilled workers. This is due not only to the fact that these families were spending more money for food than the lower-income groups, but also to their greater knowledge of nutritional requirements. The executive group was presumably more conscious of what constitutes an adequate diet and was more likely to provide it for their families—if not for health reasons, then for social status reasons, it being the "proper" thing to do to eat the "correct" foods.

Quite separate from the question of "How well were people eating?" is the question "How much were people eating?" It was found that the executive group and the skilled group were consuming slightly more than before the war, while the unskilled group were consuming slightly less. These differences are probably to be explained on the grounds that the skilled group was earning more money and hence was able to purchase more food; while the unskilled group came largely from rural areas and was tending not to replace fully the foods that had formerly been produced at home.

It was an interesting fact that the majority of housewives in this study reported their sugar rations, canned food rations, and meat rations to be adequate.[3] This was especially true of the rural group, and may reflect the fact that many rural families were supplementing their rations of canned food and meat with home-produced food. Many of the women canned fruit and vegetables in the summer; and many managed to buy meat in large quantities directly from farmers and to store it in deep-freeze lockers.

Of all the families studied, 92 per cent were consuming meat at least at the same rate as before the war. Almost half the families reported they were eating more meat than

[3] Sugar, most meats, and most canned goods were rationed throughout the United States; and most American families felt the sugar and meat shortages acutely.

formerly. The large majority had meat at least once a day. This is in contrast to the situation in many parts of the United States, where meat shortage was a constant source of complaint. The more favorable situation among Seneca war workers was probably due to the fact already mentioned— that many housewives arranged to buy meat directly from farmers—as well as to the fact that Seneca was allowed more liberal amounts of rationed foods than other areas. As one woman put it, "At least there's meat to be had for my red stamps here in Seneca. Back home, my sister writes, there isn't any meat in the butcher shops!"

Furthermore, many shipyard workers bought one meal a day at the plant cafeteria, where they could usually get a meat dish. Their patronage of the cafeteria was probably far greater than the usual patronage of restaurants by working-class people.

Seneca war workers were eating more meat, more eggs, more oranges, more butter than the average American family; and they were buying more of these foods than they did before the war. Milk consumption, while it increased somewhat, did not increase to the same extent as meat, eggs, or oranges.

Thus, on the whole, Seneca newcomers were spending much more money for food than before the war; they were eating well as compared to what they had been eating before the war, and as compared to the country as a whole. While there were some families—usually they came from rural areas—who were consuming less adequate diets than before, there was a much larger number on the other side of the ledger—families who now found themselves financially able to buy more and better food than before, and who took full advantage of the opportunity.

Because of the initial demands of the Southerners among the newcomers, the grocers in Seneca laid in a supply of white corn meal, hominy grits, Louisiana coffee, black-eyed peas, salt pork, and canned turnip and mustard greens. The grocers formed the impression, however, that the Southerners gradually changed some of their food preferences.

The grocers were astonished at the quantity of soft drinks they sold, even in winter. One store was selling twenty-five cases of twenty-four bottles each of Pepsi-Cola per week, and twenty cases of several other drinks. The other side of this story was seen in the interviewer's conversation with a lady who had been traveling all her married life with her husband, a painter. When asked whether she used much canned fruit and fruit juices, she replied, "Well, I used to, but the children like pop just as well now."

Shortages

The *Fortune* magazine poll on July 12, 1945, asked people in what one or two ways they had felt the inconvenience of the war most. Results for the country as a whole and for the Midwest were as follows:

Sources of Inconvenience	United States	Midwest
Shortages		
Food and Meat	26%	21%
Gasoline	14	12
Housing shortage	1.6	1.1
General cost of living	8	5
Rationing in general	7	—
Labor shortages	6	7
Business difficulties	4	6
Transportation difficulties	4	3

With the single exception of a greater inconvenience due to housing shortage, Seneca seems to have fared pretty much as the nation fared; and somewhat better in the matter of food.

Food, clothing, manpower, and shelter were the principal objects of scarcity in Seneca. The coming of the first shipyard workers in August, 1942, was described by a Seneca grocer as like "a swarm of locusts." They cleaned everything from the grocers' shelves in a few days, and it was two months before government agencies cleared away the obstructions that kept Seneca residents from receiving more than 70 per cent of the prewar supply of scarce items, which was the allocation of the ordinary community. Finally, Seneca was listed as a special case and given generous treatment by the rationing agencies. Being in a crucial war production job, Seneca got special favors in the allocation of food.

A catalogue of shortages in the winter months of 1943–44 reads much the same as it would read for any part of the country. Bananas were seldom seen. There was no green tea— only black. There was no Kleenex or other kind of absorbent face paper for a month. Any kind of meat was eagerly bought. If fresh meat came in at 9 A.M. it would be gone by 11. Fresh fruit that came in at noon would be sold out by 2 P.M.

The storekeepers took practically everything they could get from the wholesalers, and the buying public took whatever the storekeepers had. In the meat line, there was a large demand for brains, kidneys, and other meats low in ration points, which had seldom been sold in Seneca before.

At the department store, needles were a cent apiece, with a limit of two to a customer. Coal orders were limited to one ton at a time. Laundry service was scarce, uncertain, and unsatisfactory for the first year; then it gradually improved.

But there was no real hardship in Seneca. Conditions were better than they were in surrounding towns.

The manpower shortage was felt most acutely by retail business in Seneca, which was not prepared to compete with the CBI wage rates. Women had to be employed wherever possible. Boys and girls were pressed into service, but even they were often enticed away by opportunities at the shipyard.

Oldtimers enjoyed a joke at the expense of one of the personnel officers at CBI. He drove into a service station to have his automobile washed. He got into a conversation with the boy who was to wash the car, telling him how much money they would pay him at CBI. When he came back two hours later, the car was not washed. He complained to the owner of the service station, but got no sympathy. The owner said, "That boy lit out for the CBI the minute you left. He was my only help. Now you can just take your car somewhere else and get it washed."

It was said in the town that the CBI would hire everything that had one arm and one eye. In any event, there were few able-bodied men in Seneca available for employment by the commercial establishments of the town.

Conclusion

Wartime life for the people of Seneca, both oldtimers and newcomers, appears to have been relatively more favorable than life in stable, non-boom communities. To a greater degree than in the ordinary community, life in Seneca brought the rewards of high wages, the feeling of patriotic accomplishment, excitement, and novelty. To counterbalance these advantages in some part, living conditions in Seneca were uncomfortably crowded. But wartime shortages of food and clothing were no worse in Seneca than in the rest of the country—in fact, after the first few months, they were somewhat less severe than elsewhere. The standard of diet actually improved for most Senecans.

6.

The Children's World

It is the first day of school in September, 1943. For five hundred and fifty youngsters it is a new experience, coming to this new school building that was finished just in time for opening day. They come wide-eyed and expectant, cautious and curious. They look around for friends, but many of them are strangers, having come to Seneca since school closed in June, and they do not know other children yet.

A new world is in the making—a new children's world. From time immemorial children have created their own social world, with its customs, rhymes, games, and superstitions that pass on from one childish generation to the next—a world largely unnoticed by the adults.

What will the new children's world be like, built by children from a dozen states and a hundred towns and cities? Last June the Seneca children trooped out of school to the singsong tune of

> "No more pencils, no more books,
> No more teachers' sassy looks."

Will they pick up another rhyme this year from some newcomer?

Will the game of marbles as played in northern Illinois villages be changed by the impact of other children's cultures? "In Texas we shoot like this." "In Iowa we make the circle this way." What about the old playground game of "pom

132

pom pullaway"? Will the Seneca variation win out over the newcomers' forms?

What sort of rhymes will be learned about the cracks in cement sidewalks? "Step on a crack, you break your mother's back," or a new version from southern Illinois?

More significant for the future lives of these children—what kind of social structure will take shape in this new social world? Who will gain prestige, and how? Who will be popular, who will make friends, who will be teased, who will be bullied, who will become lonely and friendless?

Will the answers to these questions be determined entirely by the children's own qualities of friendliness, kindness, cruelty, shyness; or also by the social positions of their parents? In what ways will the social structure of the adult world affect the growth of structure in the children's world? Will sectional antagonisms arise, South against North, rural against urban? Will socioeconomic differences come to the front, dividing children of management from children of labor?

These are the questions this chapter will seek to answer, by looking at some of the children individually, and by reporting some systematic studies made on the children in grades five through eight.

CHILDREN OF SENECA

While the bulk of the children had lived most of their lives in Illinois, they found themselves playing with and sitting next to children from twenty-five other states. In grades five through eight there were twenty-five children from the southwestern states of Oklahoma, Missouri, Texas, Louisiana, Arkansas, and Arizona, and eighteen children from the southeastern states of Kentucky, Tennessee, and Georgia.

The newcomers tended to be widely traveled people, especially if they came from beyond the borders of Illinois. One youngster had lived in forty-six of the forty-eight states. A second grader had already attended fifteen different schools, and during the year moved away from Seneca. One high school girl had attended five different schools during the 1942–43 session, while another had attended fourteen different high schools.

The children who made up the school population were as typically varied a group of individuals as would be found anywhere. There was the popular child, and the unpopular; the attractive and the unattractive. There was the newcomer who disliked his new surroundings, and the newcomer who soon became adjusted and contented with his new friends. There was the child from the "better-class" home, and the child from the "lower-class" home.

There was Jeff Carpenter, for example, a red-headed, freckle-faced ten-year-old from Oklahoma, who very soon became a leader among his age-mates; and there was Samuel, his older brother, whom the other boys called a "sissy" and who was socially isolated from the rest of the group.

Jeff walks with a businesslike swagger, usually with a bunch of keys dangling from his belt. Although not a big muscular fellow he stands in with those who are. He is usually manager of the baseball team, or he keeps track of who comes up to bat next.

One day the children complained about having to sit at the table in the cafeteria every day until all had finished eating. The teacher decided that they could choose one person and ask to be excused by that person when they wanted to leave the table. The class chose Jeff.

Jeff is one of a religious family. He sings with his older brother and father and mother in a family quartet at the Assembly of God Church. He brings religious literature to his teacher. He said of his father, "If the Lord called him, he'd go right away. But the Lord hasn't called him yet."

On the Moral Ideology Test, in which the children were asked to write down things that were good things to do, Jeff wrote: "to go to church; ride horses; do dishes; pray every night; don't sass your mother; don't smoke; don't course; don't steal; no fighting."

In spirit, Jeff is still in Oklahoma. In any conversation he brings the talk around to horses and ranch life, and he keeps the class laughing telling stories about riding horses and lassoing calves. In one of the papers he wrote for his teacher, he said, "I would like to live in West Texas on a ranch and ride my horse and sing those cowboy songs and jingle my spurs and turn back my hat and yell 'Wahoo, Wahoo, Wahoo.'"

Jeff's older brother, Samuel, aged fourteen, is a home body. He likes to keep house for people. He even bakes pies and cakes. He uses the adjective "gorgeous" a great deal. On the Moral Ideology Test he listed, as good things to do, "going to Bible Study; going to young people's meeting; going to Prayer Service." And as bad things to do, "going to shows, drinking strong drinks; playing pool and many other worthly things." The extent to which his life is both female-centered and church-centered is indicated by his essay on "The Person I Would Like To Be Like When I Grow Up." Unique among the boys, he chose a woman as his ideal self, the co-pastor of his church.

"I would very muchly like to be like Agnes Stark which is a real person and about 34 years old and very nice looking, her occupation is in ministry work. She is a band director and can play almost every kind of instrument."

There was Claude Dahern, a fourteen-year-old boy from Louisiana, one of the few Southerners who took a strong dislike to their northern sojourn, and who never hesitated to express his discontent.

Claude was one of those who drew a clear line between old-timers and newcomers in Seneca, as is shown on the Moral Ideology Test in the discrimination he uses in indicating who would approve the good things a boy his age might do:

Good Things To Do	*Who Would Praise?*
1. Going to school for 9 months.	About half the pupils of our room.
2. Swimming.	Nearly everybody in our room.
3. Playing football.	About all the boys in this room.
4. Going fishing.	About ½ of the pupils of this room.
5. To belong to some organization.	About all the people in the room.
6. Being a good boy.	Maw.
7. Working.	About ⅕ of the people of this room.

Claude's essay on "The Person I Would Like To Be Like When I Grow Up" is as follows:

"I want to be like myself and nobody else when I grow up. I dont want to work very hard when I grow up. I want to take life easy, not hard. But of course I will have a business good enough to earn what money I need. I won't do like most dum guys will. I will be smart and wise. I will settle down in the State of Louisiana. It ain't hard to earn a living there. It is a good State two. I want to be tough enough to defend myseft if any northerners get tough and rough with me they will learn to Stay away. I will help the South chase all the northerners out of the South. Then I will be famous. It will be a South without no northerners in it. I will be able to handle a rifle as good as Robert E. Lee and a Pistol as good as Stonewall Jackson, and fight better than Grant."

In contrast to Claude, there was Sally Steel, a thirteen-year-old girl who made the move to Seneca with trepidation, but who soon was happy and well-liked by others.

In her autobiography Sally wrote, "I have one girl friend back in Peoria with whom I have grown up. We write to each other often. We are very close.

"I, as with all girls my age, like to have fun with the boys. Just to go to shows or skating with them occasionally.

"I don't believe I have very many enemies. At least I hope not.

I am careful with the kids I go around with. Those that I don't think are decent I speak to but that is as far as it goes.

"I hope to move back to Peoria for high school. I like Seneca but I was brought up in Peoria so naturally I would want to go back there.

"I like this school an awful lot. I'm crazy about my teachers and you couldn't beat the kids. Of course, the houses are discouraging but it is some consolation to know that it is only temporary."

Her teacher describes Sally in the following manner:

"Sally is an all-around good student. She is well liked by everyone. She is intelligent, dependable, honest, courteous, thoughtful of others. She is loyal to her school and to her friends. She is well liked by older boys and girls, especially some in high school. She is interested in music, and she is active in baseball, volley ball, etc. She loves to play. She, too, had a very hard time adjusting herself here. She was very lonely for a long time. Now she is very happy and is enjoying life. She is enjoying her school work. In her school work I would say she is above average. She is very neat, very punctual, and hasn't been tardy at all. She attends St. Patrick's Catholic Church regularly. Sally does a lot of work in the school office here and distributes milk in the school cafeteria, collects money for extra milk. People in the cafeteria have a lot of confidence in her and she knows how to go in and do things on her own. Sally is so refined!— She shows this refinement and culture in everything she does. She laughs and enjoys laughing but she keeps her laughing under control. She is very nice looking and carries herself well."

In the eyes of adults Sally is one of the most attractive children in school. She has dark, naturally wavy hair, is of average size and build, knows all the social graces and has a great deal of poise. She never pairs off with one or two people, but is always in a large group and seems to be friends with nearly everybody.

Sally writes the following for "The Person I Would Like To Be Like":

"I would like to be like my mother and my Aunt combined. My mother is 38. She is of wonderful character. A good personality, very nice looking. She has black hair which is turning grey. Green eyes, medium built and medium height. She is a very clean person. Right now she is a switchboard operator at the Seneca Shipyard's. She does smoke but her recreation consists of making friends and playing cards.

"My Aunt is 27 or 28. Light hair, blue eyes, medium height, and medium built. She is my mother's sister. She also has a wonderful character. She is a private secretary. She plays cards and also makes friends. Her fiancee was killed in action."

Geraldine Porteus, one of the more mature girls in the eighth grade, was the daughter of a leading citizen of Old Seneca. She was friendly with the newcomers, but their coming had no great effect on her.

More than most girls her age, Geraldine lives in the future, with a vivid imagination of what it will be like to be a college girl. Her "Person I Would Like To Be Like" is as follows:

"She likes sports of all sorts and is especially good at swimming and ice skating. She loves to dance. In college she majors in astronomy, higher math., and grammar. She has many friends and travels all over the Americas. She loves to camp in the open air. She also likes domestic things like cooking and sewing. While in College she models at some large store to help pay for her tuition fee. She loves flowers and nature. She is a good singer. She lives in either Minnesota, northern Wisconsin, northern Michigan or southern Canada. She is dark-skinned, blue-eyed, and has beautiful, long dark hair. She is tall and slender. She loves to see plays and shows. She reads many books."

Her catalogue of "good things to do" on the Moral Ideology Test is: "Help at home willingly; go to church and take part in it; obey your parents and teachers; learn how to play games and sports fairly; swim, skate, play other outdoor games; learn to sew and cook; keep your room tidy; be honest, polite and courteous; ride horseback."

Among the newcomer children, there were some who came from families of high social status; others from families of low social status. The boys and girls to be described below are children of families already described in an earlier chapter of this book.[1] Patsy Burnside was the child of an "upper crust" family; Grace and Ralph Plank and Curtis and Eunice Magee were the children of "working-class" families; and Susan Andrews was a member of a family who ranked "at the bottom of the heap." Each child was an individual in his own right, but each reflected the attitudes and values of the particular social class to which his family belonged.

Patsy Burnside is an active, talkative, friendly ten-year-old. She is always busy at something, but often not at what the schoolteacher would like her to do. The teacher says, "Patsy is a great talker. She'd rather talk than write." She pays some attention to the boys in her room; made a valentine for one boy, but was afraid to give it to him.

Patsy loves animals of all kinds. She has brought to school snails, turtles, fish, butterflies, grasshoppers, and tadpoles. Often she picks up a cat or a dog and brings it to school with her. Other boys and girls bring dogs and cats for her, which she keeps in school for the day and then takes home, only to be told by her mother, "You'll have to send it away; we haven't got room in this small apartment for a pet."

Patsy plays a great deal with Barbara, the daughter of an executive at about the same level in the shipyard hierarchy as her father. The girls have been told by their mothers not to play with other children until their mothers have found out if the other children come from nice homes.

Like their parents, Grace and Ralph Plank are solid citizens. They study faithfully, and are looked upon by the other children as steady members of the children's world. They both are nearsighted and must wear thick-lensed glasses.

Fourteen-year-old Grace is one of the smarter girls in the class. In discussions she is quick in seeing the answers to problems, in pointing out conflicts, and in seeing possible consequences. She is not very popular in the classroom, yet she is accepted by all.

[1] See Chapter 4.

Grace is slim, tall, not attractive looking, and is occasionally called "bean pole." She is rather athletic and was most popular during the baseball season. She was the best baseball player among the girls and often played with the boys when there was no girls' game.

Though she has an acceptable role in the children's world, Grace is closely attached to the adult world, too. Her "Person I Would Like To Be Like" shows no adolescent rebellion.

"I would like to be like a woman that was in the play 'Lavendar and Old Lace.' This woman was kind and understanding. When things went wrong she always had a cheerful word and good advice.

"I would like to be like Molly Pitcher in the way she fought for her country. I should like to be American enough to stand up for my country like she did.

"I would like to be like my grandmother that just passed away. She was a god-fearing woman who was always helping others.

"I should like to be like my mother in all her ways for she is kind and understanding and tolerant with all people.

"I would like to be like Rosiland Russel. She can act and is very beautiful.

"If one person had all of these qualities they would be blessed far beyond the ordinary."

Similarly, Grace's list of "good things to do" on the Moral Ideology Test shows conformity to adult standards:

"Respecting all teachers and elders in the school; helping mother with the household chores; helping older people with bundles and across the street; not to talk back to my parents and mind their commands; take your turn when getting mail or getting groceries; make the most of what you have and share with others; riding a bicycle on the street so that people can walk on the sidewalk; keep our feet clean so that we don't get our house and school room dirty; be neat with our clothes and act decent when in public."

At eleven, Ralph Plank is still a little boy, even though he is growing tall. He still wears short, knee trousers at a time when most of his age-mates wear long trousers. He is not very active in the school room, on the school playground, or on the playground at the housing area. He has one mutual friend. Like most boys his age, Ralph has heroes of the glamorous type. In describing the "Person I Would Like To Be Like" he writes:

"I would like to be like Joe Lewis.

But I would not like to be brown.

I want to look like Clark Grable.

But I want to sing like Gene Autry

I want to be a pilot like Clark Grable.

I want to be like Lou Costello because I want to be funny. and I want to make the gril mad at me like Cary Grant."

The Magee children are just as well-liked as their parents. Curtis, Jr., at the age of 13, is described by his teacher as being very dependable, intelligent, and ambitious.

Curtis is growing tall and slender. He writes that his favorite sports are baseball, football, basketball, hockey, racing or jumping, with football and basketball being his special favorites. He played on the grade school basketball team this year. Curtis is neat and clean and has a great pride in his personal appearance. He has a certain standard of honor or value that is noticeable. He wonders if ideas and suggestions given in discussions are really good, and he usually considers what effect these will have on other people in the group. He has a paper route in the War Homes area, and wants a larger route for the summer.

Curtis chooses for his hero the football player "Slinging Sammy" Baugh. He writes,

"I want to be like *Samuel Baugh*. He is about 28 years old. He is one of the finest men you could meet. Sam is a tall and sort of slender man. He keeps himself very neat except when he plays football. He plays for the Washington Redskins during the fall. When he is not playing football he goes to his ranch in Texas. The only recreation I know he likes is hunting."

Eunice Magee is eleven years old. She is the newcomer who is most widely accepted by the oldtimers in her age-group. She is the "little lady" type; goes to church regularly and sings in the choir.

Her list of "good things to do" on the Moral Ideology Test is as follows: "Study your lessons; go to Church; go to the store for mother; be polite to little children; be sure to help your mother every Sat. with housework; do every thing she wants you to do; take turns when you are playing with other pals; help little children across the streets."

Susan Andrews is the nine-year-old member of the Andrews tribe that live in two trailers at a private trailer camp. Both her father and mother work at the shipyard, and both of them worked at farm labor in southern Illinois before coming to Seneca. Now the five children are cared for after school by Flora, twelve years old, until their mother returns from work at seven o'clock in the evening.

Susan is a very small, frail-looking child, who often complains of illness. She is seldom neat or clean. She is very inactive at school. This may be because she is rejected by other children in her classroom, or it may be that she does not have sufficient energy to be active in games.

Susan is very irregular in her school work and in her attendance. Although the family has been living in Seneca for a long time, Susan did not begin coming to school regularly enough to be counted as a student until the latter part of March. Then she sat at a table alone at the back of the classroom. She seldom plays with other children, but stays with her older sister, Flora, who accepts her willingly, probably because Flora is rejected by her own classmates and it is a comfort to her to have Susan around.

SOCIAL STRUCTURE IN THE CHILDREN'S WORLD

Individual children were popular or unpopular, bold or shy, happy or unhappy, as in any set of children anywhere. But were there any broad differences among groups? Were individual histories related to family backgrounds? Did the unwritten rules of social class divide these children into the favored and the unfavored, as in more stable communities? Did social distinctions become more or less evident as time went on?

To answer questions like these a study was made of all children in the fifth, sixth, seventh, and eighth grades between December, 1943, and June, 1944.[2] There were 274 children in these four grades, of whom 60 were oldtimers.

The oldtimer children faced a situation as new and different, in many respects, as the situation faced by the newcomers. Before the boom, there was one group of approximately twenty children in each of the school grades. Each group had begun school together and had stayed together from year to year. There was a permanency and a stability in the pattern of social relationships between children in each group that was the result of long familiarity and a common school experience.

In December, 1943, this familiar pattern had been disrupted. There were now two groups of children at each grade level, each group numbering from thirty-five to forty, and each group consisting of a majority of newcomers. A fifth-grade child of an old Seneca family now found himself in a group twice the size of the one he had been accustomed to, where most of the boys and girls were strangers not only to him but to each other. He was as likely as not to have a teacher who was new to Seneca; and he was as likely as not to find that his best friend was now in "the other 5th-grade room."

Thus the children's world was a new world to oldtimer and newcomer alike.

[2] The data from the systematic study are taken from Hugh Gerthon Morgan, *Social Relationships of Children in a War-Boom Community*. Ph.D. Dissertation in the University of Chicago Library, 1946.

Also, Hugh Gerthon Morgan, "Social Relationships of Children in a War-Boom Community," *Journal of Educational Research*, 40 (December, 1946), 271–86.

The children were tested twice—first in January, 1944, and again in the following May. Approximately half of the newcomers had entered the Seneca school in September, 1943, while the others had entered during the preceding school year. Thus the January testing came while a good many of the newcomers were still quite strange to Seneca; and the May testing came at a time when the children had had at least one school year in which to become acquainted.

These children were tested by two well-known procedures for studying social structure in a children's group. One was a "sociometric" test, which asks each child to write down the names of his best friends, and also of those with whom he is least friendly. The other procedure was a "guess-who" test, which consisted of twelve brief descriptions of various kinds of people, and asked the children to write the names of the boys and girls who fitted the various descriptions. For example, these two items were intended to pick out the popular and unpopular children:

Here is someone whom everybody likes. People are always glad to have him or her around.

Here is someone whom no one seems to care much about. People do not notice when he or she is around.

Other items were intended to pick out boys and girls with reputations among their age-mates as being active in games, enthusiastic, good fighters, good-looking, attention-getting, and the opposites of these characteristics.

Effects of length of residence. In January, after the entire group had been together but a short time, the newcomers chose and rejected other children as friends without apparent relation to length of residence of those whom they chose. To a newcomer, all children were new, and there was little discrimination between old residents and new residents.

The oldtimer children, on the other hand, showed strong

identification with each other from the beginning. They chose many more friends from their own group than from the newcomer group.

By the end of May, there was a shift in this over-all pattern. Oldtimer children were still preferring oldtimers, but

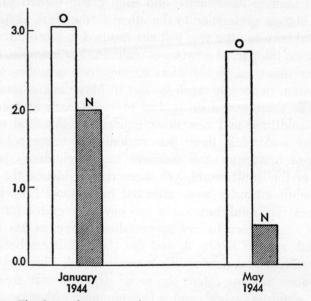

The first column in each pair represents choices made by oldtimer children; the second columns represent choices made by newcomer children. The groups have been equated for size.

Fig. 11. Friendship Choices Received by Oldtimer Children.

newcomers were now preferring other newcomers. The new children were increasingly identifying with each other, and there was a tendency for the total group to divide into two separate groups according to length of residence in Seneca.

A portion of these data are shown graphically in Figure 11, where friendship choices received by oldtimer children are shown for the two testings. The figure shows that, after the two groups have been equated for size, oldtimers received far fewer choices from newcomers in May than in January.

Data on social reputation showed the same trends. Oldtimers tended to ascribe better social reputations to oldtimers than to newcomers; and each group tended to rate itself high in preference to the other group. Here again the interval between the two testings resulted in more discrimination on the part of newcomer children. For example, newcomers' mentions of oldtimers on negative, or unfavorable, reputation items was much greater in May than in January.

While there was a great deal of social participation between oldtimer and newcomer children in the total social context, and while there was undoubtedly more cohesion between newcomer and oldtimer in the children's world than in the adult world, yet these data evidence the fact that adult attitudes were reflected in the social world of children. The adult newcomer was never integrated into the life of Old Seneca to any appreciable degree, as has been pointed out in Chapter 4, and the standoffishness between old residents and new residents was marked. This situation influenced to some extent the social structure that grew up in the children's world, and it became more rather than less evident with the passage of time.

Effects of father's income level. Studies of children in stable communities have shown that social class factors are operative in the children's world just as in the adult world. Children of high-status families tend to occupy positions of high status in the eyes of their age-mates; they are in the favorable position of being often chosen as friends, of being considered good-looking, popular, happy, good at games, and so on. Children of low-status families tend to fall at the other extreme; and there is, on the whole, a high relationship between family social position and the social participation and reputation of the child.[3]

In wartime Seneca, where social class lines were less sharply drawn, and where there was little time for a clear-cut social hierarchy to crystallize among adults, what would be the effect of social factors upon the children's evaluations of each other?

As a rough measure of socioeconomic status the father's income level was taken. The highest level included foremen and management in the shipyard, and professional men and other "better-class" people from Old Seneca. The second or middle level was that of mechanic or skilled craftsman in the shipyard, and small businessman or skilled worker in Old Seneca. The third or lowest level was that of apprentice or helper in the shipyard, and semi-skilled or unskilled worker in Old Seneca.

The study showed that children of the higher socioeconomic level had greater numbers of mentions as friends, and their social reputation was better than that of children of low socioeconomic status. Children of Group I (top) received more friendship choices from all three groups than did children of Groups II and III. Similarly, children of Group I received more mentions as "active in games" for both boys and girls, "fighter" for boys, "good-looking" for boys, and "popular" for both boys and girls. On the other hand, children of Group III received the highest scores on unfavorable items, such as "unpopular" for boys and girls, "not good-looking" for boys and girls, and "not a fighter" for boys. A portion of these data are shown in Figure 12.

The patterns of choice became clearer as time went on. In other words, social structure became more distinct during

[3] Bernice L. Neugarten, "Social Class and Friendship among School Children," *American Journal of Sociology*, 51 (January, 1946), 305–13.

the period from January to June, and father's income level became a more, rather than less, influential factor.

Relations with other factors. Several other factors were also studied in relation to friendship choices and social reputation of children. Academic achievement as measured by an objective test of knowledge was found to be associated with high friendship scores and favorable reputation. Since

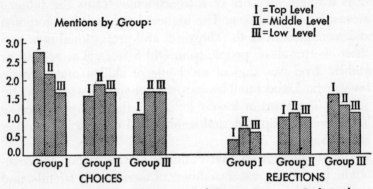

Fig. 12. Friendship Choices and Rejections as Related to Father's Income.

high academic achievement is usually associated with high socioeconomic level, it is not clear from this study whether it is favorable socioeconomic status or better academic achievement or a combination of the two that works to give a child higher status in the children's world.

Factors that were not definitely related to status in the Seneca children's world were: section of the country from which the child came, size of community from which the child came, and religious affiliation.

CONCLUSIONS

Within a few months the children's world took on a definite structure, with some children popular, wanted as friends, and bearing favorable social reputations, while other children were unfavorably regarded by their age-mates. This structure became more definite as the months wore on, until by the end of the second year of the boom it was comparable in sharpness to the structure of the children's world in a more stable community.

The structure of the children's world was a fuzzy reflection of that of the adult Seneca social world. The same general elements of prestige and social status were present in the children's world as in the adult world, though there were more exceptions to the rule among the children. For example, the children all recognized a few boys and girls from lower-income families as desirable for friends; and a few boys and girls of upper-income families were generally disliked and given low status in the children's world. Nor were social class differences as marked between Seneca children as they were between children of other communities.

On the whole, the children of Seneca had an interesting and happy time of it. They very quickly formed their own society, with its heroes and heroines and leaders and followers and strangers. Perhaps it was slightly more "democratic" than the children's world of many towns, in that it rewarded talent and good will with somewhat less reference to the social status of the child's parents.

PART III: THE ADJUSTMENT OF INSTITUTIONS

7.

Religion

Throughout the whole of its prewar life, Seneca relied upon the churches for making it something more than a cluster of houses with people living in them. The churches met the individual spiritual needs and the moral needs of their people. They brought people together for all the kinds of friendly face-to-face sociability that made Seneca a community, a place where people lived a common life. Then too, the rituals of life took place in the churches—babies were christened, children were confirmed, young people courted and took each other in marriage, the dead were eulogized and buried.

How did the war boom affect the churches? Were these effects temporary or lasting? And what role did the churches play in New Seneca? Did they do for five thousand newcomers what the churches had been doing all along for the oldtimers? Or did they fail to meet the challenge of the new situation? Or did they discover new things for churches to do—human needs to meet that had not existed in Seneca before the war?

Before answering these questions we shall take a bird's-eye view of the history of organized religion in Old Seneca.

The first population wave brought in three churches. The Catholic church was founded in 1858, the Baptist in 1864, and the Methodist in 1865. These three churches met the needs of the community during its first seventy-five years.

The Catholic parish was one of the largest in the Illinois River Valley, thanks to the Irish settlers along the canal. Later some German Catholics came in to strengthen the church further. When, in 1880, the Seneca parish priest was offered the church in Bloomington, Illinois, a sizable city, he declined it because the Bloomington parish was not as large as Seneca.

By far the largest church in Seneca, the Catholic church was a fine building, constructed at a cost of $196,000, and with a seating capacity of about six hundred. The parish consisted of some three hundred families, many of them from the surrounding countryside. There was a small parochial school with three teachers. Father Preston, the parish priest, had come in 1938. He succeeded Father Higgins, who had made the church famous throughout the countryside for its annual Fourth of July Carnival.

The Baptists had a strong church during the nineteenth-century decades when Seneca flourished. Their church grew gradually weaker after 1900, and about 1905 they finally gave up the effort to hold regular services. Some of their members joined the Methodists, while those who felt that they must continue to be Baptists went to church in the neighboring town of Marseilles.

The Methodists also flourished during Seneca's first fifty years. When their first church building was destroyed by fire during this period, they replaced it with a small but substantial brick church, which had a seating capacity of two hundred. Their organization fell away after the first world war, but they managed to survive, aided by recruits from the Baptists. Their minister preached also at the Manlius church, in the open country. When the boom began, the Methodist

membership was about a hundred, more or less, depending
on how many of the "inactive" members were counted.
Church attendance was seldom over twenty-five, and only
the interest of Mr. Ray Nichols, the leading layman, kept
the church going.

The Lutheran church was founded in Seneca in the 1920's.
It grew from the gradual migration of Norwegian Lutherans
outward from their original settlement to the north and east
of Seneca. This group had come to America in the nineteenth
century and had established its own churches and schools.
Many of the people were followers of Hauge, the Norwegian
religious reformer. There was a strong church at Stavanger,
a few miles north of Seneca. As old Norwegian farmers retired and moved into Seneca, the demand grew for a church
in town. The pastor at Stavanger, the Reverend Mr. Reynold
Wilson, then established a church in Seneca. The Lutherans
bought the old Baptist church building. Mr. Wilson preached
at Seneca as well as Stavanger. Membership in the Seneca
church was about a hundred.

This church belonged to the Norwegian Lutheran Church
of America, one of the more fundamentalist of the Lutheran
groups in its religious doctrine. It encouraged its members
to organize their social life around the church, and to keep
apart from groups that dance, play cards, and go to the
theater.

The Holiness Methodist church was an offshoot of the
Methodist church, formed about 1933 by five or six Methodist families who were influenced by a revivalist in a neighboring city, and who felt that their church had become too
modernistic in its doctrine and too Episcopal in its form of
service. Led by the Reverend Mr. Burns and his daughter,
Beatrice, who had had deaconess training, the group met in
a rented room and gradually saved money for a building of
their own.

RELIGIOUS LIFE IN NEW SENECA

Equipped with these churches, Old Seneca faced New Seneca and the task of building a religious organization to serve a quintupled population. The new population, from the point of view of religious preference, was not greatly different from Old Seneca. This fact was indicated by a house-to-house canvass of church preference made jointly by the Lutheran and Methodist parish visitors in the summer of 1944. These two ladies called at four-fifths of the War Homes

TABLE 10

RELIGIOUS PREFERENCES OF NEWCOMERS IN SENECA
Summer, 1944

Denomination	Per Cent of Families Interviewed
Methodist	25
Catholic	20
Lutheran	16
Baptist	10
Assembly of God	6
Christian	6
Holiness Methodist	1.2
Presbyterian	1
Congregational	1
Evangelical	1
Jewish	0.9
Episcopal	0.6
Pentecostal	0.5
Christian Science	0.5
United Brethren	0.4
Latter Day Saints	0.4
Others (Salvation Army, Church of God, Missionary Alliance, Gospel Tabernacle, Nazarene, etc.)	1.5
No Preference	8
	100
Total Number of Families Reporting	809

apartments and slightly over half of the Victory Court and Riverview Homes. The results of their survey are shown in Table 10. The Methodists, Catholics, Lutherans, and Baptists account for 70 per cent of the preferences.

There was a great deal of shifting of newcomers away from their former church preferences. This was true not only of people from such denominations as the Baptist, which did not have a church in Seneca, but also of Methodists and Lutherans. Table 11 shows that people in War Homes went to the Lutheran and Methodist churches even though they had not formerly belonged to these denominations. This table is based upon data gathered from a sample of War Homes residents as part of the survey of church preferences.

TABLE 11

SHIFTS OF RELIGIOUS AFFILIATION
BY FAMILIES IN WAR HOMES

| Former Affiliation | Affiliation in Seneca | |
| | Methodist | Lutheran |
	Number of Families	
Baptist	11	11
Christian	5	5
Presbyterian	2	1
Congregational	2	0
Methodist	—	5
Lutheran	5	—

Seen in terms of religious activity, the boom was divisible into two periods. The first half of the boom in Seneca was a period of evangelization and religious organization, while the last half was a comparatively stable period with an approach to the even tenor of church life as it occurs in ordinary communities.

The first year and a half saw the organization of one new church in Seneca, the completion of two new church buildings, the holding of revival meetings by several churches, the establishment of a religious organization in War Homes, and the development of several women's church groups in the housing projects.

At first it seemed that the housing projects might develop religious organizations independent of the churches in the town. For several months a group was active in War Homes. It was led by Mr. Curtis Magee, a member of the World Missionary Alliance, and was called the War Homes Christian Fellowship. The group held a Sunday school in the morning, Sunday evening vespers, and Wednesday evening prayer meetings, all meeting in War Homes. The Sunday school was announced as "of the people, for the people, and by the people." This group, never exceeding thirty in number, found friends in Old Seneca in the Holiness Methodist Church, and joined with this group in pushing the construction of a church building. This building was completed in the autumn of 1943, at a cost slightly exceeding $5,000. The Holiness Methodist group had been raising money toward the building for several years and, aided at the close by their friends in the Christian Fellowship, they built the church debt-free.

These two groups joined in a tent revival in the autumn of 1943, in a vacant lot near War Homes. They were assisted by some religious-minded Chicago laymen. After the close of the revival, when the Holiness Methodist building was completed, the War Homes Christian Fellowship disbanded and most of the members went to the Holiness church. This church did not grow large. It reached a total of thirty-five families, of which two-thirds were newcomers.

One other religious project was carried on in a housing area independent of the town churches. This was a children's Bible class conducted on Friday afternoons by a lady in Victory Court, with the assistance of Miss Moreland, the Lutheran parish visitor. The class flourished for a time during the winter of 1943–44, with about sixty children. The leader was a member of the World Missionary Alliance. Eventually this class was discontinued, partly at least because some parents disliked the leader's tendency to proselytize. Week-day Bible classes were offered thereafter by the Lutheran and Methodist churches.

The Assembly of God. The most energetic evangelistic movement of all led to the building of the Assembly of God church in the winter of 1943–44. In the summer of 1943, Ross and Agnes Stark, husband and wife, both ministers of the Assembly of God Church, came to Seneca with their two boys. The Starks were church-builders. They had two churches already to their credit and were out to build their third.

Ross and Agnes Stark grew up in Quincy, Illinois. Both became active in the Assembly of God Church and both became ministers. They were married in their early twenties, and had two children before they came to Seneca.

Ross Stark was the more attractive of the pair. He looked like a movie star—tall, well-proportioned, with black hair, brown eyes, regular features, and a dapper black mustache. At the age of forty he looked nearer thirty and people could hardly believe that he had a son in the Navy. Agnes was a vigorous, strong-featured woman. She liked to preach, and she did preach more frequently than her husband, who looked after the business affairs of the church and did a great deal of pastoral visiting.

Coming to Seneca to start a new church, they had to find a way to earn a living, since they did not expect much of a salary from their church. Ross got an appointment as school truant officer, which gave him ample opportunity to get around and see people. Agnes devoted all her time to church work.

Seneca was to their liking. At the end of the boom, Mr. Stark said, "These have been the happiest years of my life." He and his wife had created a church from the ground up. They had found their kind of people, who wanted their kind of religion.

This new church drew its members largely from among newcomers who had formerly been Baptists or Methodists— working-class people with a simple fundamentalist belief in the Scriptures. Since the Assembly of God was a tithing church, the money soon began to come in for a church build-ing. In a few months, a lot was purchased on Main Street and excavation was begun, part of the labor being donated by church members. A one-story cinder-block building was constructed. The second story, containing the church audi-torium proper, was to be constructed later. The building cost $6,000, and was free of debt shortly after it was com-pleted.

Attendance at the Sunday evening meeting, the principal meeting of the week, ran from a hundred to a hundred and forty. About seventy families, totaling some three hundred persons, became identified with the church, though none of them joined the church formally. The church was not "set in order" by the church authorities and hence could not receive members. This policy was purposeful, for with the future of the church uncertain it seemed better for the larger organization to carry the responsibility than for it to be turned over formally to the local people.

At a typical Sunday evening service, there was a choir of twenty with an orchestra of four wind instruments. In the audience there were always several infants in arms and a dozen young children. The visitor coming in from the fresh outside air felt his nostrils contract with the sharp odor of human bodies.

The preaching was preceded by an hour of testimonials interspersed with hymns. The piano played softly during the testimonials, to suggest what the next hymn would be. The testimonials began with people speaking rapidly and became faster and louder as they proceeded. At the end of the crescendo, the women would often weep.

"I want to testify how the Lord helped me. Just this last week I had a bad sore throat, I prayed, 'Lord, heal me,' and He healed me."

"Bless the Lord. I've been in trouble and doubted but the Lord was patient. When I cried to Him, He heard me."

"I hear you, Lord, oh, pray for me, brethren and sisters, so when He calls me, my lamp will be filled with oil. I'm on my way to heaven."

"I want to be filled with the Holy Ghost, so full that my ears will bubble over."

"I want everybody to know my sweet Jesus—everybody."

"When I was first anointed and filled with the Holy Ghost, and joined the church, I wasn't so much thinking would I be healed of my thyroid. No, I was thinking would the Lord wash all my sins away. Well, He did, and I was healed into the bargain. Bless His holy name."

Throughout there was a constant fire of comment from the ministers and congregation:

"Allelujah." "Heavenly Father, Amen." "Yes, that's right." "Bless her, Lord." "God, hear us."

The songbook was entitled *Full Gospel Songs* and was published by the Gospel Publishing House of Springfield, Missouri. Songs sung during the evening were: "Are You Washed in the Blood?" "Beulah Land," "I Love to Tell the Story," "Jesus Is Calling," "There Shall Be Showers of Blessings," "Whiter Than Snow."

Sister Stark preached on the subject of prayer. She said,

"Maybe you won't like me after this sermon. Maybe some of you don't like me now. But what about the Sunday school teachers that don't go to the evening prayer meeting? Three parents spoke to me about it. How do you think they feel to have their children taught by a teacher that does not go to prayer meeting? Now, how many Sunday school teachers are going to prayer meeting next Thursday? Hold up your hands."

She read the text where the disciple said, "Lord, teach us how to pray." "They didn't ask to be taught how to sing or to preach. You can't preach unless you are called to preach, but everybody can pray. The Lord said, 'Don't be like the Pharisees and pray to be seen of men.' Jesus said, 'Don't pray that-a-way.'"

She said prayer has three stages: communion, which is the up-go, petition, which is the in-go, and intercession, which is the out-go.

"Communion says, 'I love you, Lord,' not 'I love you 'cause you saved me,' but just as your child says, 'I love you, mama' not because it wants you to give it something either. 'Our Father, which is in heaven, hallowed be Thy Name,' that is the communion aspect. Then there is the in-go. 'Give us our daily bread.' And the out-go, 'Lead us not into temptation.'"

She called on all who felt the need of prayer to come forward. About four-fifths of the congregation did come, knelt at the altar and prayed audibly, each his own prayer. One voice rose high, groaning, "Oh Lord, hear me."

This church had activities scheduled five or six nights a week. A typical schedule was:

Sunday, 10 A.M.—Sunday School
11 A.M.—Preaching
7:30 P.M.—Testimonials and Preaching
Tuesday, 7:30 P.M.—Bible Class
Wednesday, 7:30 P.M.—Preaching
Thursday, 7:30 P.M.—Prayer Meeting
Friday, 7:30 P.M.—Young Folks' Meeting

In addition, there was choir and orchestra practice before and after meetings.

Finances seem never to have been much of a problem in this church of tithers. In the summer of 1945 five departments of the church each had a bank account. There were

accounts for Building Fund, Sunday School, Church, Young
People's Organization, and Parsonage Fund.

The Lutheran church. The Lutheran church also carried
on an active evangelistic campaign. The pastor of the Seneca
and Stavanger churches, as soon as the war-boom started,
asked his denomination for help to build up the church in
Seneca. He felt that the time had come to set up the Seneca
church with a full-time pastor. Home mission funds were
given by the Norwegian Lutheran Church of America; the
president of the state organization of the Church worked to
get collections taken in the Lutheran churches of the area.
Soon enough money was available to provide a pastor and a
parish visitor for Seneca.

Mr. Wendell Huber came to be the new pastor in October,
1942. Shortly afterward a parish visitor, Miss Annie Moreland, came to work with Mr. Huber. The two spent the first
two or three months in almost full-time door-to-door calling.
One day Mr. Huber made sixty-five calls. Later on, he busied
himself more with other pastoral duties, while Miss Moreland combined visitation with Bible study classes.

Wendell Huber was the first resident pastor the Lutheran
church had had. He was a big, dour young man. Over six feet tall,
all muscle and no fat, he appeared older than he was because of
the stern lines in his face. His mere presence announced that life
was a serious business. He came from Oklahoma, and the stories
about him said that he had gained a reputation as a "fighting
preacher," one who would fight another man if necessary for his
religion.

Wendell Huber put his slender blonde wife and his three tow-
headed children into a parsonage which the church had just
bought, and then he began a three-year stint of evangelism. He
laid the success of his work to his emphasis on "personal evangelism"—visiting and working with people as individuals—and to his
church doctrine of sticking to the fundamentals of the Bible. "We
don't go down a lot of by-paths," he said.

Wendell Huber and his church provided the tone of stern authority that many of the shipyard workers wanted in their lives. He opened his church to them, but on his own and his church's terms.

Whether Pastor Huber was happy in his work at Seneca was a question, but one which he would have said was irrelevant. He did his duty. Probably he was somewhat out of sympathy with the large-scale building and spending that were going on in Seneca in order to further the large-scale killing that was going on in the world. He took his turn at blessing the ships that slid down the launching ways, but he was an incongruous figure amid the fanfare and frivolity and champagne foam of these occasions. Once he wrote and spoke the following poem at a launching:

INVOCATION

Eternal God, almighty Lord,
Thou Lord of hosts by all adored,
We give Thee thanks for Thy great love,
For mercies showered from above.

We thank Thee, Lord, for victories
By land, by air, and on the sea.
We pray for faith and strength that peace
May come, and come indeed from Thee.

Speed forth the day that ends the strife,
And war replaced by love and life.
Lord, make us yielded to Thy will;
Though faith burns low, be with us still.

Into Thy hand this ship we place;
Go with it with Thy truth and grace.
And this we pray from hearts that yearn,
God, grant that ships soon homeward turn.

The church grew rapidly, and soon the Sunday morning attendance came to average almost a hundred and forty, which filled all the pews and overflowed into chairs at the rear. Sunday school enrollment was about two hundred, with fourteen classes. About half of the attendants at the Lutheran services were shipyard people. In the Lutheran Ladies' Aid Society, 30 per cent were newcomers. The church conducted Mission Circles in War Homes, Victory Court, and Riverview Homes. In the summer of 1944 two deaconesses were employed to teach a Vacation Bible School. In January, 1944, the church held a five-day series of evangelistic services with an out-of-town speaker.

The membership of the church grew from about a hundred at the start of the boom to about a hundred and seventy-five at the peak. This was the only church that received a large number of formal accessions to membership. In addition there were many other families who identified themselves with the church but did not transfer their memberships from their previous places of residence.

Like the other churches, the Lutherans raised money. They bought a parsonage, and in two years paid the $6,000 that it cost. By January, 1945, they were paying all the minister's salary and were entirely self-supporting, except for the parish visitor's salary, which continued to come from Home Mission funds.

On a typical Sunday morning the church was full at 10:30 and the organist started playing the processional. Hardly a half-dozen of the congregation were little children, and almost half were men. The choir consisted of four women in robes, four men in business suits, and eight little girls and one little boy in surplices. A leaflet handed out by the ushers showed a photograph of a church interior with a young man kneeling in a pew, and the motto, "My house is a house of prayer." The order of service included three prayers, four hymns, and several responses as well as the sermon. The sermon was on the Apostle Paul, and was preached in a simple, unvarnished speech with a number of homely phrases, such as, "It may seem that Paul had a nerve to say that—to set himself up as an example."

The Luther Hymnary contained a statement from the president of the Minnesota Synod, three creeds (Apostles, Nicene, Athanasian), the Augsburg Confession (explaining the Lutheran rejection of certain Catholic practices, such as retirement of men to the priesthood and women to nunneries, and eating no meat on Friday) and "Luther's Shorter Catechism." In addition it gave forms for morning and evening worship, long blessings for use at meals, and of course the beautiful old German hymns.

The Methodist church. The Methodist church, with a quarter of the newcomers having a Methodist preference, was the least active of the churches in evangelization. Whether this was a conscious policy or due to the rapid turnover of ministers is not clear, although the latter factor was certainly of considerable importance.

The Methodist church was the only church that did not have continuity of leadership during the boom. There were three different ministers in three years, and three different parish visitors in two years.

The minister who was in Seneca when the boom started was occupied for most of the year before he left with a personal decision to become an Army chaplain. He departed in July, 1943, and the church was without a minister for a short time until a former pastor, Mr. Thomas, came for a month during his vacation from his duties at another church. Mr. Thomas organized the Sunday school for the following year, and then was followed by Mr. R. L. Danielson who came from Colorado. Mr. Danielson was supplied with an assistant who was paid with outside funds by the Missionary Society of the Methodist Church. First he had Miss Hobbs, a deaconess, and then Miss Bugbee, a missionary on furlough.

After nine months Mr. Danielson was transferred to a

church nearer Chicago so that he could continue his post-graduate studies at Northwestern University. In his place came Mr. Telfer, who carried on for the last year of the boom. At the same time Miss Bugbee left and Miss Harriet Carlton came as Mr. Telfer's assistant.

At the beginning of the boom the Methodist church was quite weak, but it picked up considerably, with the help of some of the residents of War Homes. The Ladies' Aid Society grew until about half of its members were newcomers. Most of the Sunday school teachers were newcomers. In the spring of 1943 the men of the church started a Sunday Evening Club to provide constructive social and educational programs. The first meeting was addressed by Mr. Sam Campbell, the naturalist, who gave an illustrated lecture on the Great West. Following him were Dr. Morris Fishbein, of the American Medical Association, and two travel lecturers. The Club was discontinued for the summer and not revived.

When Mr. Danielson came in September, 1943, average attendance at church services was about fifty. This increased with the growing population, and reached about ninety by the fall of 1944, when it stayed constant until the close of the boom. Mr. Danielson promoted the young people's work, and he organized a visitation campaign in War Homes and Victory Court led by laymen in the churches.

A church beautification program was begun under Mr. Danielson and continued by Mr. Telfer. The entire interior of the church was renovated, and a new altar, a divided chancel, new pews, and a new furnace were provided. The parsonage was also renovated. The cost of the project was about $8,000. The money was raised locally except for $2,500 which was contributed by the Mission Board of the Methodist Church and by the Rock River Conference Mission Fund. The annual church budget was increased from about $2,000 to $3,500.

On a typical Sunday the Methodist church service started at 11 A.M., with the auditorium about half full. The ushers handed out a program leaflet bearing on the front page a line drawing of the church. Of the ninety people present, about twenty were young children, and about twenty-five were men. There was an organ prelude, and then a call to worship by the choir. The choir consisted of about fifteen women and girls, and two or three men, including the minister who sang with them in the anthem. There were three responses from the congregation, reading from the hymnal, an anthem and two choral responses, and three hymns.

The sermon was a challenge to "Live by your dreams," with a text taken from the story of Joseph and his brothers when the brothers planned to kill Joseph and throw him into a pit, saying, "and then we shall be done with these dreams." The minister alluded to the need for opposition to commercial interests in gambling and liquor, which profit at the expense of Seneca's moral and spiritual welfare. The service was much different from that of the Holiness Methodist church; one might say more Episcopal and less Methodist.

The announcements told of the Youth Fellowship meeting on Sunday evening, a meeting of the Women's Society of Christian Service, choir practice, a district conference for Methodist youth, and a bake sale sponsored by the Youth Fellowship to raise funds to pay for the candlesticks they were presenting to the church. The minister made a plea for the congregation to subscribe to the church publications and said that sample copies could be obtained after the service. Each person received from the ushers, on leaving, a leaflet by Deets Pickett entitled "Vigilance, the Price of Liberty." This was an appeal to church members to interest themselves in government, especially in local government problems, and particularly in the work of the Methodist Board of Temperance.

Although the Methodist church did not grow as much as the Lutheran church, it got a new lease on life from the newcomers. Two-thirds of the attendants at church services were newcomers. In 1944, four of the nineteen members of the Official Board were newcomers. A newcomer became superintendent of the Sunday school. Out of a total of sixty-five members of the Women's Society of Christian Service, twenty were newcomers.

The Catholic church. The Catholic church was much less changed by the boom than were the other churches. Being relatively large at the start (about three hundred people paying pew rent) and having a good-sized building, the church was able to accommodate a considerable number of newcomers without having to change very much. The parochial school, which had been taught by three sisters, was expanded by the addition of one more sister, but this used up all available space; and enrollment was closed when the school was full. Father Preston could have used an assistant; but all the potential assistants were assigned to take the places of the twenty-five priests out of 196 in the Peoria diocese who went into the armed services.

Probably the Catholic church reached with some regularity about a hundred families of newcomers. Masses were said at 6:00 and 7:30 A.M. on week days and 8:00 and 10:00 A.M. on Sundays. The ten o'clock mass was attended largely by farmers.

On a typical Sunday there were about three hundred and fifty at the ten o'clock mass, consisting of about one-third children, one-third women, and one-third men. The choir consisted of the older girls from the parish school. There were eight altar boys. The smaller girls from the parish school sat in front on one side of the church, the boys on the other side.

Father Preston announced an afternoon prayer service for those in the armed services. He urged his hearers to attend this service and add their prayers. "Sometimes I get very impatient with those whose homes have not yet been touched by war, who have sacrificed nothing. War bonds? Those are not sacrifices, they are investments! Now if you must go on Sunday to the movies, go at seven o'clock, and come to this service this afternoon." There was a brief sermon. The collection was for the Catholic University of America at Washington, D. C.

INTERPRETATION AND EVALUATION

In Table 12 are given some estimates of the numbers of families reached by the various churches, together with the numbers who were in Seneca and expressed a preference for these churches. This table refers to the situation at the peak of the boom, in 1944, and does not take account of families who came and went before and after this period.

The table indicates that the Methodists, with the largest potential field, reached relatively fewer newcomers than the Catholics and Lutherans. The Assembly of God and Holiness Methodist groups are, of course, in a special category, for relatively few newcomers had previously been affiliated with these denominations.

The table shows that the majority of shipyard workers went unchurched. There are undoubtedly several reasons for this. In the first place, many of the newcomers felt much like people on a vacation who also take a vacation from church life. Some of this group retained a real allegiance to the home church, and they did not affiliate with a church in Seneca.

TABLE 12

EXTENT TO WHICH NEWCOMERS WERE REACHED
BY THE CHURCHES

Church	Number of Newcomer Families in Church	Number of Newcomer Families Preferring This Church
Catholic	100	320
Methodist	60	400
Lutheran	60	250
Assembly of God	70	90
Holiness Methodist	20	18
Total	310	1,078
Families with other preferences (principally Baptist) or with no preferences		530

NOTE: These estimates are based on figures supplied by the churches and on the church preference census reported in Table 10. It is estimated conservatively that there were about sixteen hundred families of newcomers in Seneca for longer than three months in 1944.

Secondly, many of the newcomers were rough, uncouth people, who, while expressing a church preference, had had no real church affiliations previously; and who now were preoccupied with war work, war earning, and war spending, and were not in a mood to be evangelized.

A third factor is undoubtedly the generally cool relations between oldtimers and newcomers, as described in an earlier chapter. A large proportion of oldtimers in Seneca considered themselves to be socially above the rank-and-file of the newcomers; and neither these oldtimers nor the average newcomers felt very much at ease with one another. While all might *worship* in the same church without uneasiness, there would be embarrassment and awkwardness at church suppers, social meetings at the homes of church members, and meetings of the women's societies.

For example, Mrs. Rosten, wife of a buffer living in War Homes, was asked about going to church. She said,

"No, we shipyard folks don't go to church in Seneca much, they froze us out. I went three times to the Methodist church but nobody ever spoke to me or looked at me. Then I went to the Lutheran church on Easter Sunday but nobody noticed me there, either."

A large, talkative, and rather blustery woman living at Riverview Homes, who talked gustily about her experiences, said,

"If I'd a' knowed when I came we'd be here two and a half years, I'd a' thought I never coulda stood it. But now—I've met some of the finest folk here, from all over. We came from near Peoria. We came in three suitcases, and now my husband says it'll take a truck to move all our things. . . . Seneca folks has treated us like mud. Me'n another shipyard woman went to the Lutheran church 'n Sunday school—I was a Lutheran before I came. It was right after the big fire that burned the store building on Main Street. Some o' the ladies in the Sunday school class said 'There's lots of other places we could a' had that fire, where it'd done some good,' and looked at us. Another lady said, 'that trailer camp.'

"Well, then I tried the Methodist church, but they didn't seem to want us either—didn't ask us back. Finally, I went to Assembly of God, the new church, and they treated us like human beings. I felt at home there."

In addition to these factors, and before making any evaluation of the services rendered by the churches, it will be useful to bring another factor into consideration—the social status levels of the various churches in relation to the social status levels of the newcomers.

Social status in relation to church affiliation. Inquiry among oldtimers showed that the "upper crust" of Seneca were about evenly divided between the Methodist and Catholic churches. Of course, both churches, together with the Lutheran church, had members reaching all the way down Seneca's rather short social ladder, but there was no question that the social reputation of the Methodist church was slightly above that of the Lutheran church, while the Catholic church was known to have all kinds of people, high and low on the social scale.

When the boom came, several of the shipyard management families, who lived in War Homes, became friendly with some of the oldtimer Methodist families and started going to that church. The Methodists drew relatively few of the shipyard workers from the lower ranks of the job hierarchy, and these few were the exceptional ones who were striving for upward social mobility, and were using community activity and the Methodist church to get up a step on the social ladder.

The Lutherans, through their active door-to-door calling, attracted a good many people who were somewhat lower in the shipyard hierarchy than the Methodist group. Still, they drew a number of people in supervisory or white-collar positions, and who averaged only slightly below the Methodists in social status. Since their program was more intellectual than that of the Assembly of God, the Lutheran Church had only limited appeal to many newcomers of lower social status.

The War Homes Christian Fellowship organized a group of people who felt at home with one another socially and were drawn together by similar religious attitudes. This group consisted almost entirely of manual workers in the shipyard, who mixed easily with the oldtimers in the Holiness Methodist church.

When Ross and Agnes Stark came to build the Assembly of God, their message appealed to workers in the shipyard at the levels of apprentice, helper, and mechanic. It was this working-class group to which the Assembly of God and several other rapidly growing fundamentalist churches made their appeal; and to which they owed their growth in the two decades after World War I.[1] Known in social-class parlance as the "upper-lower class," this group furnished enough members to the Assembly of God in Seneca to make it larger than the Methodist church almost overnight.

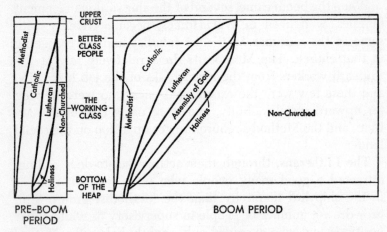

Fig. 13. Church Membership in Relation to Social Status.

The Catholic church drew Catholics to it, regardless of their social-class position, as is usually true of Catholic churches.

Thus the social ladder among the churches began with the Methodists at the top, went down a half-step to the Lutherans, and down a full step farther to the Assembly of God and the Holiness Methodist groups. The Catholic church was off to the side, with a social distribution among its members corresponding closely to that of Seneca as a

[1] Charles S. Braden, "Sectarianism Run Wild," in Wm. K. Anderson, ed., *Protestantism* (Nashville, Tennessee: The Methodist Publishing Company, 1944), pp. 110–22.

whole. This picture of the churches in relation to the social hierarchy is represented in graphic form in Figure 13.

Evidence of the status differences among the churches was afforded by a comparison of church preference with occupational status. This was done for those War Homes residents who gave their church preferences in the summer of 1944, and who had been living in War Homes since the spring of 1943. The occupational status is that of 1942–43. Some of those with lower status were promoted later. This was a rather stable group, most of its members having worked in the shipyard almost from its beginning. It also contained relatively more people of higher occupational status, since these people were given preference in assignment of housing space in War Homes.

TABLE 13

OCCUPATIONAL STATUS AND CHURCH PREFERENCE
OF WAR HOMES RESIDENTS

Church Preference	Occupational Status			
	Semi-skilled and unskilled	Skilled	Foreman, supervisor	Managerial, professional
	Numbers of Families			
Methodist	17	20	11	11
Catholic	15	11	11	10
Lutheran	11	8	8	3
Assembly of God	5	7	1	0
Holiness Methodist	3	2	0	0

Table 13 shows that those expressing Methodist or Catholic preference tended to have higher occupational status, while those with Assembly of God and Holiness preference tended to have lower occupational status.[2]

Analysis of the membership and attendance at the women's societies of the churches provided further data regarding social status and church affiliation. For example, the names of all the women present were noted at one regular meeting of the Women's Society for Christian Service of the Methodist church in the spring of 1944.

Of the twenty-three women present, six were from the shipyard, and all six came from War Homes. The husbands of five of these women held executive or professional positions, and the husband of the sixth was a foreman. All six of the new women were, thus, of relatively high social status—the group served by the Methodist church in Seneca.

Furthermore, in contrast to the experience of Mrs. Rosten, who said she had gone three times to the Methodist church without anyone's speaking to her, was the experience of the fieldworker in this study. The first time the fieldworker went to the Methodist church, a stranger, she was greeted cordially by several people. In short order she was made a member of the Women's Society for Christian Service, and she was invited to take as much part as she would in the work of the church. But she, a former teacher and a well-educated woman, was recognized by the leading Methodists as "our kind"; and she, in turn, recognized her kind of people in them. Mrs. Rosten, on the other hand, whether or not she was actually snubbed as she described it, might well have sensed the invisible but inviolable social difference between herself and the other women; and might well have felt "frozen out."

One of the Protestant ministers, when asked whether he

[2] These figures, since they refer to *church preference* and not to *church attendance*, do not answer the question of whether people of the various statuses actually attended the churches in these proportions.

noted any differences between the people who came to his church and those who went to the other churches, said,

"We get the high-class people. The Assembly of God and the Holiness Methodist get the riff-raff. They come to us once or twice and we always try to make them welcome, but they sense a difference and do not come back. These are sociological facts. They are true. I don't say that I like them."

Another minister said, "The Holiness Methodists are doing a good work, reaching a class of people we cannot reach."

The fact that the Assembly of God and Holiness churches "did not count" among the higher-ups came out clearly one day in 1944 when a meeting was called of community leaders to consider the problem of juvenile delinquency. This meeting was called by the director of personnel at the shipyard, who acted when there had been a number of reports of delinquency of boys and girls in Seneca. Some thirty people were present, and the leader had apparently intended to invite all the people who might have a professional interest in the problem. There were the housing director, director of recreation, superintendent of schools, chief of police, county welfare worker, Boy Scout leader, members of the Community Recreation Committee, and many others, including the Catholic priest and the Methodist and Lutheran ministers. But the Assembly of God and Holiness Methodist ministers were not there, had not been invited, and no one mentioned them. The Reverend Mr. Stark had even been ignored in his alter ego of truant officer. The fact that these two churches had so many activities for their young people, and that they forbade dancing, movies, and gambling, might justify the omission of their pastors from a meeting on juvenile delinquency, on the grounds that their boys and girls were poor candidates for delinquency. But the more probable explanation of the absence of the two ministers is that they were simply overlooked by those who intended to invite to the meeting "everybody that counts."

Finally there was the V-E Day service. A United Victory-in-Europe service was announced. Here, it might be thought, the various people of the various churches would be united by a common bond. It turned out, however, that the Catholics and the Lutherans held their own separate V-E Day services, leaving the Methodists, Assembly of God, and Holiness Methodists to join in the Union service at the Methodist church. The Reverend Mr. Telfer, the Methodist minister, took the lead in organizing the program.

The church was quite full. The mimeographed program called for a prayer by a member of the Holiness church (his name was misspelled), and a duet by members of this church; a solo by a Methodist; and "Thoughts on Victory" by four people—Ross and Agnes Stark of the Assembly of God, Mr. Curtis Magee (representing the Holiness pastor who was ill), and Mr. Telfer. But Mr. and Mrs. Stark were out of town, and a member of their congregation substituted for them. Mr. Magee was present, sitting well toward the front, but he said he had just come in from a trip, was very tired, and asked to be excused. Mr. Telfer therefore made the principal speech.

One of the leading women of the Methodist church, when asked whether there were many members of other churches present, said that it was rather dark in the church, the lights were not on full, people hurried out after the meeting, and she recognized very few from other churches.

These scattered observations all substantiate the hypothesis that participation in the Protestant churches was regulated in part by considerations of social status.

Evaluation. It seems clear, then, that any evaluation of the work of the various churches should take into account the social status factor. This is especially important in evaluating the record of the Methodist church. This church, with what must have seemed the largest potential harvest of souls, did not draw any more newcomers than the Lutherans and fewer than the Assembly of God.

The District Superintendent of the Methodist Church was interested in Seneca—fully as much interested as were the supervisors of the Lutheran and Assembly of God churches in that region. He had more money to use in Seneca than did the other churches. When he brought Mr. Danielson to Seneca he underwrote a salary higher than that of any of the other ministers, and told him that here was an opportunity to build a great community church. There were Presbyterians, Congregationalists, Baptists among the newcomers, he said, who could find no church of their own denomination. The Methodist church should open its doors to them, and make itself a community church.

The Methodist church seems to have succeeded in becoming a community church, attracting Baptists, Presbyterians, and Congregationalists, but it became a middle-class community church, with its appeal to lower-class people largely limited to those with desires for upward social mobility. Consequently, its place in the community prevented it from growing as rapidly as the churches with more of an appeal to lower-class people. The program of the Methodist church was *social* and *educational*—that is, middle-class in its appeal; whereas the bulk of newcomers were lower class.

The Lutheran church appealed to a solid group of people, both middle class and lower class, who wanted a *spiritual* program combined with social activities of a simple, strictly moral sort. Its potential audience was somewhat greater than that of the Methodists, judging from the social characteristics of the newcomers as a group. Why the Lutheran church did not draw greater numbers of newcomers is probably due to the fact that the original membership of the Norwegian

Lutheran group in Seneca, being predominantly rural, morally puritanical, and Republican in politics, did not mix well with the majority of shipyard workers, many of whom were partially urbanized, Democratic in politics, and addicted to movies, mild gambling, drinking, and rough language.

The Assembly of God and Holiness Methodist churches offered a *fundamentalist*, highly *emotional* religious experience, with a simple social life along strictly moral lines. While they drew their congregations from lower-class people, and while the largest group of newcomers were lower-class, still their puritanical moral code could be expected to appeal to only a portion of this class. The fact that they reached a larger proportion of their potential members—because of their vigorous proselytizing—resulted in congregations somewhat larger than that of the other Protestant churches in Seneca.

The Catholic church went its universal way, serving all kinds of people as it was accustomed to doing, and capitalizing on its excellent church building.

Given more time, the churches would no doubt have made more headway. The people would have felt the need for individual spiritual help in personal crises. They would have formed social ties with church people, and they would have seen the values of joining church associations. Seneca's war boom was too brief for the churches to exert their maximum effect.

The churches served those who wanted to be served, and in ways to which they were accustomed. Church patterns of Old Seneca persisted. So persistent and inflexible were they that they left a gap that was filled by a new church with a new pattern, the Assembly of God, which appealed to fundamentalist believers among the working class.

While there was relatively little change in the ways of the various churches, there were significant results in the vitality of the churches due to the boom. As in the case of business institutions in Seneca, the anemic and run-down churches received a transfusion with results that continued after the boom. This new supply of energy did not come alone from the dollars that flowed into their treasuries and enabled them to improve their property. It came also from the work of newcomers in the church and from a renewed spirit on the part of oldtimers. This was especially notice-able in the Methodist church, where a number of members who had been losing interest returned and took hold again when the church began to prosper. Thus every one of the old churches was in strong condition financially and its mem-bers were active and optimistic at the close of the boom.

8.

Business

Seneca's war boom contrasted sharply in its effects upon business with the nineteenth-century boom that started the town off. It was a contrast between old age and youth, between conservative skepticism and unbounded optimism. Gone were the entrepreneurs of Seneca's earlier days, the young men who risked their own capital and borrowed as much as they could in order to build businesses. In their places were their sons, now grown old in the family business, who looked at the war boom with weary eyes. These old men accepted the new business with complaints about the extra work it made and the difficulty of finding help. They invested capital grudgingly in new equipment, and as they pocketed their profits they spoke with desire for the end of the boom, when they could take long summer vacations again.

None of them expected the boom to be anything more than a brief episode in Seneca's history, and in this attitude they were no more than realistic. Still, it was the conservative attitudes of Seneca businessmen as well as the facts of population increase, swollen payrolls, rationing laws, and wartime shortages that determined the answers to the questions that will be considered in this chapter. Did all kinds of business expand at the same rate as the population expanded? Did methods of doing business change? What was the net effect upon business in Seneca after the boom was over?

182

Before the war Seneca's business district had been de-
teriorating for twenty years. An old resident said,

"It was a ghost town before the boom. Half of the stores were
empty. All the store buildings needed renovation. The building
later occupied by the Seneca Grill was in such bad state that it
dropped loose bricks to the danger of the passers-by."

Although the statement that half the stores were empty
is an exaggeration, it is true that at least eight empty buildings were remodeled and opened to new business establishments during the boom, while one other building, too far
gone to be reclaimed, remained empty and continued to
crumble and sag in silent contrast to the face-lifting under-
gone by the rest of the business district.

A survey showed forty business units in Seneca before the
boom. These included one general store, six grocery stores,
four taverns, two hardware stores, three grain elevators, a
lumber yard, two small eating places, one drug store, three
garages, five filling stations, a funeral home. There was no
clothing store, no jewelry store, no motion picture theater.

Two students of small towns have attempted to predict
populations of such towns from the number of business units
they contain. They have devised mathematical formulae
from the data on several thousand such towns, and all that
need be done is to count the number of business units in a
town like Seneca, put this number in the proper place in
the formula, and calculate the expected population.[1] On this
basis, one formula gives an expected population for pre-
boom Seneca of 950, and the other formula gives 1060.

[1] T. Lynn Smith, "The Role of the Village in American Rural Society,"
Rural Sociology, VII (1942), 10–21. Smith's formula is $Y = 119.6 + 20.9X$,
where Y is the predicted population and X is the number of business units.

Vincent H. Whitney, "The Estimation of Populations for Unincorporated
Places," *American Sociological Review*, II (1946), 98–103. Whitney's
formula is $Y = 324 + 18.5X$.

These predictions are for stable towns in stable times; and obviously would not apply to the relation between business and population in a boom town. Yet it is interesting to see how far below the expected number of business units Seneca could fall during its boom and still meet the essential demands of its population.

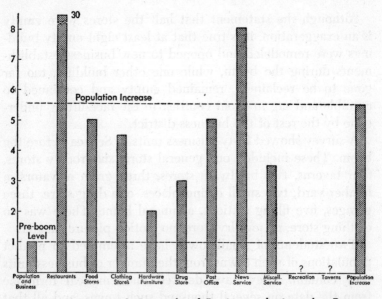

Fig. 14. Estimated Growth of Business during the Boom.

In December, 1943, the number of business establishments had grown to 53; and eventually it reached 65. For a population of 6,600 the expected number of business units would be 310 according to one formula and 340 according to the other.

In addition to the eight empty buildings that were remodeled, two new buildings were constructed—a small grocery near Victory Court, and a new store building to replace one destroyed by fire during the boom. Thus there was very little physical expansion of business. Instead, the available space was used as fully as possible, and a few private houses were turned temporarily into places of business.

Real-estate values and rentals were low by city standards. Twenty-five dollars a month was a reasonable rent for an average-sized store. One of the better two-story buildings sold for $4,000 at the end of the boom.

The expansion of various kinds of business, compared with the expansion of population in Seneca, is shown graphically in Figure 14.

The only statement that can be made about every business in Seneca during the boom is that practically every businessman made much more money than he had been making in prewar years. In some categories the number of establishments increased. Other categories had no increase in number but a manifold increase in volume of business. Still others had no more than a healthy upswing in trade and profits. We shall describe what happened in several types of business.

RESTAURANTS

Two small eating places cared for Seneca's prewar diners-out with a total business averaging about sixty meals a day. Anyone who had to "eat out" was considered an unfortunate person. A small number of men by reason of bachelorhood or business duties were deprived of the pleasures of "home cooking" and kept the restaurants going.

At the height of the boom the Seneca Grill alone served a thousand meals a day and the seven other public eating places accounted for another thousand meals. Thus the restaurant business expanded some thirty- to fortyfold. And this leaves out of consideration the cafeteria and the canteen at the shipyard, where six thousand meals were served daily, and thousands of workers got everything from a cup of coffee to a full meal.

The people whose food needs were responsible for this enormous expansion in the restaurant business were four or five hundred single men and women working in the shipyard, and another hundred working in the housing projects and in Seneca business establishments. These people lived in furnished rooms in the village, in the War Homes dormitories, or they commuted to work in Seneca from the surrounding farms and towns.

Eating places varied enough to suit almost everyone's taste.

The Seneca Grill was a modern restaurant housed in a remodeled building, complete with new, up-to-date restaurant equipment and machinery.

The first new business of the boom in Seneca was the Seneca Grill. The owner was Mr. Glenn Toops, manager of the Hay Barge Company. Early in 1942 he took over an empty building on Main Street and made of it a thoroughly modern restaurant. There was an air-conditioning unit, washrooms for patrons, stainless steel trimmings at the front, plate glass windows said to have cost a thousand dollars, and Venetian blinds to keep out the afternoon sun on hot days. Mr. Toops brought Miss Lydia Finley from Kansas to help manage the business, with Mrs. DeMoss as kitchen manager and chief cook.

The Grill opened for business in May, 1942, in time for the beginning of construction work at the shipyard and housing projects. From that time, for more than three years, the Grill was busy all the time it was open. The usual business was a thousand meals a day. In the hectic months of August and September, 1942, when construction work was at its peak, the Grill was open for twenty-four hours a day.

When Mr. Toops went into the Navy in the summer of 1943, Mr. Lee McCormick replaced him as manager. All told, there were twenty to twenty-two employees most of the time, and the

Grill was often closed on Sundays because of shortage of help. The waitresses started at $16.25 per week and worked up to $23.00 per week plus tips. (Tips were neither plentiful nor generous in the smaller cities of the Midwest.)

In the spring of 1945 Miss Finley bought the business from Mr. Toops. She sold it, in turn, a few months later. By autumn, when the boom had almost completely faded out, the Grill seldom had more than a dozen patrons at a time, and Seneca boosters were wondering anxiously whether this asset to Seneca business was going to remain indefinitely. Business settled down to a level of two hundred meals a day during 1946. The Grill was then closed all day Sunday, and Saturday after 2 P.M.

The Ship Ahoy, a tearoom in the home of Mrs. Irwin, was situated on the bluff overlooking the village. With her boy gone into the Navy, Mrs. Irwin said, "It is better to do something," and she started to serve luncheons and dinners. She catered especially to family parties and wedding parties. For Sunday dinner she usually had her tables full of people who wanted a quiet, leisurely dinner for a dollar.

Johnson's Restaurant, a pre-boom business, had been run for years by Mr. Johnson and his family, who made a few "improvements" in keeping with the times, but mostly went along as usual.

Van's Eat Shop was a small ordinary restaurant operated by William Vangelisti, who started in business in Seneca about 1940, and moved to a new location in 1943.

The J-B Hamburger-Eat was a white-tile interior room, about twenty-five by thirty-five feet. The menu consisted of six kinds of sandwiches, short orders, and a regular dinner for sixty-six cents which included meat, potatoes, salad, dessert, and coffee.

The Hollywood Inn, a tearoom on the main highway, closed late in 1943.

Red's Quick Lunch, a hole-in-the-wall with seven stools

at the narrow counter, specialized in chili. It was run by an Old Seneca resident who formerly had a popcorn stand.

The Victory Sweet Shop, the confectionery and news service store, added sandwiches and short orders to its soda fountain menu.

Seneca restaurants felt the pinch of wartime rationing restrictions less than restaurants in more stable communities, for there was no prewar base from which to estimate their normal level of business. Thus they could not be readily cut to the official fraction of their former consumption of rationed foods. Probably the rationing authorities favored Seneca as a war-production center, and allotted more liberal quantities of meat and butter to the restaurants than were parceled out to the more stable communities. Butter was never absent from the Seneca restaurants, and it was served in a prewar-size pat, about twice as much as what people felt lucky to get in nearby cities. A steak could nearly always be obtained at the Seneca Grill—T-bone or a small steak—for seventy-five cents or a dollar.

The fieldworker compared the Seneca Grill noon menu with that of restaurants in the city of Morris, which had about the same population during the boom. The Morris restaurants usually carried one "honest-to-goodness" meat at a meal, whereas the Seneca Grill usually carried four. On a typical day the Seneca Grill had roast beef, lamb chops, meat loaf, and liver (in addition to chicken giblets, fish, and spaghetti with meat sauce), while Kindelspire's at Morris had veal, liver, and fish.

FOOD STORES

In Old Seneca there were six food stores which gave their owners a very modest living. They relied heavily upon the farm trade, though this trade had lessened considerably in

the decade of the thirties. Two of these stores sold fresh
meat, but there was no store limited to the sale of meat.

Five of these six stores, owned by Marshall and Heaton,
Wicks, Raibley, Sand, and Tendall, continued to do business
throughout the boom. The sixth, belonging to Jensen and
Nelson, was a general store. These proprietors sold out to
Mr. Hummel, a newcomer, who closed out the grocery business and turned the store into a clothing business in the
spring of 1944.

Marshall and Heaton was one of the best-established businesses
in Seneca. The following is a typical advertisement, appearing in
Ship and Home:

Dealers in
Everything Good to Eat
Fancy Groceries a Specialty
Phone 125—It's Music to Us
MARSHALL AND HEATON

A name plate over the entrance to the store read, "Archie and
Jerome." "Archie" was Mr. Marshall, a man in his sixties, tall,
heavy, ruddy-faced. His associates in the store called him Archie,
even down to Bud, the high-school boy who clerked after school.
"Jerome" was Mr. Heaton, in his early fifties, a small, quiet, accommodating man, who started working for Mr. Marshall as a boy
of fourteen, and later became a partner.

The store was posted as Class 2 under the wartime Office of
Price Administration classification, which means that its annual
business was between $50,000 and $250,000.

Before Mr. Marshall went into the grocery business he was clerk
and buyer for a Seneca dry-goods store. This was in the days
when there were eight or ten dressmakers in the village. The
merchants went to Chicago department stores for samples of dress
goods; and each lady ordered her own exclusive "pattern" of six
to seven yards, the store's astute buyer watching to see that there
were no duplicates. Young Archie soon became an expert not only
in surah silk, taffeta, mohair, and Valenciennes—but also in the

hang of skirts and the pitch of feminine hats. To this day, when he goes to Chicago, he spends his spare time not in "Stop and Shop," Chicago's finest food store, but looking in Marshall Field's or Carson's windows. "Even now, I can't help noticing the fit of a lady's coat, the length and hang of a skirt," he declares, "well, not length, they don't *have* any length nowadays."

Once established in the grocery business, Mr. Marshall proceeded to enjoy himself by specializing in cheese. He used to buy rich, ripe American cheeses in large quantity.

"I was known all over this part of the country for my cheese," he said sadly, and showed the fieldworker a three-pound hunk of ripe Wisconsin Daisy Cheese, which he graciously allowed her to sample. "I don't sell this, but keep it for my own use. Can't get any more. The government takes it all now, before it has a chance to ripen.

"I used to go into Chicago for cheese and I'd go to a man I knew who used to be quite a cheese man. He knew I liked good cheese. It was none of your processed cheese. It was the real stuff. He'd take me down in the basement with a sampler and I'd sample the cheeses and I'd pick the ones I wanted. I'd bring home twenty or thirty cheeses, and the word would go around that I had them, and the pile would go right down. I used to sell three or four a week."

In the early days the farmers accounted for about half of his business. He took their butter and eggs, and provided their groceries; and at the end of the month he would add up the figures to see what they owed. He would "carry" some farmers for six months, until they sold their corn and grain.

Some of Mr. Marshall's Seneca customers used to order fifty dollars' worth of butter at one time and keep it all winter. Of course they wanted him to pick out the best batches when they came in. One could keep country butter in those days by wrapping it and salting it down in a cold room.

When the boom came, Marshall and Heaton had a reasonably modern store, but they immediately prepared for bigger business and less help. They arranged their stock for self-service, and bought a large "walk-in" refrigerator.

There were serious food shortages during the first few months of the boom, when the town was rationed to receive only 70 per cent of the meat and certain other supplies which had been sold the year before. People had to go to the neighboring cities for much of their food. But increased quantities were soon released to Seneca, and the supply of goods at Marshall and Heaton's was usually better in quantity and variety than it was in most city stores. For example, Franco-American spaghetti, a new prepared food which came in cans, was released to Seneca and to a few other high-priority war-industry areas before it was made available to the general public.

Business hours were expanded. Before the boom, the store had closed at 6 P.M. daily, Thursday afternoons in the summer, and all day Sunday. But during the boom the store was open daily until 7 or 8 P.M., until 10 P.M. on Friday and Saturday nights, and for about two hours Sunday mornings. Delivery service was stopped in November, 1942, and not resumed until after the boom.

When the boom was over Mr. Marshall was ready to return to old times. "My farm trade has never left me," he said, "and things will be like they always were. We won't make as much money, and we won't work as hard, either. I like to have a fishing trip every summer—that's the only vacation I ever take. I've missed my fishing for three years now. I go up to northern Wisconsin. If we had another boom I would just quit. I don't think I could go through it again. It took something out of me."

All five of the Old Seneca food stores doubled or tripled their business, the limiting factor in their expansion being sales help. They added women and boys and girls, mostly oldtimers; and most of them remodeled their stores for self-service. These grocers estimated that 50 to 75 per cent of their business at the peak was with shipyard people, and that they lost a substantial portion of their former country trade, because the farmers could find no place to park their automobiles and had to wait too long to be served.

There were ten new food businesses opened in Seneca during the boom. Only two of them were located in the business district, the others being established near the centers of new population.

The *Supermarket* was started in the summer of 1942 by Mr. Harris, who had been in the grocery business in Chicago. He and his wife gave all their time to their Seneca business. They rented a building in the business district and fixed it up for self-service. Although they specialized in groceries and meats, they also carried a small line of general merchandise.

Sampson's Royal Blue store was located near the entrance to Victory Court. Mr. Sampson, discharged from the armed service in 1943, built a small store at that time and enlarged it the next year. He did a thriving business for the remainder of the boom.

Miller's store was opened in April, 1944, in the house of Mr. Miller, a Dupont employee, across the street from the entrance to Victory Court. He sold a general line of groceries, including some fresh meat, which he bought already cut; and he had as much business as he and his wife and a part-time clerk could care for.

The *S & S Market* was established in 1943 in the home of Mr. Sherrill near the War Homes Trailer Park; and it continued to the end of the boom.

The War Homes Canteen was a small store operated on a concession basis in the War Homes administration building. It changed proprietors, and was finally run by Mrs. Cohen, wife of a shipyard employee. Under this management the store carried a line of canned and packaged goods, some fresh fruits and luncheon meats, as well as confectionery and soft drinks.

The *Antique Shop*, on the highway opposite Kiner's Trailer Camp, was owned by Mr. and Mrs. Sampson (brother of Mr. Sampson of the Royal Blue). The Sampsons turned from their antique business to serve the residents of Kiner's Camp with a delicatessen and a soft drink stand. The boom over, they planned to return to their dealings in antiques.

The *Hollywood Service Station,* on the highway near the Hollywood Trailer Camp, had a line of work clothing, auto accessories, soft drinks, and a few packaged foods.

Tommy's Vegetables opened late in 1944 in a new brick building constructed after a fire. This store was opened by Mr. T. Girot, of Morris, who had provided dealers and residents with vegetables from a truck service before the boom. Mr. Girot sold mostly fresh fruits and vegetables, with a small line of packaged goods.

Martin's store operated on a concession basis in Riverview Homes. Mr. Martin was a shipyard employee, while Mrs. Martin for a time managed the Co-op store at Victory Court. When they moved to Riverview Homes late in 1944 they applied for a concession to open a store there. Finally they were provided by the FPHA with equipment and they opened their store in March. Thus they had only about three months of business. They sold groceries, and occasionally fresh meats, which they bought from an out-of-town market.

Victory Court Co-op. In Victory Court there were a few people who had been active in retail cooperatives before coming to Seneca. Since Victory Court was located a mile from the nearest store, they immediately began to work through their Tenants' Council for the establishment of a Cooperative Store. Housing management encouraged them. Mr. Brim, the Housing Manager, had aided in the development of cooperatives in his previous work with Farm Security Administration projects.

There were several months of protracted discussions, during which time Sampson's and Miller's stores were opened at the gates of Victory Court. Gradually, however, the group organized and was ready, about December, 1943, to sell stock in a Cooperative Society. The stock was five dollars a share, with a limit of twenty shares per person. The housing project would provide space and light and heat, in return for a percentage of the gross sales. The goal was set for $2,000 as capital.

By January of 1944 a total of $1,375 was pledged, and only about half of the tenants had been visited by the solicitors. Eventually about $2,000 was pledged for capital stock. Then there were delays in organizing the Society, and it was not until May that the money was called for. With considerable difficulty a total of $1,200 in cash was then secured. The store was opened in June, 1944. The first manager proved unsatisfactory, and was succeeded in a few days by Mrs. Martin, the wife of one of the more active members of the committee who had organized the Society.

Business was good right from the start. Gross sales were about $1,200 a week. Heaviest sales were in bread and milk. Meats were not carried until late in 1944, and then only for about three months.

Mrs. Martin resigned as manager in October, 1944, because she was moving to Riverview Homes. At this time the assets of the Society were worth $1,600. There followed a period of some confusion while a new manager was sought. The store was supervised during this period by several of the directors, especially by Mr. Robert Maxwell, who has been described in an earlier chapter.[2] There was some dissension at this time because the wife of one of the directors wanted to become manager and the others would not have her. Eventually, a young man from Marseilles, Mr. Jim Traeger, became manager.

The Co-op closed in April, 1945, after about ten months of existence. At its liquidation it paid handsome returns to its members.

[2] See Chapter 3, "A Place to Live."

Expansion of food business. It is possible to estimate the expansion of the food business in Seneca as follows: The five pre-boom stores multiplied their volume by two or three times. Ten new stores were opened. All the new stores were small, except the Supermarket and the Royal Blue, and most of them operated for less than the full duration of the boom. All together, they may have done half to three-fourths as much business as the five old stores. Thus the total expansion was probably four- to fivefold. This is about what could be expected, since Seneca's population increased fivefold.

The Seneca food stores seemed to be perpetually short of merchandise. This was not due to the restrictions of rationing so much as to difficulty in getting goods from wholesalers. This was especially true for the new stores, which had to make new contacts with wholesalers during a period of wartime shortages.

One of the oldtimer grocers said, "We take everything the wholesaler will leave." This describes the state of affairs quite well. Seneca workers were on a buying spree. They would take anything that was edible, at almost any price, though they often grumbled at Seneca prices and said that they could do better at chain stores in Ottawa.

Food prices seem not to have been exorbitant in Seneca, compared with other towns, although about half of the dealers were fined in the fall of 1944 for exceeding the price limits set by the Office of Price Administration. Profits were made, to be sure, but these profits came from an expanded volume of business rather than from increased profit margins.

Every one of these food merchants worked harder than he had ever worked before. Stores were kept open until 8:30 and 9:00 at night, and a good part of Sunday. Wives and children and relatives were pressed into service as clerks.

The boom also modernized and urbanized the food business in Seneca. Not only was self-service established in most of the stores, but the grocers learned to cater to urban food expectations. Pre-boom Seneca rarely saw fresh vegetables except in season. The merchants kept only potatoes and root vegetables, onions, cabbage, and perhaps lettuce on Saturdays. In the winter there were no tomatoes or asparagus, no fresh peas or beans, no spinach or greens—much less such things as broccoli, green peppers, strawberries out of season, and Pascal celery. This was still true in the winter of 1942–43. Then the customers began to demand, "Why don't you carry fresh tomatoes sometimes?" At first the grocers replied, "Oh, Seneca won't pay the price for foods out of season." But as soon as they experimented with these more expensive things they realized that they were no longer dealing with a low-income group. The shipyard worker demanded the best he could think of, and was ready to pay for it.

It was, then, a learning experience for Seneca food merchants, and they may be expected to continue their "modern" methods in postwar Seneca, if their customers appreciate these methods. It is difficult to predict whether these changes will attract or repel the farmers, upon whom Seneca must rely again for whatever it can gain of postwar prosperity.

CLOTHING STORES

Old Seneca had relied for its clothing and dry-goods business upon one general store, Jensen and Nelson's, founded in 1910. Most people went to Ottawa or beyond for their clothing, and used the Jensen and Nelson store for small purchases or emergency needs. It had been a long time since the dry-goods business flourished in Seneca.

Hummel's Department Store was the successor to Jensen and Nelson. Mr. Nelson died in the fall of 1943, Mr. Jensen was ill, and Mrs. Nelson was an invalid. Wishing to retire from business, they began to sell out their stock and advertised their store for rent early in 1944. Mr. Hummel, a salesman from Chicago, came by to sell them new stock. He asked their price, and the bargain was quickly consummated. He turned the former general store into a clothing and shoe store, run by himself and his wife. The business was sold at the end of the boom to Mr. Jack Herbert, who thus became the first man to start a business in postwar Seneca.

The Seneca Department Store was opened at the beginning of the boom by two sisters who had a clothing store in Beloit, Wisconsin. Mrs. Lord and Mrs. Moriarty came to Seneca, rented a building and had it remodeled, and stocked it with men's clothing. There was such a demand for women's and children's clothing that these were added. Business was excellent throughout the boom.

No merchants were more popular with oldtimers and newcomers than Mrs. Lord and Mrs. Moriarty, the sisters who ran the department store. Toward the close of the boom they received many picture postcards from departed customers addressed to "The Sales-Ladies, Seneca Department Store," or to "Susan and Babe" which were their names for each other. One customer wrote from Madison, Wisconsin, that she had lost the sweater she bought of them, could she have another just like it?

The two ladies slept in furnished rooms, but they practically lived in their store. After closing time in the evening they continued to sit in their store, often visiting with friends around the little stove in the back on which they could make tea.

Every Saturday afternoon their husbands, Mr. Lord and Mr. Moriarty, drove down from Beloit, Wisconsin, often arriving as late as 2 A.M. Sunday morning. The Beloit rationing board gave them just enough gasoline to make the trip. There was never any left over for a Sunday ride.

Merchandising was easy in Seneca, once the goods were on the counters. The problem was to get enough sheets, pillow cases, children's clothes, and men's work clothes to meet the demand. When a new shipment arrived, the shipyard workers chose the best there was. Bargains in "seconds" were of little interest to them. One woman told Mrs. Lord, "I never earned money before, now I am just going to spend it."

They had all classes of customers. There were the Mexican laborers who had come to Seneca temporarily to work on the railroad, and who came in to buy goods to send back home as gifts. At first the business was transacted by sign language, until the salesladies learned a few Spanish words and the Mexicans a few English words. There was the young woman who came in "pickled" from the Brown Derby Tavern, and boasted about her experiences as a dice girl and owner of a gambling joint in the days before she came to Seneca. Then she asked to "charge" her purchases. When met by a firm refusal she grew angry. "I'll have you know I have a charge account at Marshall Field's, and who do you think you are, by God!"

The Seneca Department Store closed its doors on June 30, 1945, and the two ladies went off for a long vacation with their husbands, their first vacation in three years. Mrs. Lord said, looking back over the experience in Seneca, "It has been intensely interesting. I only wish I were qualified to write a book about all the people I've seen and the experiences I've had here."

To estimate the expansion of the clothing business we know that two stores took the place of one; the clothing business of the old store probably doubled; and the business of the new store probably exceeded that of the old. Thus we may estimate a four- to fivefold expansion.

HARDWARE AND FURNITURE

There were two hardware stores and one furniture store in Old Seneca, and none was added during the boom. The Harris Hardware Store was established about 1875 by the father of Henry Harris, the current owner. Gerbert Brothers' hardware business was established by the father and uncle of the current owners. The furniture store was owned by the Pfeffer Brothers, who also operated a funeral home.

These businesses expanded less than any other kind of business in Seneca, for two reasons. One was that the newcomers nearly all moved into furnished quarters, which were maintained for them by the government maintenance crew. Thus few people needed to buy furniture or household tools. The other reason was that wartime shortages reduced both the quantity and quality of hardware and furniture, so that stocks were limited, and people made their old equipment last as long as possible rather than buy new, but inferior, articles.

The *Harris Hardware* company was run by Mr. Henry Harris, already introduced to the reader in Chapter 1.

When the boom came, Henry Harris was sixty-three years old. He was a tired man. The wartime shortages of hardware stock found him unready to make the quick decisions necessary to secure goods, and unwilling to do business with the makeshift materials that came his way. He often complained about the quality of the goods he had to sell.

"The wholesalers unload old junk on us," he said. "They will sell only assortments, and about one-third of the assortment is things you can't use. You have to buy the assortment, or else they won't sell you anything."

He showed a dustpan made of stiff cardboard with wooden pieces nailed on the sides and a wooden handle nailed on.

"What should this sell for?" he asked. The fieldworker said, "Oh, maybe ten cents."

"Well, that's about right. But I paid forty-five cents plus two cents postage on it. I'm selling it for twenty-five cents and ashamed to take the money. I'm going to close my doors if I can't get any more good stock. I won't sell the stuff they give me now."

In former years Mr. Harris had three times the amount of stock he had during the boom—in fact, "everything a hardware store could or should have." He estimated that 90 per cent of his business during the boom came from shipyard workers. "The Seneca people can do better to keep their old stuff," he said, "but the shipyard workers must have something new."

Despite his reluctances, Henry Harris kept his store going all through the boom. He met his customers, and watched the crowds go past his window, with a weary and tragic face that seemed beyond change. He refused to open his store on Sunday, just as he had refused years before when it was popular to keep open on Sunday for the sake of the farmers.

At the close of the boom, Mr. Harris said, "The war boom's been a good thing for the town, all right. Anybody that's not made money these last three years, it's his own fault. But the younger generation has got used to spending lots of money. When they don't have it to spend, what'll they do? They'll steal and rob, that's what they'll do.

"Some of the folks leaving say to me, 'Dad, what you going to do for a living when we've all gone?' I tell 'em, 'Well, I got along all right for forty-seven years before you came, and I guess I can do it again.'"

Mr. Harris looked on the boom with something of a jaundiced eye. Yet nobody can suffer financially in a boom town, and Mr. Harris was no exception. In addition to increased business and increased profits, he owned the cornfield in which Victory Court was built, and he received a good price from the government for it.

When the boom was over nobody was happier than Henry Harris. He closed up his store and went West to visit his son. Two months later he returned with some of the fire of youth back in his eyes. He told people that his son was coming home from the West to go into business with him. Soon he could sit back and take it easy, as his own father had done, and watch the business go on in his son's hands.

A few weeks later he came home one evening from the store, ate a good supper, settled down in his easy chair to read the paper, and died within a half-hour of a heart attack.

In spite of the wartime difficulties of the hardware and furniture businesses, they did expand. We estimate that their business approximately doubled.

DRUGSTORE

There was one drugstore in pre-boom days, a modern one which had been established in 1940 in a remodeled building. The owner, Mr. Trowbridge, also had a store in Marseilles. The Seneca store discontinued its soda fountain before the boom, but otherwise had the variety of goods that a modern "drugstore" carries, including a lending library and a magazine stand.

When the boom started, Mr. Koch from Minnesota was brought in as manager, and he later bought the store from Mr. Trowbridge. The inventory was increased by about $3,000 when the boom came, and Mr. Koch estimated that three-fourths of his trade was with shipyard people. Five clerks were employed at the height of business.

Mr. Koch said, when the boom was over, "I have enjoyed it immensely, even apart from the chance to make money. I never worked so hard before in my life—but I've enjoyed the *bang!*"

A threefold increase of business seems to be a conservative estimate of the expansion in this field.

NEWS SERVICE

The news agency for Chicago papers was run by Mr. Barsi, in the Victory Sweet Shop. He started in business in Seneca in 1918.

Before the boom Mr. Barsi sold about one hundred and fifty Chicago papers a day. At the height of the boom he sold about eleven hundred papers, and Van's Eat Shop also sold them from its counter. Mr. Barsi established five paper routes, with four girls and a boy as his carriers, all from shipyard families. The expansion in newspaper sales was about eight-fold, and would have been greater but for the shortage of newsprint, which limited the number of papers delivered to Seneca. Mr. Barsi sold about eight hundred Chicago *Tribunes* on weekdays and two hundred and fifty Chicago *Suns*.

One day the fieldworker saw Mr. Barsi mowing his lawn. "First time I ever saw you at home," she commented.

"Aw! I don't have no time to stay at home," he said, "I'm making money, of course, but I ain't never got no time to enjoy life. Why, I can't even read my own papers no more!"

CURRENCY EXCHANGE

There had been no bank in Seneca since 1933. A currency exchange came in with the boom.

The notice on the wall read:

"The Seneca Currency Exchange is not a bank. We do not loan money. The only source of revenue we have is the fee we charge for cashing checks, handling silver, and money orders. In other words, the only commodity we have to sell is currency and silver. That is why we charge for it."
Rates were:

Silver Exchange Rate
Currency (paper money) for silver—more than five dollars—one per cent.
Loose silver for wrapped silver—one-half of one per cent.
Wrapped silver for loose silver—no charge.
Wrapped silver for currency—no charge.

Checks Cashed
One to five dollars—charge is five cents.
Five to fifteen dollars—ten cents.
Fifteen to thirty dollars—fifteen cents.

Thirty to forty-five dollars—twenty cents.
Forty-five to sixty dollars—twenty-five cents.
Sixty to eighty dollars—thirty-five cents.
Eighty to one hundred dollars—forty-five cents.

In addition to cashing checks and exchanging currency and silver, the Exchange sold money orders (on a Streator Bank), provided a notary public, received Western Union telegrams, and collected payments for telephone, gas, and electricity bills.

Owner of the Seneca Currency Exchange was Mr. Saul Samors, who had a garage business in the neighboring city of Streator. He employed a manager, and eight or nine clerks on the peak business days of Friday and Saturday. On these days the Exchange operated a branch office at the shipyard. Checks cashed on Friday and Saturday amounted to $85,000 to $100,000 at the peak of the boom.

The Currency Exchange closed when the shipyard closed, though its functions were carried on by a new bank, one of Seneca's first new businesses after the boom.[3]

MISCELLANEOUS SERVICES

Of the usual services, prewar Seneca had two barber shops, two beauty shops, a cleaner's agency, a laundry agency, a shoe repair shop, and seven automobile service stations. Additions during the boom consisted of one barber shop, one beauty shop (but one of the old ones was closed), a watch repair shop, a cleaner and tailor, one shoe repair shop, two cleaner's agencies, and two or three ephemeral shoe shine stands.

Barber shops and beauty shops were kept busy throughout the boom, whereas business had been slow before.

Mr. Peter Andersen moved his cleaning and tailoring busi-

[3] The establishment of the bank is described in Chapter 14, "Aftermath."

ness from Oak Park, Illinois, to Seneca. The Peerless cleaners of Ottawa already had an agency run by Mrs. Eckhardt, wife of a Dupont employee. Mrs. Eckhardt came to Seneca in 1931, and had kept this business since then. The Blue and Gold Laundry and Cleaners of Joliet sent in a truck to Victory Court to pick up laundry and clothes to be cleaned. Two other cleaning establishments from Ottawa set up agencies in Seneca.

Mr. Frank opened a watch repair and jewelry shop. He had stores in Streator, Champaign, and Rantoul, Illinois. At the close of the boom he transferred his stock to his other stores. "I made good money while it lasted," he said.

Old Mr. Brinker, introduced in Chapter 1, had had his cobbler's shop in Seneca since about 1900.

When the boom started, Mr. Brinker was seventy-eight years old and just about ready to sell his business and retire.

But Seneca could not do without a shoemaker when the boom, combined with shoe rationing, multiplied the shoe repair business several times. Johann Brinker grumbled about there being five shoemakers working at other jobs at the shipyard where they could make more money; yet he kept on mending shoes. This was his post of duty and he stuck by it, working longer and longer hours as the rows of shoes lengthened on his waiting shelf. When his rheumatism bothered him he complained a bit and hoped for warmer weather, so that the bees in his beehives at home would become more active. He said his bees stung him in the knees, which was good for his rheumatism.

While Sherman's Quick Shoe Repair Shop was established in 1944 (and remained until the end of the boom in 1945), Brinker still felt compelled to keep his business going. So he worked and passed his eightieth birthday during the boom. Probably he was the oldest man at work in Seneca, and certainly the oldest man working at an essential job.

When the boom was over, he found a man who wanted to take over his business. One day Mr. Brinker turned over the key of his shop to his successor and went home to his wife, his bees, and his garden.

The garages and service stations in Seneca had no such falling-off of business as happened in the ordinary town during the war. On the contrary, business expanded because of the hundreds of automobiles coming daily to the shipyards. Many drivers bought their gasoline in Seneca.

Most of the garages and service stations were shorthanded, and consequently kept their gasoline pumps operating only part of the time. Some of the owners themselves took jobs in the shipyard, where they could make more money than in their own businesses, and kept open only during their hours off work at the yard.

Andrew Brown of the Hollywood Garage and Service Station added to his help by employing his sister-in-law, and two men who worked part time helping him sell gasoline and service cars. He said,

"I sold two and a half times as much gas as before the boom and could have sold five times as much if the cars hadn't come in a bunch, mornings and evenings. They couldn't all get waited on fast enough, so some went on to Marseilles and Morris."

These miscellaneous services multiplied their business two to five times.

COMMERCIAL RECREATION

Prewar Seneca had as commercial recreation one poolroom with three tables, and five taverns.

The coming of the boom brought a movie theater, a bowling alley, and an "amusement center," which provided dancing to the music of a juke-box, a penny arcade, and slot machines. Thus commercialized recreation may be said to have come into Seneca as a result of the boom.

The Barge Theatre, with 268 seats, was built by the Anderson Theatre Circuit, which operates motion picture theaters in several nearby towns. The Seneca Recreation Center, offering bowling and games of various kinds, was opened in September, 1943, and was closed the following summer. Playland, opened by two Ottawa men in 1944, contained a number of games to be played for a penny or a nickel, a food bar, and a floor space roped off for dancing.

Throughout the boom Seneca was limited to the five taverns that existed there at the beginning. No new liquor licenses were issued. When a fire burned out two of the taverns in January, 1943, one owner moved to the old Interurban Station, two blocks off Main Street, and the other came back to his former location on Main Street just as soon as the building was repaired. A sixth tavern and roadhouse was located outside the village limits, on a dirt road near War Homes.

The taverns did a big business in the late afternoons and evenings, and especially on weekends. Any estimate of the expansion of the liquor business would only be a guess, but it must have been greater than the expansion of most other kinds of business.

TRANSPORTATION

To accommodate increased automobile traffic, the old gravel road leading from Main Street to the entrance of the shipyard was made into a three-lane paved highway. A second paved highway was constructed from Main Street to another entrance to the shipyard, for the use of traffic from the south.

The railroad increased its Seneca service. Before the boom one eastbound train (for Chicago) and two westbound trains stopped for passengers. At the height of the boom three eastbound trains stopped, including the crack Peoria-Chicago afternoon "Rocket." One additional westbound train stopped in Seneca. The Seneca station reported a fivefold increase in receipts. Station employees were increased from two to four men; the railroad station was doubled in size, and a cement platform was laid.

Through bus service was increased from four eastbound and four westbound buses a day to five daily. The Santa Fe Bus Company reported receipts at the Seneca stop of $1,374 in the year ending February, 1942, and $5,253 in the year ending February, 1943, which did not include a full year of the boom. Commuter service was provided by private bus companies in Ottawa, Streator, and Morris. Victory Lines, Inc., of Ottawa, operated five morning and six afternoon buses to Seneca.

There was virtually no taxi service in Seneca, although a local resident occasionally used his car for taxi purposes.

COMMUNICATION

Before the boom the Seneca post office was in Class 3, and employed two workers. It was moved up to Class 2, and employed five full-time workers and one on part time. There was no delivery in Seneca before or during the boom, but branch offices were established in War Homes, Victory Court, and Riverview Homes.

Christmas of 1942 caught the post office unprepared. People lined up on the street to mail their Christmas packages and to call for incoming mail. There were no branch offices at that time. Incoming Christmas mail piled up like a mountain in the back room, and the post-office staff fell far behind.

When that emergency was past there were new ones ahead. Helen Higgins, the chief clerk, worked ten hours a day and alternate Sundays. There was never any letup. One of the problems was the dead-letter pile. These letters had to be kept for six months before they could be sent to Washington for disposal, and there was no place to store them. The great turnover of shipyard workers was responsible for the dead letters. People would go away without leaving a forwarding address, and their correspondents would put no return addresses on their letters.

During the last months of the boom Helen Higgins was kept busy readdressing and forwarding mail. She said,

"We'll miss them. I've made lots of friends I'll keep always. I get many greeting cards from people whose names I don't even remember. I'm afraid we'll be awfully poky without them. It was *very* interesting, all those new people and new experiences."

The total volume of mail was multiplied about five times by the boom.

The pre-boom telephone service was handled by two day operators and one night operator. Four day operators were used during the boom. The number of telephones in the Seneca exchange increased from 306 in 1941 to 417 in 1943. This excludes the shipyard, where CBI had 260 telephones and three switchboards of its own, in addition to its teletype.

Both the CBI and the FPHA had direct, private telephone lines between Chicago and Seneca. Calls over these two lines did not go through the Seneca exchange.

Telegrams had been handled before the boom by the railroad station. The telegraph office was now moved to the Currency Exchange. On the average this office handled twenty-five or thirty telegrams daily. Again, this excludes CBI, which had its own telegraph facilities.

ORGANIZATION OF THE BUSINESS COMMUNITY

The Commercial Club was organized in February, 1942, to help get the shipyard located in Seneca. Previous to the boom there was no organization of businessmen in Seneca.

An earlier organization, known as the Business Men's Club, had died out seven or eight years before the war.

The Commercial Club consisted of about forty members, including ministers, doctors, and teachers as well as businessmen. A board of directors, consisting of ten or twelve men, met monthly at the office of Graves' lumberyard or Hogan's coalyard. There were no regular meetings of the total membership, and annual dues were not collected after 1943. Thus the new businessmen had relatively little to do with the organization and it is not surprising that most of them, when asked whether they were active in the Commercial Club, said, "I never heard of it."

Yet the Club, although it operated mainly through its board of directors and without widespread participation, was not altogether inactive, and it sponsored a number of community projects. When WPA support for the public library was withdrawn in 1942, the Club arranged a special election to vote on a special tax levy to support the library; it promoted the War and Community Funds; it was instrumental in obtaining a branch office of the Rationing Board in Seneca; it was instrumental in getting the sewer district extended and in selecting the site for the new well for the water supply. In general, the Club tried to meet needs that arose in connection with the boom; and watched for opportunities to improve physical conditions in Seneca through the various government projects that came along.

At the close of the boom, the Commercial Club was reorganized into the Community Club, aimed at wider participation of Seneca residents, and aimed at "keeping Seneca on the map." The activities of the Community Club will be described in a later chapter, "Aftermath."

Although the newcomers in Seneca business were not officially welcomed by the oldtimers, they certainly were not given "the cold shoulder." The oldtimers seemed, on the whole, so busy and so burdened with their increased business that they did not have time to look up from their work and recognize the fact that they had new associates and new competitors.

There was one striking exception to the general ignoring of newcomer businessmen. Ray Nichols, earlier described as Seneca's leading citizen, went out of his way to welcome them. One of the new men said, at the close of the boom,

"You know, that Mr. Nichols certainly helped a lot of people. Why, I was here, a stranger, trying to get a store fixed up in an empty building, and feeling lonely and blue, and he came in the second day and held out his hand and said, 'I'm Ray Nichols. Is there anything you need? Just call on us if we can do anything for you.' And he came in every couple of months after that to ask how I was getting along."

This man, like many others, felt that Ray was genuinely interested in him. If Ray himself made money on the business they might have together, he did so without effort, and without arousing criticism.

Ray Nichols cooperated not only with new businesses, but also with the governmental agencies as, one by one, they entered the Seneca scene.[4] His cooperation set a pattern that was followed, though sometimes with grumbling, by Old Seneca people generally. If Ray had refused to cooperate, many of the local leaders would also have refused; and the task of extending Seneca's institutions to serve the newcomers would have been much more difficult.

NET EFFECTS ON BUSINESS IN SENECA

By the end of 1945 the boom was definitely over, and business in Seneca was back to "normal." The newcomers in Seneca business had been of two types. The first group con-

[4] See Chapter 13, "Government."

sisted of experienced businessmen and women from outside
Seneca who saw an opportunity and came for the duration of
the boom. Such people as Mrs. Lord and Mrs. Moriarty of the
Department Store belong in this group. The four Jewish businessmen—Samors, Frank, Harris, and Hummel—all left when
the boom was over. This is hardly to be ascribed to anti-
Semitic sentiments among Seneca residents, although these
sentiments were present, but rather to the fact that these men
had more permanent business interests elsewhere.

The second group were the local people who ventured into
business in a small way while retaining another source of
livelihood. Miller and Sherrill, who opened grocery stores in
their homes, are representatives of this second group. None
of these local people remained in business after the boom.

There were, then, very few new businesses; and such new
names as appeared on store fronts—such as the drugstore and
the clothing store—were those that would have resulted from
the normal retirements, deaths, and removals of any other
five-year period.

The moving picture theater was closed but later reopened.
The boom-time grocery stores were all closed. The Seneca
Grill remained alone among the new restaurants, but it was
changing hands rapidly in a way that worried people who
hoped that Seneca could continue to boast of a modern, air-
conditioned restaurant. Mr. Andersen remained with his
cleaning establishment.

The net effects on business are to be found in the financial
condition of the local businessmen, in the physical condition
of their places of business, and in their methods of doing business. In the first two of these respects there was a great improvement. Everybody who was in business in Seneca made
money. According to local gossip several men were rescued
by the boom from the verge of bankruptcy. Nearly every
store was substantially remodeled and modernized, and thus

Seneca will look reasonably modern and prosperous for a decade, at least.

In their methods of doing business all the storekeepers became more "modern." Time will tell whether self-service, new lines of goods, year-round fresh vegetables, and other "modern improvements" are suited to the conditions of life in postwar Seneca.

Viewed in the perspective of Seneca's business history the boom seems to have been little more than a temporary period of hectic prosperity. Businessmen came out of it in an optimistic frame of mind, with their properties in good physical condition and with their business methods somewhat modernized. But there were no changes in economic structure and processes, such as concentration of capital, or development of the cooperative movement.

9.

Recreation

"The trouble with these high wages is—there's no chance to spend it." This complaint of a young shipyard worker expressed the sentiment of many others, young and old, that life was dull in Seneca. With long working hours, there was not much time for amusement, and even when time was available there was not "much to do" in a town as small as Seneca.

Yet some compensations were necessary to balance the frustrations and discomforts of living in crowded quarters, being limited on food and gasoline, living in a small town, and being a stranger in the community. One compensation was high wages, which meant big savings and a good start in life after the war for many families who could trade present satisfaction for anticipated rewards. But for many others, probably the majority of people, there had to be some present rewards beyond high wages to maintain their morale and keep them steadily at work.

A present reward needed by most people is recreation, and consequently the recreational program of Seneca was a strategic part of the over-all situation.

For the married men it was largely a question of recreation for their wives and children. Men were working overtime, getting big money, and they could afford to do without some of their normal leisure-time activities temporarily. But they needed sleep, often in the daytime, which meant that the children had to be kept away from their small living apartments. And they needed the ease and security that are provided by wives who are comfortable and happy.

The single men and men without families had more direct personal need of recreation. Living in a small cubicle in the dormitory, or in a rented room in a private home, they needed places to congregate in their spare time. And they needed ways of releasing the tensions that build up in men under these conditions. Otherwise they would become excitement-hungry and disturb the peace of the town; or they would quit their jobs and go elsewhere.

A country town of twelve hundred is hardly equipped with the facilities or the institutional experience to provide recreation for a community of six thousand, most of whom are living in crowded quarters and lack the means of transportation to larger towns.

When the boom started, Seneca had a small school gymnasium; also a weed-grown field called Crotty Park, which had once been used as a softball diamond but had since gone to waste and become infested with "chiggers." There was a pool hall but no moving picture theater. The churches provided much of the organized sociability for old and young, but none of them had more recreation space than a basement or back room where dinners could be served. A library had been started with WPA funds in 1938.

The Masons had a lodge hall and were fairly active. The Rebeccas, a Masonic women's organization, had broken up some years earlier. The Knights of Columbus had a small organization. Delta Theta Tau, the women's sorority, provided social as well as philanthropic activity for its own group. The American Legion Women's Auxiliary held parties occasionally.

There was a well-organized Boy Scout troop, a Camp Fire Girls group, and youth organizations in the Methodist, Catholic, and Lutheran churches. The Future Farmers of America and the 4-H Club included mainly rural youth.

The children had the run of the countryside. For the boys the river was an inexhaustible source of adventure. Men and boys could go hunting and fishing. The family could always climb in the automobile and go the few miles to Ottawa for a movie.

This was adequate for a small town, but it was a weak foundation for the kind of recreational program needed by a war-boom community. The small town had to grow a set of institutions befitting an industrial city. Among others, it had to produce a kind of organized recreation for which the oldtimers in Seneca had neither the experience nor, in most cases, the desire.

During the course of the boom there were four types of recreational development in Seneca. First, the existing community facilities were expanded, including the churches, youth organizations, and library. Second, the housing projects organized their own recreational programs. The housing project programs and certain community activities came together in due time into a single program with federal support. Third, the CBI Company established a large-scale recreational program for its employees. Fourth, commercial recreation expanded.

The stories of the first two developments will be combined, and the other two will be told separately.

COMMUNITY RECREATION WITH GOVERNMENT ASSISTANCE

Planning for recreation was started almost as soon as ground was broken for the first housing units. This planning was stimulated by federal government employees in the Federal Public Housing Authority and in the Office of Community War Services. The Housing Authority was active because its staff felt responsible for the development of good living conditions in the housing projects. The Regional Office of Community War Services in Chicago had on its staff a consultant on recreation whose business it was to help war-production communities meet the recreational needs of expanding populations.

The Housing Authority staff encouraged the formation of Tenants' Recreation Committees. The Recreation Committee of War Homes, and later a similar committee for Victory Court, organized a large part of the recreation for these housing projects. One WPA recreational worker served in Seneca during the winter and spring of 1943. Hence the first year's recreational activities in the housing projects comprised a volunteer program, organized by the tenants, with the help of one paid WPA leader. Space was available in the recreation halls of the administration buildings, both at War Homes and at Victory Court. In addition, at War Homes there was one lounge in each block of apartments, and four lounges in the men's dormitory.

A typical week's program is shown in Table 14. All the leaders, except Mrs. Heath, whose name is in italics, were volunteers; and all but one of them were War Homes residents.

The recreation projects became the most active and probably the most successful of the things done by the Tenants' Councils. When the Community Recreation Project was set up with federal funds, it had at the very start a base in the work of the Housing Project Recreation Committees, and it built upon this base. Several volunteer workers were simply placed on the payroll when the government money became available. Still, there was a good deal of discouragement and conflict over the work of these Tenants' Council Committees. All attempts at organizing teen-agers were failures. The kind

TABLE 14

Schedule of Recreational Activities in War Homes, February, 1943

Activities	Leader	Location	Day	Hours
For Adults				
Social Activities	Neva Heath	Recreation Hall	Mon.-Tues.-Wed.-Thurs.	6:30–11:30
Orchestra	Group Practice	Lounge	Wednesday	8:30–11:30
Art	Rex Cleveland	Lounge	Thursday	7:30–8:30
Dance	Adm. Fee $.28	Recreation Hall	Friday	8:30–12:00
Vesper Service	Rotating	Recreation Hall	Sunday	4:00
Boxing	Bill Foli	Lounge	Time to be arranged	
Dramatics	H. J. Mead	Lounge	Time to be arranged	
For High School Students				
Boxing	Bill Foli	Lounge	Mon.-Wed.-Fri.	7:30–8:30
Social Activities	Neva Heath	Recreation Hall	Mon.-Tues.-Wed.-Thurs.	3:30–9:00
Shuffleboard, Ping-pong	Mrs. J. Madura	Recreation Hall	Tuesday	4:00
Folk and Square Dancing	Neva Heath	Recreation Hall	Tuesday	7:30–9:00
Art	Rex Cleveland	Lounge	Tues.-Thurs.	7:30–8:30
Camp Fire	Mrs. L. Beals	Lounge and Rec. Hall	Thursday	4:00–5:30
Vesper Service		Recreation Hall	Sunday	4:00
For Young People 8 Years of Age and Older				
Social Activities	Neva Heath	Recreation Hall	Monday	3:30–5:30
Boxing	Bill Foli	Lounge	Mon.-Wed.-Fri.	7:30–8:30
Art	Rex Cleveland	Lounge	Tuesday	7:30–8:30
Active Games	Neva Heath	Recreation Hall	Tuesday	4:30–5:00
Sewing	Mrs. H. Rhodes	Lounge	Tuesday	4:00–5:00
Folk Dancing	Neva Heath	Recreation Hall	Wednesday	3:30–5:30
Quiet Games				
Story Period	Mrs. V. Sitze	Lounge	Friday	4:00–5:00
Vesper Service	Rotating	Recreation Hall	Sunday	4:00

of recreation that demanded initiative on the part of the participants usually failed. The most successful affairs were dances, motion pictures, dinners, and bingo parties.

Recreational groups did not form to any great extent on a close neighborhood basis. The lounges in War Homes, one to each block, had been planned as recreational centers for the "one big happy family" that was expected to form in each block. But this did not happen. Occasionally someone would have a party for friends in the lounge, usually with liquor and enough noise to bring complaints from all the neighbors. But generally the lounges were not used for social purposes. Certain lounges became headquarters for projects of the entire housing project, such as Red Cross and Nutrition Clubs. Others were converted into living quarters.

There were a few exceptions to the rule that neighborhood social cliques did not form. The 200 block in War Homes, consisting entirely of members of the management of CBI, formed something of a social unit. In other areas a few neighbors would find themselves congenial and would form an informal social clique, in which wives lunched together, and couples played cards together in the evenings.

The government-financed recreation project. The informal social cliques of the type just described and the loosely-organized Tenants' Recreation Program with WPA assistance were not judged adequate to meet recreational needs by FPHA and OCWS officials who were responsible for morale-building in war-industry centers. These people urged the Seneca Village Council to request funds for a recreation program from the Federal Works Agency.

Since none of the oldtimers in Seneca had ever had experience with a community recreation program, the project had to be "sold" to the village council. And that mission was carried through, only to have the Seneca request rejected by the Washington Review Board of the FWA, on the ground that people earning as much money as the shipyard workers should pay for their own recreation. However, the request was finally granted, after the Chicago offices of several government agencies bombarded their Washington offices with telegrams urging favorable action. War Public Service Project Number 11-M-66 was approved, to provide $12,725 for ten months starting July 1, 1943. This money was to pay the salaries of a director and four or five assistants, and to pay for equipment.

At this time Mayor Smith named the Seneca Recreation Commission to supervise the expenditure of funds. The Commission had the following membership:

Robert Hogan, coal and grain dealer, Chairman

Mary Coulter Bell, Counselor for Women, CBI, a local girl, Secretary

Walter Colby, Director of Public Relations for the shipyard, Vice-chairman

Emmett Sand, local businessman, Treasurer

In addition there was an Advisory Committee on Recreation consisting of oldtimers and newcomers.

The Commission employed as director Mr. Jack Gentry, a big bluff Irishman, affable, friendly, and a great talker. He came from an Illinois city, where he had been secretary and business manager of the park system.

Mr. Gentry issued the following statement as soon as he arrived:

"My work in this community will be to assist and cooperate with the various groups who are already functioning, to help them determine what forms of recreation are desired, and to see that the people of the community are provided with a program of their own choice."

This was probably the kind of statement that any professional recreation man would make on coming to a new job, whether he meant it or not. Gentry seems to have meant it, and therein lay both his strength and his weakness.

The program that resulted is illustrated by the "Social Calendar" for Victory Court, which was printed in *Ship and Home* in October, 1943.

SOCIAL CALENDAR

Friday	Oct.	1	Social Evening—Movie—Free
Saturday		2	Bingo, 8:30 to 11:00 P.M.
Monday		4	Boys' Boxing Class, 7:00 P.M.
Tuesday		5	Youth Council, 8:00 P.M.
Wednesday		6	Victory Court Council, 8:30 P.M.
Thursday		7	Victory Court Bible Class
Friday		8	Stag Party for Men—Recreation Center for Men
Saturday		9	Bingo—War Homes
Sunday		10	Visual Vespers—a free religious movie, 7:30 P.M.
Monday		11	Boys' Boxing

Regular weekly affairs were repeated during the month, together with the following "special" events:

Wednesday	Oct.	13	Dance—Music by Moonlight Serenaders
Thursday		14	Free Family Movie and Community Singing
Sunday		17	Family Pot Luck Supper, 6:00 P.M.
Wednesday		27	Dance
Friday		29	Youth Hallowe'en Dance
Sunday		31	Hallowe'en Party for Victory Court Children—6:00 P.M.

War Homes had a similar program. These were largely activities that had been initiated before the recreation program came into effect. Two handicraft classes were put into operation, one in War Homes and the other in Victory Court. Classes were scheduled for various age groups. Playgrounds at War Homes and Victory Court were supervised every afternoon and all day Saturday.

Several new elements were added to the recreation program in 1943–44. An ice-skating rink was prepared, with music and a shelter house, on a pond near War Homes. "Visual Vespers," a Sunday afternoon religious movie, was carried through most of the year at Victory Court. Attendance at these showings was usually over a hundred.

An important element in the recreation program was the Men's Recreation Center, established late in 1943 in a new building at War Homes. It was furnished attractively; and the men who lived nearby in the dormitories used it for lounging, reading, and card-playing. The Center was most used just before and just after the evening meal. Otherwise, it seldom drew more than a dozen men. The following report was typical:

On a week-day evening, about 10 P.M., the visitor, on entering the building, found three boys, aged 12–14, lounging in the reception room. They all had cigars stuck in their mouths, their chairs tipped back against the wall, and exhibited an air of bravado qualified by a degree of uncertainty. Obviously they were expecting to be expelled at any moment. In the large club room, one man was listening to the radio at one end, and another was reading a newspaper at one side. Otherwise this room was empty. The small card room or "poker room," as it was generally termed, had a game going with eight players. There was no one in the arts and crafts room.

Just as the Men's Recreation Center failed to draw more than a few men, so the recreation program as a whole failed to draw many participants. The program looked good—on paper—and there seemed to be a wide variety of activities for persons of varying interests. The truth was that relatively few people engaged in the program, and participation was desultory.

In November, 1943, for instance, Mr. Gentry was describing his program to one of the fieldworkers:

"Mr. Gentry showed me a calendar on which he had listed all the activities which he and his staff had participated in for the month of September. He called out the Wednesdays, for example, and told me that on Wednesday, the 1st, he and his group staged a dance at Victory Court. On Wednesday, the 8th, he met with a youth council picnic; on Wednesday, the 15th, his staff staged a dance and movie program at Victory Court; on Wednesday, the 22nd, he and his staff helped with a youth council party; on Wednesday, the 29th, he and his group helped with a Victory Court dance.

"Then he turned to a copy of *Ship and Home* issued on October 2. Included in this housing newspaper was a social calendar which listed the events for October. Gentry had checked off on this list all the activities in which he and his staff participated. These included activities on 23 of the 31 days of the month."

Yet a prominent Seneca resident, in criticizing Gentry's program to the same fieldworker, said, "Gentry himself gave out a figure the other night that since he has been in Seneca he has had an average of twenty-six people a day participating in some kind of activity that was specifically sponsored by his staff. Twenty-six people a day! What kind of average is that, I ask you?"

In the fifteen months that Gentry stayed with the job in Seneca he made many friends, and he alienated many others. But at no time did anyone say that Jack Gentry was cramming his own recreation program down Seneca's throat. Rather, the most frequent criticism of him was that he was all promises and no performance; that he took credit for everything that was going on in recreation, even though he had started little of it; that he failed to give adequate direction to his poorly trained staff—direction that was needed in getting an organized recreational program going among a group of people who were not accustomed to such a program.

Gentry came to Seneca under less than optimum circumstances. He was hired quite suddenly, and before everyone who wanted to be consulted in the selection of a director had been consulted. For example, the Advisory Committee on Recreation was not informed by the Seneca Recreation Commission that Gentry had been employed until after the deal was closed.

After his first three months, Gentry knew that he was not satisfying some of the local leaders. He said at that time that much of his difficulty in Seneca was due to his having a different approach to recreation from what was expected. He said there were too many people in Seneca who were interested in laying down the law on different things and in directing the lives of people. He, however, believed in letting people go ahead and develop ideas of their own while he sat back and advised them. He wanted to encourage community initiative.

Still, a number of influential people in Seneca who had been unfavorable toward Gentry were veering in his direction. Interviews at this time with Florence Nichols, head of the nursery-school program, and Frank Johnson, superintendent of schools, showed them both to be fairly well satisfied. Johnson said there were a lot of things in Gentry's favor. And he pointed out that Gentry was having difficulty in finding assistants, just as Johnson was having trouble in finding teachers. Eddie Danciszak, Supervisor of Sports in the CBI recreation program, had a very good opinion of Gentry and his program.

In March of 1944, however, Frank Johnson was asked by FWA representatives what he thought about the recreation program and he told them he thought it was a failure. The OCWS consultant on recreation came to Seneca and tried to improve the situation. Since the period of the initial grant was drawing to a close, the project must either be stopped or there must be a new request for funds.

The OCWS consultant supported Gentry and pointed out that he had been handicapped for three reasons. First he did not have adequate space and equipment; second, he had lost his two ablest assistants (one had gone to a better job, and the other had resigned because of ill health); third, he could not pay high enough salaries to attract good people.

The OCWS representative commented to one of the authors:

"The local people were largely in favor of just abolishing the program. Many of them said that nothing was going on and they thought it was just a waste of federal money. They argued that there was no point in enlarging the budget to secure additional workers when it was impossible to secure people for the present positions. I took the opposite position and was able to swing the people to my side. I argued that Gentry had not been able to get an adequate number of staff members because he had not been able to offer enough money. Everywhere I go, in Seneca and Chicago, people throw up the fact that we had such a good child care program in Seneca and such a poor recreational program. They can't understand that the child care people have had good staff workers, adequate space, and good equipment all along. These are the things that we have been unable to get in recreation, and these are the things we have been unable to get the money for."

Johnson, reporting these discussions, said:

"It was not easy for Mr. W. (the OCWS Consultant) to get the Seneca people to favor an extension of the program. We put through the request all right, but it was more or less on a trial basis. We are going to consider it a test of the Seneca Recreation Commission to see just what they can do with it. The new budget will give them enough money, enough space, and enough workers to carry on an A-1 program. At the end of six months, we will know just where we stand on this recreational issue. If the Commission succeeds, everything will be fine. If it does not succeed, then there will be no excuses. I went on record as favoring this trial period. I was in favor of giving to Mr. Gentry and his staff everything they needed in the way of new staff members, additional salaries, equipment, and space, just to see if this kind of program would really work. At the end of the extended program, I don't want anyone to have any excuses as to why the program did not succeed."

The new grant, for a period of a year starting May 1, 1944, carried $18,997. It provided increased salaries for all staff members, including a salary of $3,600 for the director. This increase in the director's salary met with the private objection of several Seneca people.

The OCWS consultant worked with Gentry to build up a strong summer staff, viewing the summer program of 1944 as the critical test. Playing fields were prepared; and equipment secured for a first-rate program. Early in June, Gentry organized a two-day training institute. The OCWS consultant came down to assist and he took a great deal of initiative. For example, he made a long-distance telephone call in Gentry's presence to try to get a certain man as boys' work director for the summer. The staff was to consist of six to eight people, operating four playgrounds.

When the authors visited this institute, one of them said to Gentry that it looked as though he would have a fine program. He replied casually, "It'll be very good or it'll be a big flop. It's in the laps of the gods now."

The 1944 summer program can be described in part through Mr. Gentry's report to the Seneca Recreation Commission.

TO THE CHAIRMAN AND MEMBERS OF THE SENECA RECREATION COMMISSION AND TO THE MEMBERS OF THE SENECA RECREATION ADVISORY COMMITTEE

The month of July brought the tempo of our activities into step with the contemplated program for the summer with one or two exceptions. We were unable to obtain the services of a male Director of Special Activities. It was in the original summer program set-up and for which money was allocated in the Federal control budget. Five or six men qualified for this position were contacted, men professionally trained, such as High School Athletic Directors and Coaches and one man who was recently discharged from the army after serving 19 months as an Athletic Officer. Of the individuals contacted only one apparently would have come to Seneca, but at the last minute this party asked for a salary of $300 a month which our control budget did not permit. The Commission may have been able to adjust the control budget with the Federal Works Agency in Chicago and brought this figure up to around $250 but your Director felt that they would not entertain the suggestion for an adjustment bringing it up to $300. As a whole, however, this deficit in personnel was absorbed by the staff.

We report with regret the loss of services of Miss Wilma Thomas who was in charge of the Victory Court program. The Director has temporarily employed a Mrs. Preston for the Victory Court program, being convinced that the continued success of the program should not be retarded by lack of help to Mrs. Banos who by this time, under the influence, advice, and training of Miss Thomas, has developed into a capable play supervisor. We are also losing Miss Mathier and in this connection the Director attempted to employ a Mrs. Russell who is a resident of the new Riverview project and has had many years of experience in this work. However, Mrs. Russell the other day indicated to the Director that she was not definite in her decision to join the staff feeling that due to her age she would be unable to stand the long hours and the arduous work attending to our summer program.

The craft program under Mrs. Evelyn Pugh is now in full swing and the increase in traffic indicates the attraction this program holds in the community.

The Director has given considerable thought to the matter of giving service to the new residents of the Riverview Project and believes that service should be inaugurated to those residents within the next week or ten days which brings back into the Commission's concern the necessity for putting Crotty Park in shape to be used; and here are the things the Director thinks are essential for services in Crotty Park. First of all, the area is alive with jiggers and other parasites. I believe this situation could be corrected by mowing the play area of the park, letting the cuttings lay on the ground until they are completely dried and then burning over the area, following which it would have to be completely raked. I have attempted to obtain advice as to how to handle these parasites and this seems to be the most effective way. However, how to get this work done is a poser to the Director. I would like to ask the Commission and the Advisory Committee for suggestions to the end that this work could be done. (Crotty Park of course is directly adjacent to the Riverview project and no traffic hazard would present itself by directing the children to use an entrance which could be made at the south end of Crotty Park and approximately in the center of the west border of Riverview project.) It would of course be necessary to make some arrangements for storage of equipment. I believe that the Housing Management might be receptive to the suggestion of temporarily loaning the wooden building used as a warming building during the ice skating activities. There is of course the question of moving this building but possibly cooperation in this matter might be obtained from the Shipyards. The only other problem of which the Director has not a solution would be the matter of some type of temporary toilet accommodations. In this respect it is hoped that the Commission and Advisory Committee may find the answer.

TOTAL TRAFFIC FOR THE MONTH OF JULY

Boys—4,292   Girls—2,869   Adults—2,382   Total—9,543

TRAFFIC FOR PREVIOUS TWO MONTHS

Boys—7,900 Girls—5,293 Adults—4,345 Total—17,538

The traffic figures given in this report are, again, evidence of lack of participation in the recreation program. How the traffic counts were obtained is not clear, but whatever the method of counting, the traffic for the month of July—when schools were closed, and when one might expect a great increase in attendance at playgrounds and other recreational activities—showed only a small increase over May and June for the boys and girls of Seneca; and showed a slight decline for adults. This was in spite of the all-out effort to prove the success of the program, and to establish its worth during the summer "testing" period.

Too, if we consider the traffic figures in light of the over-all population of Seneca, it appears that a relatively small proportion of persons were participating. In June, 1944, school enrollment stood at 882; in September, at 947. Estimating an average, then, of 900 boys and girls as potential participants, and estimating 25 potential "recreational days" in July, the total potential traffic would be 22,500. The actual traffic figures shown (total of 7,161 for boys and girls together) indicate that somewhat less than one-third of the school population was involved in any part of the recreation program. A similar estimate for the adult population would indicate a much smaller proportion of adult participants.

However well these figures compare to similar figures for recreational programs in other communities, certainly in the eyes of the Seneca resident the program was not succeeding. When the six months' trial period for the renewed recreation program was over, in October, 1944, there was general agreement that it had not succeeded even reasonably well.

But Jack Gentry had some staunch friends on the Seneca Recreation Commission, and they did not have the heart to fire him. To ease the situation, the Commission resigned in a body, and Mayor Smith named a new Commission, with Frank Johnson as chairman. The membership of the new Commission was somewhat more varied than before. With the superintendent of schools as chairman, it included a representative of CBI management, a member of the Village Council, a member of the Commercial Club, a representative of the labor unions, and a representative of the Tenants' Council of one of the housing projects.

To Frank Johnson, the chairman, fell the job of asking for Gentry's resignation. Jack Gentry left in November, 1944; and Hal Redus came in as the new Director of Recreation in December, at a salary of $300 per month.

Mr. Redus had been overseas in Red Cross work, and immediately before coming to Seneca had been Community Recreation Director at Centralia, Illinois. He made a few changes in his staff, but mainly carried on with the program that was already going. He had the good will of practically everybody, and he retained that good will. But the end of shipbuilding was imminent, and everybody knew it, and nobody wanted to launch a big new program of any sort.

Frank Johnson said, after Redus had been on the job a month:

"I don't know whether Redus will pull through or not. He's too hesitant about going ahead, he's too easy with his staff.—I told him I would fire members of the old staff in the name of the Committee if he was holding back because of the trouble it might create, but he says he can't let them go until he can replace them, which may be right."

Johnson went on to say that the new Recreation Committee was not very effective. It was too large. "We have had three meetings, and as yet no agreement on anything."

Three months later, Johnson thought that the recreation

program was getting along very well. "If Mr. Redus had come here when we first started we would have had a good recreational program all along."

It was late in 1944 that the idea was proposed of a community building for Seneca. The recreation consultant of OCWS favored it, and pointed out that such a building was usually allotted to a community if it reached a size of 2,000 new housing units (Seneca reached 2,150 units). Plans were drawn for a building with a large auditorium, and the village council applied to FWA for funds. The Chicago office of FWA approved the project, and village officials were notified by telegram that the project had been approved in Washington.

But the construction of the building was never begun. Actually, the project was stopped by U. S. Navy officials in Washington. They planned to use Seneca only a few more months, and consequently they knew that the building could not be ready in time to be of use to shipyard workers. Yet they did not want to announce the imminent end of the boom. Consequently, they quietly pigeonholed the project in Washington, leaving people in Seneca mystified and somewhat frustrated. The most disappointed were Old Seneca residents who wanted a community building because they hoped to convert it into a high school auditorium after the war. They looked for someone to blame, and they fixed on housing management as the ones who probably stifled the project.

By April, 1945, it was clear that there was no basis for a further federal grant for recreation. But there was an unexpected balance in the fund, and the period of the old grant was extended to June 30, 1945.

Speaking in May, Redus evaluated his program as follows:

"This program has been a flop—not at all successful. Maybe it was because of what happened before I came, but I wouldn't say that. I would give two reasons for the failure: first, the Advisory Committee is too large and the members have done nothing at meetings but argue among themselves and nothing has been accomplished; second, I have not had sufficient staff members and I have not had good staff members. Miss Thomas is wonderful and if I had three others like her, it would have been wonderful."

The Seneca Recreation Commission formally disbanded about July 1, 1945, and divided the recreational equipment evenly between the two school districts (high school and elementary school) with the provision that community groups were to have free use of this equipment. The piece of equipment most used by community groups thereafter was the motion picture projector.

The library. Part of the community's recreation program, but entirely under the control of Old Seneca, the public library had an interesting history. It was started in 1938 as a WPA project. The librarian, Mrs. Lois Zimmerman, was employed full time, and a collection of books was begun. WPA support was withdrawn in July, 1942, but the library was maintained by local efforts, stimulated by the beginning of the boom at that time. A drive among Old Seneca residents in the winter of 1942–43 raised $500 for library expenses. At this time there was no solicitation of funds in War Homes because the housing manager would not permit solicitation of funds for any purpose. The village council, after a special election to authorize a special tax levy for the library, issued tax warrants for $600 to help pay expenses.

There were over fifteen hundred books in the library in 1942, and these were supplemented during the boom by donations from various sources. A thousand books discarded by the Chicago Public Library were added. From the "Books for Victory" drive in Evanston, Illinois, fifteen hundred books were given to Seneca. (These were books that were left over after those of probable interest to soldiers had been picked out and sent overseas.) From the State Library a supply of three to five hundred books were borrowed on long-period loans of several months to be replaced by others when the loan period was over. Thus the total number of books in the library was about forty-five hundred; but many of them were of slight interest to Seneca readers.

In addition to the library's shelf collection, there was a mail service from the State Library, which supplied readers with technical and scientific books when specific requests were made for them.

The library was directed by a Village Library Board with Frank Johnson as chairman. The budget of $1,450 for 1943 was increased to $2,500 in 1944, aided by a contribution of $800 from the National War Fund whose campaign in Seneca took the place of the 1943 library drive.

The librarian who had been on duty only from 2 to 5 in the afternoon, and who had been paid $50 a month, now had her hours lengthened from 11 A.M. to 5 P.M. (with a corresponding increase in salary); and the library was kept open Tuesday and Thursday evenings until 8 P.M.

Circulation figures grew steadily during the boom. In October, 1943, there were 1,607 books circulated, 1,222 to adults and 385 to children. There were 27 new registrants during the month, and 1,050 registrants altogether. In March, 1944, circulation reached 2,063. In January, 1945, circulation was 2,516.

A few magazine subscriptions were entered and a few new books bought. In April, 1944, the Library Board reported that it had bought a new *Webster's Unabridged Dictionary*, and had subscribed to *Time* magazine, *Better Homes and Gardens*, and *Reader's Digest*. Among the new books purchased in 1944–45 were Audubon's *Birds of America*; James Gray, *The Illinois* (River); Nicolay, *MacArthur of Bataan*; Gilmore,

How To Build a Model Navy; Brien, *Smoke Eater*; Kjelgaard, *Forest Patrol*; De la Roche, *The Building of Jalna*; Cronin, *The Green Years*; Ernie Pyle, *Brave Men*; Inaife, *Lake Michigan*; Stone, *The Immortal Wife*; Goudge, *Green Dolphin Street*.

Mrs. Zimmerman was a sociable person, and she encouraged a number of women to make their visits to the library a social occasion. They would sit and chat with her when she was not busy, or with friends who came in, or with strangers whom Mrs. Zimmerman introduced to them. The majority of adult readers were women, and most of them expected the librarian to select books for them, usually novels.

Mrs. Zimmerman resigned in May, 1945, and her place was taken by Miss Louise Peddicord, who lived on a farm near Seneca. In the spring of 1946 the library was still running smoothly, being open from 1 to 5 daily. At this time the library contained about five thousand volumes. All the books belonging to the State Library had been returned. The library subscribed to six magazines, including *Time, Better Homes and Gardens, Parents' Magazine,* and *Reader's Digest*. The annual budget was $1,850, of which $1,000 came from taxes and the remainder from gifts.

Shipyard Recreational Program

Very early in the boom, the CBI set up a recreational program under its Department of Public Relations. The recreation staff consisted of two men, a supervisor of sports and a supervisor of activities, who worked through an organization known as the Shipyard Recreational Association. There was an executive committee consisting of ten employees, each representing a department; and each working in turn with a department committee. The program was planned to be carried on through the initiative of the employees, with the supervisor there to furnish facilities, but not to teach or to introduce new types of recreation.

Early in the program an interest questionnaire was circulated among the workers (with the results shown in Table 15), and the program that grew up attempted to build upon these interests.

TABLE 15

RECREATIONAL INTERESTS OF SHIPYARD WORKERS

Activity	Number Interested	Activity	Number Interested
Bowling	850	Wrestling	115
Basketball	325	Dart Ball	20
Hobbies	110	Ping-pong	285
Billiards and Pool	475	Track	95
Band	90	Tennis	245
Orchestra	120	Calisthenics	125
Drama	100	Touch Football	165
Singing	230	Apparatus	35
Baseball	725	Tumbling	65
Softball	900	Commando Training	200
Golf	380	Refereeing	71
Horseshoes	625	Umpiring	213
Volley Ball	160	Score Keeping	67
Handball	80	Publicity	67
Soccer	75	Hiking	241
Swimming	550	Badminton	85
Boxing	200		

Others added by workers in questionnaire replies:

Quiz Programs	3	Fencing	2
Horseback Riding	30	Photography	3
Trap Shooting	11	Casting	7
Bridge	7	Checkers	10
Fishing and Hunting	170	Cribbage	1
Bicycling	6	Ice Skating	21
Dancing	55	Religious Activities	2
Flying	43	General Exercises	2
Football	21	Bocci Ball (Italian Game)	24

The *sports program,* under Eddie Danciszak, ranged from large league activities to small individual games and small group sports, including ping-pong, chess, cards, dominoes, volleyball, boxing, and horseshoes. Sixty-four workers engaged in a golf tournament. There were 110 bowling teams in the shipyard league. These teams, totaling some six hundred workers, were formed in leagues according to towns neighboring Seneca in which the shipyard workers lived. There were leagues in Marseilles, Morris, Ottawa, Streator, and LaSalle. (There was one bowling alley in Seneca at the time.)

Night softball games were engaged in by twenty-four yard teams organized into three different leagues; and by the one big team representing the entire shipyard.

In 1943 the shipyard organized a baseball team managed by John "Bud" Clancy, formerly with the Chicago White Sox. This team played fifteen games. Home games were played on a field in the shipyard. On one occasion "Dizzy" Dean played with the shipyard team.

The distribution of recreational facilities within the shipyard was based on a unique plan. Twenty-five recreational stations were distributed around the edge of the shipyard. Regardless of where a man worked, he was always near one of these recreational stations. Each station was a storehouse for recreational equipment, and a volunteer worker was responsible for the equipment at each of the twenty-five stations. He checked the material out to workers at lunch time or after the day's work was over.

A number of large areas for recreation surrounded the edge of the "berth" section of the shipyard. These areas—four in number—were large enough for standard-sized softball fields and were used for large game activities. In these areas there were also volleyball, badminton, and croquet courts, horseshoe pits, and other similar provisions. One area was even equipped with outdoor tables for ping-pong.

Some activities were prohibited because of possible injury to essential workers. These included such games as soccer, touch football, tumbling, commando training, regular football, and fencing. Because of the nature of the work being carried on in the shipyard, a ban was placed on photography and on any form of aviation.

The *activities program,* under Robert Ruff, was concerned with drama, hobbies, orchestra, band, singing, chorus groups, and so on. The electrical department's male chorus often supplied music at ship-launching ceremonies. The shipyard orchestra, an organization of some fifteen pieces, played for a number of events in Seneca, including dances and banquets. The LST Minstrels, a show with an all-shipbuilder cast, toured the towns in the neighborhood.

Perhaps the biggest handicap to the recreational program was lack of transportation. Many workers came to the shipyards in groups of four and five riding in one car, and the individual in the group had to come and go with the group. This kept down the number of people participating in the recreation program. Almost as big as this problem was the one of having few local indoor facilities. The program had to be extended to nearby towns where bowling alleys and gymnasiums were available.

The shipyard recreational program was financed initially by CBI and by dues from the members of the Shipyard Recreational Association. The dues, a dollar per person, were paid only once, early in the program, in order to buy equipment to get a program started. About two thousand workers paid dues. Funds from gate receipts at ball games and other large-scale events practically covered the expense of the program, except for the salaries of the two supervisors, which were paid by CBI.

Some idea of the way the employees took responsibility for

the recreation program can be gained from the following report concerning the bowling leagues:

Sports Release from: November 26, 1943
Shipyard Recreational Association
Shipbuilding Division
Chicago Bridge & Iron Company
Seneca, Illinois

. . . We must introduce the President and Secretary of our Shipyard Recreational Association Bowling Leagues before we can explain the activities of this fine organization.

Our president, Ernie Knottek, is employed as an Electrician in the Electrical Department of our shipyard. He is married and has two sons in the U. S. Army and a daughter at home.

His experience in bowling dates back to the year 1925. Ernie's average for the last three and one-half years is 196.

After talking with his fellow workers, here in the shipyard, he took the responsibility of organizing bowling leagues under the supervision of the S.R.A.

At the same time that Ernie was elected president, Carl Imhoff was elected secretary. Carl is the Supervisor of the Blue Print Department, coming to the shipyard from the Chicago Bridge & Iron Company office in Washington, D. C.

He has had ten years' experience in bowling, his average for the past four years being between 160 and 165. It is largely through the unceasing efforts of Ernie and Carl that our bowling leagues were organized. To cope with the gasoline situation, leagues were formed in the surrounding towns of Ottawa, Marseilles, Morris, LaSalle, Peru, and Streator. The following tabulation will give an idea as to how many, when, what, and where—of our bowling leagues: [See page 238.]

We have also formed Women's Bowling Leagues. Monya Renner, of the Electrical Department, was elected president. She is quite capable of filling that office, as she is very sports-minded as well as being very popular with her fellow workers.

MEN'S LEAGUES

City	Name of Alley	League	No. Players
Ottawa	Illini	Three 8-Team	172
Ottawa	O'Brien		
Streator	Bee's	One 8-Team	72
Morris	Morris Recreation	One 6-Team	36
Marseilles	Palace DeLuxe	Seven 6-Team	252
LaSalle-Peru	Playmore	One 8-Team	48
			580

During the year 1941, Monya made a 23,000 mile tour of the "South" with the Peoria Farrow Chix. She has played professional softball in every state in America. In 1942 she was a member of the Peoria Farrow Chix when they won the Women's State Softball Championship. It was in the summer of this same year that she was in Chicago for the world championship!

WOMEN'S LEAGUES

City	Name of Alley	League	No. Players
Morris	Morris Recreation	One 6-Team	30
Marseilles	Palace DeLuxe	One 6-Team	30

With the cooperation of the Bowling Team Captains, the different departments in our shipyard, and the Supervisor of Sports, Eddie Danciszak, we feel we will have a very enjoyable and successful season.

The First Annual Sports Banquet of the Shipyard Recreational Association was held November 22, 1943, in the shipyard cafeteria, with 231 people present. Music was furnished by "Harm" Galley's Shipbuilders, the shipyard orchestra.

The toastmaster for the evening was Mr. Jim Flynn, a shipyard worker who was chairman of the Executive Committee of the

Shipyard Recreational Association. In the opening remarks Mr. Flynn welcomed people to the banquet and announced the recent organization of the shipbuilders' orchestra. Following this introduction he introduced Mr. C. W. Hines, general manager of the Shipbuilding Division of the CBI. Mr. Hines gave the official welcome to those present. Mr. Hines announced that on the next day, November 23, the Shipbuilding Division would launch its 40th ship. Mr. Hines announced that the shipyard was at the present time 22 days ahead of schedule. He paid tribute to the many workers who had a part in this, and he said that the recreation program itself contributed a great deal toward making this production schedule possible. He said that these 40 ships had been built at a much lower cost than what the Navy had expected to be possible. In this introductory talk Mr. Hines paid tribute to Mr. Danciszak for his work in the recreation program and then announced that Eddie was leaving the shipyard around the first of the year to enter the Army.

In talking about Eddie's work, Mr. Hines said that he did not think Eddie ever went home. He said that he had been at the shipyards at 1:00 A.M., 3:00 A.M., 5:00 A.M. and so on and that he had always found Eddie around some place. He said that the same thing was true for Walter Colby and other members of the general staff. He said that midnight movies had proved to be very popular with men at the shipyards and that he had heard and witnessed some of the baseball games going on at 4:30 and 5:00 o'clock in the morning.

Special awards were given to the best participating contributor to any one team and to the outstanding athlete at the shipyard. Medals were given to two women welders who had been on hand for every baseball game scheduled for the 5:30 period in the mornings.

The speaker for the banquet was Mr. Arch Ward, Sports Editor of the *Chicago Tribune*. Mr. Ward made a very funny speech in which he told numerous jokes about the *Chicago Tribune*, the *Chicago Sun*, and Eleanor Roosevelt. The general theme of his talk was competition and he linked together sports competition, industrial competition, and battle front competition.

Dances were arranged frequently by committees from one department or another. For example, on December 17, 1943, the Hull Department sponsored a Christmas dance in the Ottawa Armory, with music by "Harm" Galley's Shipbuilders. On December 13, 1943, the executives and department heads of CBI gave a dinner dance in honor of naval officers stationed at Seneca and the board of directors of CBI at the Ottawa Boat Club. Music was provided by "Harm" Galley's Shipbuilders. On November 4, 1944, a Shipyard Women's Dance was held at Ivyway Gardens, near Marseilles. This affair was promoted by Mary Coulter Bell, Counselor for Women of the CBI.

A big Christmas party was held on December 16, 1944, in the Ottawa Armory, with dancing, door prizes, and entertainers. Over a thousand people attended. Santa Claus (Robert Maxwell) was there to pass out the prizes to holders of lucky numbers.

The first (and only) annual picnic of CBI employees was held on Sunday, June 4, 1944, in Starved Rock State Park. Approximately twenty thousand people attended the picnic, and were entertained by vaudeville acts, free dancing, open-air movies, boxing bouts, and games. Nineteen-year-old Miss Helen Hagi, of the neighboring village of Ransom, was elected by the servicemen who attended the picnic as "Shipyard Queen."

All in all, as industrial recreation programs go, the Seneca program seems to have enjoyed better than average success in the face of less than favorable conditions.

COMMERCIAL RECREATION

The largest addition to pre-boom commercial recreation was the Barge Theatre, built as soon as the boom commenced and opened in November, 1942. This theater was owned by the Anderson Theatre Circuit and managed by Harvey "Doc" Arlington. The seating capacity was 270. Showings were continuous from 1:30 to 11 P.M. and there were six different programs a week. On Saturday evenings at 11 P.M. a "midnight show" offered a new program, different from the one shown earlier in the evening.

The pictures shown during the theater's Anniversary Week, November 15 to 22, 1944, were:

Hers to Hold—Deanna Durbin and Joseph Cotton
Tail Spin—Alice Faye, Constance Bennett, and Nancy Kelly
Reap the Wild Wind—Ray Milland, John Wayne, Paulette Goddard
Remember the Night—Barbara Stanwyck and Fred MacMurray
King of the Cowboys—Roy Rogers and Smiley Burnette
The Star Maker—Bing Crosby and Louise Campbell

On Labor Day, 1943, a bowling alley was opened by the Packard Bowling Association, with Ralph Koerner as manager. The alleys were open from noon to midnight seven days a week. They were patronized mainly by young people, including many high school students. The bowling alley did not succeed, perhaps because most of the newcomers interested in bowling were involved in the bowling leagues already established at the shipyards. In less than a year it was transformed into a general recreational establishment called "Playland." Playland was managed by Dan Nichols, formerly manager of Van's Eat Shop. There was a soda fountain, a dance floor with juke-box music, a penny arcade, pinball machines, and rooms on the second floor for private bingo parties and the like.

As already described, Seneca's five taverns of pre-boom time had to meet the demands of the new population without addition to their number, because the authorities refused to issue new liquor licenses. The "D and W" (Downey and

Walsh) was a cigar and candy store that was reported to operate a "handbook." This was a temporary venture by the proprietors, who conducted a well-known gambling establishment in Ottawa.

A typical weekend in Seneca is described in the following account of such a period in late September, 1943: On Friday night the town seemed quite crowded with cars parked on both sides of the street all the way through town. The new bowling alley was jammed with young people, including a number of high school students. They seemed to be amateurs at bowling, but they were enjoying themselves. There was no rough language or anything that might be considered indecent during the evening at the bowling alley. As the evening wore on the bowling group divided into two parts. The younger group went next door for ice cream, and the older group went to the taverns.

There seemed to be more high school boys and girls in Seneca on Friday night than there were on the following Saturday and Sunday nights. On Saturday night between 9:30 and 1:00 o'clock there were distinctly fewer people in town. It was easy to find a parking space and there were approximately half the number of cars lining the streets. The bowling alley was just as crowded, and there were about as many high school boys and girls there as on the night before. It soon became apparent that many of them were simply waiting for the midnight show to begin. Several boys came in and asked several of the girls if they wanted to go car riding before the midnight show. These offers were all turned down except one. Again the group divided up when they finished bowling and part went to the ice-cream parlor for refreshments and several went to the taverns.

Following the group into a bar, the fieldworker found it filled with patrons, and in a room adjacent to it, which had seats and tables much as a drugstore does, full families were eating and having beer and other drinks with their meals. The lateness of the hour did not seem to make any difference in the number of small children accompanying their parents. Slot machines were in evidence and in constant use. The crowd in the tavern seemed orderly on the whole, and were busy with eating, drinking, and general conversation.

The midnight show began not at midnight but some time after eleven o'clock. There was a long line of people stretching out into the street, most of whom seemed to be high school students. They were a well-ordered crowd and seemed to be having fun.

Sunday night there seemed to be half again as many people as on Saturday night but not as many as there were on Friday night.

As early as twelve o'clock Saturday noon there were men staggering down the main street of Seneca. There were also men in various stages of intoxication on the streets on Sunday morning as early as 9:45. They seemed to be minding their own business and at least progressing toward some known destination. A policeman was in evidence at all times in Seneca on Friday, Saturday, and Sunday nights.

Seneca's night life, while relatively sedate from the point of view of a city-bred observer, was reputed to be quite lively by Seneca residents. An elderly man, in a white-collar shirt, was purchasing a money order at the post office and confiding his opinion of Seneca to the clerk.

"Why, it's a wild town. Wild, that's what it is. I was writing my wife, 'You should come and see, then you'd believe me.' I'd like to have her spend one week-end here, Thursday night to Monday."

Father Preston told the following story. He spoke to an urchin emerging from the movie house long after the curfew whistle had blown. "My lad, it's time you were at home." "Yes, Father Preston, I'll go." But he started into a convenient tavern door. "Here," called the priest, "that's not the way home." "No, Father, but I want to go in and tell my father and mother I'm going home."

RECREATION FOR YOUTH

Before the boom Seneca had one troop of Boy Scouts. Its leader was Mr. Oliver Hippard, who had charge of a patrol boat on the river. An additional troop was organized in 1944, consisting of boys from the housing projects. It had a membership of forty boys at its peak. A Cub Pack was also organized in the housing projects.

Girl Scouts and Brownies were organized in the spring of 1944, and developed under the leadership of Mrs. Pugh, recreation worker. The membership of these groups was distributed as follows in the fall of 1944: Seneca Village, 11; Victory Court, 12; War Homes, 10; Trailer Camp, 12; Riverview Homes, 3.

The Victory Court Youth Council was organized in 1943, but it never really "took hold." The boys and girls turned out fairly well for a few parties, but they did not become organized for effective work. Nevertheless, the Youth Council held occasional meetings through 1944.

In March, 1944, an organization was promoted to include young people fourteen years of age and on through high school, from the entire community. It was named the Se-Vi-Wa Tribe (Seneca-Victory Court-War Homes). Meetings were held during the spring in the War Homes recreation hall. The organization died out over the summer.

The church youth organizations were quite active, meeting regularly at least once a week. These organizations expanded with the expansion of the churches, but otherwise continued with much the same kind of program they had conducted before the boom.

The end of the boom found the youth organizations in much the same shape as they were at the beginning. Expansion had been temporary. Programs were much the same as they had always been.

FRATERNAL AND SOCIAL ORGANIZATIONS

The Masons became quite active during the boom, with the coming of members from other towns to work in the shipyard. The Rebecca organization was not revived, although there was some talk of it. The Knights of Columbus carried on, much the same as usual.

Delta Theta Tau Sorority carried on as usual, and added a very small number of new members, including the visiting nurse, Doris Randolph.

One new social club was organized and incorporated as the 429 Club. This organization was developed by members of Local 429 of the Boilermakers' Union, and its headquarters were in the basement of the union headquarters. Creation of the social club enabled the organization to offer such recreational facilities to its members as a bar and card tables.

SUMMARY AND EVALUATION

Recreational facilities in Seneca were expanded generally, with the enlargement of existing organizations and the creation of new ones. War Homes and Victory Court each organized a recreation committee. The shipyard organized a program for its employees. The federal government subsidized a program in the housing projects. The churches and other Seneca organizations expanded their programs. Commercial recreational facilities were provided.

On the whole, boys and girls fared quite well, as far as recreation was concerned. They had the river and the countryside to explore; there was ice skating in the winter; playground and arts and crafts equipment were provided for them; there was space for parties and dancing; there were Boy Scouts and Girls Scouts and church youth groups. The school offered opportunities for chorus, band, dramatics, and athletics. The library offered a fair collection of children's books.

Teen-age youth were not organized, but they had plenty to do. They had movies, bowling, dances, and school activities, and most of them had part-time jobs.

For the men there were outdoor sports at the shipyard, cards at the Recreation Building, bingo, dances, dinners, and victory gardens at the housing projects, and fellowship with other men in the church, labor, and fraternal organizations.

For the women who were socially outgoing and active, there was a variety of organizations to choose from. The churches, Red Cross and health classes, the Mother's Club of the nursery school, and the housing project recreational organizations all were opportunities for women who wished to utilize them. Women could join the men in attendance at dinners, picnics, sports events, dances, the movies.

Evaluation. On paper it appears that the recreational opportunities were rich and varied. Actually, few adults took much part in recreation. The men were usually working overtime, and few of them were looking for much recreation. The women were not so well cared for. Many of them, with relatively little housekeeping to do, had time on their hands and did very little with it.

The recreational activities that proved most popular were either of the spectator type, such as movies and sporting events, or those that offered the simplest type of basic stimulation, such as bingo, dancing, dinners, and the taverns.

This was no different from the recreational activities of working-class people in a thousand cities and towns, who were likewise busy with war work, and who differed from the Seneca people only in that they continued to live where they had been living before the war.

Recreation did what was necessary in Seneca. There was very little demoralization. Productivity of labor improved at the shipyard. People were not too dissatisfied.

Why, then, is the judgment of the observer negative on recreation in Seneca? Why does the observer say that, compared with other aspects of life, recreation in Seneca was not a success? The reason for the adverse judgment on Seneca's recreation is probably twofold. First, an opportunity seems to have been lost for a vital, constructive, recreational program instead of something that merely muddled through. Second, the people who took the lead in the program did not enjoy it, and did not want to stay to see it through.

The causes that lay behind what actually did happen in Seneca, as well as the failure of other things to happen, are several.

First, there was the prevailing lack of interest on the part of the old-time residents in an organized recreational program. The attitude seemed to be the typical rural one that recreation was a personal matter, to be found and paid for by the individual himself, and not to be considered a community responsibility.

Second, once a handful of prominent Senecans were convinced of the need for a recreation program, they had no precedent or pattern to follow. The people of Seneca did not know how to run a community recreation program. In contrast, they did know how to run a school program, and they were able to expand their schools with little difficulty. The village council, when it created the Seneca Recreation Commission, was creating a body analogous to the school board. But the new Commission did not have behind it the

experience with operating a community recreation program
that small communities have with operating school programs.
Furthermore, it was much more difficult to find an able,
well-trained director of recreation than it would have been
to find an able, well-trained school superintendent.

Inexperienced and unconcerned about the need to take
responsibility for recreation, and lacking local leadership, the
community of Seneca did just about what would have been
expected.

Another source of difficulty was the split among the residents of Seneca on the moral issues of recreation. There were
some people who did not believe in dancing. Many others
opposed bingo and card-playing, as gambling games. With
these differences of opinion, and living so closely together,
people sometimes disagreed and then did nothing about
recreational organizations, where in a normal community the
various groups might have separated and led their own
recreational lives.

Still another difficulty was the fact that a very large proportion of the workers had had no previous experience with
community recreation. They were accustomed to organizing
their leisure time within large kin groups, but not to organizing for play with people who had been total strangers up to
the present moment.

10.

Schools

The schools in Seneca had to expand. They needed more rooms and more teachers and more money. To get these things the school board had only to ask the government, but this was not an easy thing for men who distrusted the "New Deal" and feared the encroachment of federal government on their community life.

Whether the schools themselves would be changed in other ways than mere size was a question that interested the authors. They made observations and they interviewed teachers to find out whether the curriculum was modified, whether methods of teaching were changed, and whether new elements were added to the school program.

THE SCHOOLS BEFORE THE BOOM

In 1940 there were two school buildings, located on the same grounds. The elementary school building was the same one that was described at its dedication in 1884 as "a magnificent structure costing $10,000." A visitor accustomed to appraising school buildings described it in 1942 as a "two-story building, very old, poorly designed—a firetrap." The classrooms had old-fashioned desks screwed to the floors in rows. The windows were few and narrow. The wooden stairs creaked. There were six classrooms for eight grades. Two of the rooms had a single teacher for two grades.

The school program was typical of the rural villages of the Midwest. The basic skills were stressed and there was much readin', 'ritin', and 'rithmetic. The children "sat up tall"

from early morning to mid-afternoon, when, with the ring-
ing of the bell in the school steeple, they would "rise, pass,
and go out."

Of the six elementary school teachers, five had their homes
in the village and four had been reared there from childhood. Their professional training varied. At least one teacher,
who had been in the Seneca school for many years, had
begun her teaching career upon completion of high school.
One or two others had graduated from two-year normal
school; and one had achieved the bachelor's degree. The
teachers were paid approximately $1,000 for nine months of
teaching.

The high school was next door to the elementary school.
Its twenty-year-old building was fairly adequate by modern
standards. It contained five classrooms, a large study hall,
and a combination gymnasium and auditorium. With 130
students the building was quite well filled. About half of the
pupils came in from farms in the surrounding country.

In addition to the conventional college preparatory course
(convential, although few Seneca pupils ever went to college), there were courses in agriculture, home economics,
and commercial work. The high school teachers were college
graduates. No more than one or two out of six were native
Senecans. The average salary was $1,425 for a nine-month
school year.

There were separate school boards for the elementary and
the high schools, as was common in Illinois, but they employed one superintendent to direct both schools.

The superintendent was Frank Johnson, a young man
who had come to Seneca fifteen years earlier, fresh out of
college, as science teacher and athletic coach in the high
school. Well-liked in the community, he had settled down
and married a local girl. Finally he was made superintendent
after a succession of men who stayed for very short periods.

President of the elementary school board was Dr. Coulter, who during the boom was the only general medical practitioner in the village. When Dr. Coulter presented the eighth-grade graduates with their diplomas he could remember having brought most of them into the world some fourteen years earlier. Of the five other men on this school board, two were local businessmen, and three were employees of the Dupont Dynamite Plant.

The high school board had as its president Mr. Andrew Brown, who owned a service station at the intersection of Main Street and Highway 6. There were two farmers on this board, a retired employee of the Bell Telephone Company, and two employees of the Dupont Plant.

Since Frank Johnson was doing a job as superintendent that pleased them all, the board members left things as much as possible to his direction. Their attitude was expressed by Mr. Harris, the secretary-treasurer of the elementary school board, who said with great satisfaction that the board had very little business to do and very few meetings.

This policy of "leaving the schools to the superintendent and the teachers" was shown also in the fact that there was no Parent-Teacher Association. There was no formal organization or association to bring teacher and parent together. Informally, there was a good deal of contact between the two groups in church and in neighborhood visiting. The elementary schoolteachers, especially, being nearly all old-time residents, were accessible to most parents without the formality of an organization to bring them together. The high school teachers were more distant from the parents, a fact that they alternately resented and enjoyed. One teacher commented on the freedom that the lack of a P.T.A. gave her. "We don't have parents poking around all the time," she said. But another high school teacher complained of the loneliness of her life. "I speak to everybody and everybody speaks to me," she said, "but I'm never invited anywhere. When I first came, I used to sit in my room and cry evening after evening, I was so lonely. But I got over that. Now I go away as often as I can on weekends."

The St. Patrick's parochial school had a small brick building, with three teachers and forty-five children. Most of the more prominent Catholic families sent their children to this school for the first eight grades, after which they were entered in the public high school.

THE FIRST BOOM YEAR

School opened in September, 1942, with almost twice as many pupils in the elementary grades as were there the preceding June. Table 16 and Figure 15 show the increases in enrollment through the boom.

TABLE 16

SCHOOL ENROLLMENTS AND NUMBER OF TEACHERS

Date	Elementary School		High School		Parochial School	
	Enrollment	Teachers	Enrollment	Teachers	Enrollment	Teachers
June, 1942	175	6.5	131	6.5	45	3
September, 1942	304	8.5	163	6.5	94	4
June, 1943	416	12.5	195	9.5	95	4
September, 1943	540	16.5	223	11.5	95	4
June, 1944	630	19	252	12.5	95	4
September, 1944	700	22.5	247	14.5	95	4
June, 1945	474	20	202	13.5	95	4
September, 1945	197	12	152	11	45	3
June, 1946	176	12	133	11	45	3
September, 1946	180	11	146	10	43	3
September, 1947	199*	11	144	10.5	63	3.5
September, 1948	211*	11	147	10.5	65	3.5
September, 1949	222*	11	130	10.5	76	3.5

* Includes kindergarten of 15–20 children.

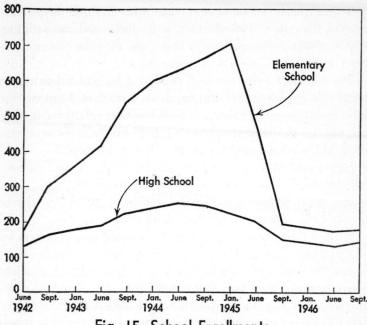

Fig. 15. School Enrollments.

The first need was for more space for classrooms. This was provided by the FPHA, which turned over two lounges of the men's dormitories for classrooms, and loaned for a school building the temporary wooden structure that had served at War Homes as construction headquarters. There were eight classrooms in this, the "Temp School." Some rooms were small, others were narrow and long. The sixth grade children had to pass through the fifth grade classroom in order to get to their room. The children in the dormitory lounges were required to approach the buildings quietly and to enter on tiptoe, because night workers were sleeping. "If you aren't quiet, the workers can't sleep. Then they won't be able to work, and if they can't work, they can't build ships and we will lose the war."

These quarters had to carry the schools through the first year of the boom, while work was started on a new building, which it was supposed would meet the needs of the expanding community.

The hiring of extra teachers proved to be less difficult than had been expected. Several teachers were found among the wives of shipyard workers. Others were recruited from rural schools in the neighborhood of Seneca. Salaries were increased to about $140 per month for elementary school teachers and $175–$200 per month for high school teachers. Mr. Johnson, who had spent part of his time teaching science in the high school, gave up his teaching duties and spent all his time administering the school program.

At first there was some antipathy toward new teachers by old teachers, partly due to the fact that new teachers were normally employed at a higher salary than old teachers had been getting. But Superintendent Johnson raised the old teachers' salaries even after they had signed their contracts, so as to keep their salaries in line with what the new teachers were getting. This quieted much of the unrest among the oldtimers on the teaching staff, although it was not until they were completely in the minority, in the following year, that they ceased to make the new teachers feel like outsiders.

The attitude of the old toward the new teachers was a part of the general attitude of oldtimers in Seneca toward newcomers. Newcomers were instantly labeled as "riff-raff" and the label stuck until they proved their right to be accorded the same status as oldtimers.

The newcomers among the children were at first said to be slow and stupid and to have a poor background. Oldtimers among the teachers cited individual examples among the new children to prove their claims. But the facts were generally so clearly at variance with this view of the newcomers that the old teachers soon quit making such remarks. Instead, they would often comment on the valuable experience that some of the newcomers brought with them to the classroom, because they had traveled a good deal, or because they came from another part of the country.

Still, the early attitudes died slowly. As late as the close of the first boom year the teachers went to the annual school picnic, which came at the time of the eighth grade graduation, with the conviction that they would have to associate with parents far below them on the social scale. The parents all came to the picnic, and brought food for a picnic dinner. The teachers thus had a chance to taste the food prepared by the mothers of the children, and in this way to evaluate their social status. Several teachers remarked after the picnic that they had been agreeably surprised by the excellent quality of the food. "I thought these new people were 'truck' and I hesitated to eat the food they brought," said one old-timer among the teachers, "but they brought excellent food, and well-cooked. I wondered how they could do it on their hot plates in those War Homes."

With the growth of the schools the school board members had to give more time to the program and to assume heavy responsibilities. They could no longer count on Frank Johnson to meet any situation that might arise. He had to have their help in determining new policies.

The first difficulty was that of financing the school program. The tax money that would have carried the schools through the year was all used up by January. This meant that the board must make a decision to borrow money. For these men who had been accustomed to running a school on money that was clearly in sight this was a difficult decision. They were trustees for their fellow citizens. If they got their school district hopelessly in debt their neighbors would hold them responsible.

There were two sources of revenue to meet the debt they were creating. The surest source was the promise of the Federal Public Housing Authority to pay money in lieu of taxes on the value of the property it held in Seneca.[1] The board members could feel quite certain of getting money from this source, but this was not enough. The second source was direct grants from the federal government. Such grants were by no means assured when the board first faced the problem of operating the schools through the year 1942–43. Such procedures were too much for the nerves of the secretary-treasurer of the elementary school board, Henry Harris, who resigned his position to a younger man who could do business in this way.

Moreover, negotiations had to be undertaken with the government to get a new school building. While the government agencies planned and built the school, the local board had to take responsibility for its maintenance. They showed none of the pride in getting a new school building that might have been expected. People were apprehensive of what might happen after the boom. The new building might become a white elephant, expensive to care for yet too good to discard.

Thus the members of the school board had to learn some new ways of looking at the problem of school finance, ways that were not easy for them to learn, since they involved dependence on the federal government for aid. They also had to have more frequent meetings, and to give more time to a job that had previously been a very light one.

When the annual school board election came in 1943, there were four members whose terms expired. Only Mr. Harris refused to run for re-election. The interest in the election was so light that nobody filed a petition, and the names

[1] The FPHA paid a total of $76,734 in lieu of taxes to all local taxing bodies up to June 30, 1945.

of the candidates had to be written on the ballot. Dr. Coulter was re-elected president of the board with seventeen votes, and Mr. Harris' successor was elected with nine votes.

The newcomers did not participate in the school board election, although they could have done so. Even in April of 1944, when many of them had been living in Seneca a year and a half, they showed little interest in the election. At that time the candidates for positions on the board were slightly more active. The men whose terms expired all filed petitions for re-election with the exception of one member of the high school board, and there were two new candidates for his place.

Newcomers and oldtimers alike acted as though the schools belonged to Old Seneca. Perhaps the general satisfaction with the schools on the part of the newcomers had something to do with this attitude. If they had not been satisfied they might have become more active in school affairs.

Community-school relationships remained on a casual basis. With many teachers living outside of Seneca, and with a large new population, the relations between the teachers and the parents of the pupils became extremely tenuous. Yet there was no move to establish a formal basis, such as a Parent-Teacher Association, for bringing parents and teachers together.

The St. Patrick's parochial school expanded to its limit of ninety-five pupils by adding one more teacher; and it remained at this level throughout the boom.

THE SECOND BOOM YEAR

The second year of the boom opened with newcomer children outnumbering oldtimers two to one in the elementary school, and equalling oldtimers in the high school. Space was now adequate, however. The high school used several rooms in the old elementary school building; while the new building housed the first eight grades in sixteen rooms.

The new building had, in addition to sixteen classrooms, a large all-purpose room—auditorium, gymnasium, and cafeteria—a kitchen, a nurse's office, a superintendent's office, and a teachers' rest room. It cost about $110,000—approximately twenty-five cents a cubic foot. There was no basement, and the roof was cheaply constructed to last only a few years. Nevertheless, it was far better than anything the children had seen in Seneca.

To get a building so commodious the superintendent and the consultant from the OCWS had had to do some pious misrepresentation. The Federal Works Agency had asked them to plan to use the building in two shifts, one group of children coming in the morning for a half-day, and the other group coming in the afternoon. Mr. Johnson and those he consulted from the FPHA and OCWS agreed that they should insist upon giving the children a full school day. Consequently, they all agreed in doubling their actual estimates of the number of children they would have in school .(Later the FWA changed its policy, and recognized the necessity of a school program as good as could be obtained in the average community.)

After a few months of school in the autumn of 1943 it began to look as though school would have to be run in two shifts anyway, because the population continued to increase. There were over a hundred children in each of the first two grades, with only two classrooms for a grade. Extra teachers were employed to assist with these children, but they had no extra space. When it became clear that a new housing project (Riverview Homes) was to be built, Johnson had to ask for still another school building.

Salaries were raised again for the teachers, until the elementary school teachers were getting $1,500 for a ten-month year, while the high school teachers were paid from $1,600 to $2,000 for a nine-month year. By this time the school boards had quit worrying about finances. Government grants were coming through regularly to supplement the regular tax money and the money paid in lieu of taxes by the FPHA. Thus the program was costing Seneca taxpayers no more than before the boom. School expenditures for the boom years are given in Table 17.

TABLE 17

SCHOOL EXPENDITURES IN SENECA *

	1941–42 Pre-Boom	1942–43	1943–44	1944–45
Elementary School	$22,000	$44,921	$48,528	$69,577
High School	23,045	29,645	47,976	54,348

	1945–46 Post-Boom	1946–47	1947–48	1948–49
Elementary School	$37,466	$52,464	$52,000	$36,000
High School	32,200	39,790	39,000	51,000

* The post-boom increases of 1946–49 are mainly due to the purchase of the elementary school building from the government and the construction of an addition to the high school building.

Throughout the boom, the school curriculum remained substantially unchanged, except for changes in methods that some of the younger teachers brought in. However, the equipment of the new elementary school lent itself easily to a more varied daily program, and the atmosphere became somewhat more that of a "progressive school." School projects, such as a war-saving-stamp campaign and a "clean-up Seneca" campaign, were started in the first year of the boom, but were not pushed aggressively in later years.

School-community relations remained in a nebulous state.

There was some discussion among the teachers of the possibility of getting better acquainted with the parents, but nothing came of it. One of the new elementary school teachers said in a teachers' meeting, "I know that the teachers in Seneca will not like it when I say this. But the people of Seneca would like some kind of opportunity to meet the schoolteachers. I don't know whether that calls for home visitation or for an open house, but it certainly calls for something." Mr. Johnson would have liked to have his teachers visit the homes of children, but he did not push the idea when he found that most of them resisted it.

With the opening of the new school it became possible to operate a school lunch program, aided by the government subsidies then available for such programs. About half of the children bought their lunches at the cafeteria.

THE THIRD YEAR OF THE BOOM

The school year of 1944–45 opened with on overcrowded school. Riverview Homes had been completed during the summer and new families were moving into Seneca every day. To meet the need for more classrooms a temporary six-room building was authorized by the government, but construction did not begin until September. In this emergency the FPHA agreed to the temporary use of the men's recreation building at War Homes, or the "men's poker building" as it was called in fascinated tones by the children. Four elementary school classes were put into this building.

School enrollments increased to their all-boom peak at Christmastime, after which there was at first a slow decline and then a rapid drop in the late spring of 1945. The new building became available in January, 1945, almost too late to be of much use, although it was occupied for several months.

Post-Boom

September of 1945 saw school enrollments back to their pre-boom size. The sixteen-room elementary school was continued in use, while the school board began negotiating with the government for its purchase. The new six-room building was taken down during the summer.

Finances were temporarily in good shape, for the FPHA payments in lieu of taxes carried over into the new school year. And to improve the financial situation even further, the maximum payments from the State Distribution Fund came in the year 1946–47, based upon enrollment in the peak year 1944–45. Thus it was possible in 1946–47 to pay $15,000 from current income to the federal government as the purchase price of the new school building. (The purchase of this building was approved by the voters at a special election in October, 1946, by a vote of 169 to 7.) Seneca thus emerged after the boom with a new school building, without having borrowed a cent to pay for it.

Other additional expenses were also met from the increased school income without immediate resort to a rise in the local tax rate. Teachers' salaries were maintained and even increased further. The kindergarten was taken over by the school board from the nursery school and made a regular part of the school program.

In brief, Seneca grew accustomed during the boom to spending more money on education without paying higher taxes. But there were disadvantages that at least partially compensated for these gains. The greatest disadvantage was the loss of pupils from the neighboring farm territory. When Seneca schools became so crowded during the boom, many farmers sent their children to other high schools. This situation continued after the boom when two neighboring towns established consolidated high school districts and voted into their districts territory that would normally have belonged to Seneca. For example, the new Morris school district came within three-quarters of a mile of Seneca. Thus Seneca lost potential territory for its own high school district. At the same time, Seneca was expanding its school plant and increasing its school costs to such a degree that taxes must eventually be raised.

In evaluation of the school program it may be said that this institution gave general satisfaction to the newcomers. Although people often complained about the service in the food stores, about the recreation program, and about the coldness of some of the churches toward them, they seldom complained about the schools.

This does not mean that the school program accomplished all that might have been desired in a war-boom community. The Seneca schools were no better than average, but they accomplished all that the parents expected of a school.

The relative success of the schools in meeting the crisis of a war boom is to be credited to a fortunate combination of a good superintendent and an institution that was capable of expansion within the pattern set by its prewar experience. Frank Johnson was an able school administrator, and a man whose personality enabled him to meet new and difficult situations without undue worry and loss of efficiency.

Frank Johnson was a big, slow-spoken young man, with sandy hair and complexion and a shy smile. He came to Seneca from Iowa, as a teacher of chemistry and basketball coach. In his first few years at Seneca he married a girl from a well-established local family; they built a comfortable house, and Frank went to summer school several summers until he obtained his Master's degree in education.

Then Frank Johnson was made superintendent of the elementary and high schools, while he continued to teach chemistry and to coach the basketball team. Frank seemed content to live his life in a small town. He apparently had no great desire to move to a larger place and start climbing the ladder of achievement in the teaching profession. As his children were born, and as he became interested in a farm he and his wife had bought, it seemed certain that he would stay in Seneca all his life, and that he would be content to keep school in the traditional manner. His ambition was to raise his family properly, to make a comfortable living, and to do a competent but not an exciting job of school administration.

While the coming of the war boom disturbed the school program markedly, still the institutional machinery was there, and it was simply a matter of enlarging a program that was already going. In the main, Frank Johnson knew what to do, and so did his school board. There were a few new things to learn, and Johnson learned them. He learned how to deal with government agencies—how to request money for a new school building, and for expansion of the school program. He grumbled sometimes at the extra work, but he never had any doubts as to what should be done.

More difficult for him was the task of making up his mind and discovering his role in several of the new projects which the boom brought to Seneca. For example, he was hesitant about asking his school board to sponsor the nursery school. Doing something entirely new was more difficult for him than doing the usual thing on an expanded scale. He became a member of the Housing Authority, and eventually he became chairman of the Recreation Commission. These appointments he accepted with reluctance, for he was naturally conservative, and he did not like to be in on the start of new things.

In spite of Frank Johnson's reluctance to take the lead in new projects, he was drafted for these assignments because his judgment was generally thought to be sound and because he was independent. He could be counted on to speak his mind, as he did, on occasion, to the FPHA, the OCWS, and the CBI. He could speak firmly and critically to representatives of these agencies without offending them. Thus he became a kind of anchor man for any project which got into difficulty. At times when some people became excited and confused, he remained cool. Unlike Florence Nichols, who had the missionary zeal to start a new institution, the nursery school, Frank Johnson started nothing new; but he gave stability to new things which other people started.

Frank Johnson's greatest contribution to Seneca lay in his conduct of one of the crucial institutions. If the schools had been inadequate, people with children would not have stayed in Seneca. To make the schools operate in a satisfactory way did not require genius, but it required common sense, character, and professional know-how. Frank Johnson possessed these things.

To make the task less formidable, the public school was a simply designed institution that could be increased in size without involving any new and complicated social problems. The one new problem was mastered by the school boards and the superintendent readily enough—how to ask Washington for money.

11.

Nursery Schools and Child Care

The idea of caring for children below school age anywhere except in their homes was a new one to 90 per cent of Seneca's newcomers and to practically 100 per cent of the oldtimers. Seneca did not have a kindergarten nor did any of the neighboring towns except the county seat of Ottawa. Nursery schools were unknown to practically everybody in Seneca except a few newcomers from large cities where WPA-supported nursery schools had made their brief appearance during the previous decade. And with relatively few mothers working in Seneca during the early part of the boom, there was no obvious need for a child-care program.

The fact that a child-care program did develop in Seneca and that it centered about a nursery school was the result of two things. The first was "sleeping fathers"—men who worked on the night shift and slept in the daytime. To sleep in the cramped quarters of the housing projects with young children running about was an impossibility; and therefore something had to be done to get the children away from home during a part of the day. The second thing that brought about a child-care program was the activity of Florence Nichols, who, almost singlehanded, introduced and built up a nursery school.

Florence Nichols was born and raised in one of Seneca's "best families"; and her brother, Ray Nichols, already described in Chapter 1, was Seneca's leading citizen. As a member of Seneca's small social elite, Florence was generally admired and respected; and her warm, affectionate approach to people added to her popularity. She had been teaching school for some years in Joliet, Illinois, but she kept her residence in Seneca, returning home practically every weekend and often during the week.

Florence Nichols found a great deal of satisfaction in her participation in the Chicago Area group of the Association for Childhood Education. She attended its monthly meetings faithfully, and enjoyed her association there with leaders in her profession. Though she was not herself a leader in the group, she tried to make herself more competent in her profession through participation in this association, and through reading the latest professional literature. Thus she had an unusual combination of secure status at the top of Seneca society, a high degree of professional training for the education of young children, and a profound devotion to her profession.

Miss Nichols had attended the meetings of the Association for Childhood Education in the spring of 1942, in which plans were discussed for the care of children in war-industry centers in Illinois. This was before the coming of the ship-yard to Seneca, and before Miss Nichols had any thought that she herself would have an opportunity to figure in a child-care project.

While spending the summer of 1942 at her home in Seneca, Miss Nichols was visited one day by the WPA Supervisor for Nursery Schools in Northern Illinois. The supervisor wanted to find out whether a child-care program was needed in the newly developing housing projects. With Miss Nichols she went to visit the Trailer Camp, where Mrs. Sharp, one of the residents, had formed a play group for preschool children. It happened that an FPHA representative and the consultant on recreation of the Office of Community War Services were in Seneca that day, and a discussion was held, ending in some preliminary plans for a nursery school, provided the need for child-care should become urgent. There were WPA funds available for child-care centers, and it was planned to request money from this source.

Another meeting was held in August, with the same people in attendance, plus Mr. Hollenbeck, Assistant Director of Personnel for the CBI. Mr. Hollenbeck expressed his interest in a child-care program. Miss Nichols at this time made a formal offer of her assistance to carry on such a project. During this same month Miss Olga Adams, kindergarten teacher in the University of Chicago Elementary School, visited Miss Nichols, and studied the situation with her.

Meanwhile the War Homes project was completed, families were moving in, and the number of young children increased every day. Miss Nichols and the wife of a new resident who had been a kindergarten teacher visited all the families with young children to find out how many of them would send their children to a nursery school. About the same time Miss Nichols was named chairman of the Child Care Committee of the Seneca Council of Civilian Defense. She put on her committee a number of prominent Old Seneca residents. She also had representatives of CBI and housing management, and some of the leaders of the War Homes Tenants' Council. It was characteristic of Florence Nichols to believe her project to be so important that important people would be interested in it. Hence she did not hesitate to ask the influential people of Seneca to work on her committee.

At the initial committee meeting early in October, 1942, she had her brother present to give prestige to the occasion. The WPA Supervisors of Nursery Schools for the state came to explain to the committee some of the responsibilities they were about to assume.

The Seneca Committee opened a play school in October, in the recreation room of the War Homes project. There was a staff of two people, a teacher and a housekeeper. Since

WPA funds had not yet been released for the project, the CBI paid $100 a month toward the expenses of the school for three months, in order to get the program started.

Meanwhile plans were made to turn the play school into a more ambitious nursery school project, with better equipment, more teachers, and a noon meal. Some equipment was secured from the nearest WPA storehouse, and children's furniture was contributed by a private school near Chicago. The FPHA agreed to furnish heat, water, and light, as well as floor space. Mrs. Bartlett of the nearby town of Granville was employed as teacher. She had been a nursery school and public school teacher, and she had good basic training in nursery school work.

On her weekends and holidays Florence Nichols worked for the school, visiting mothers of potential pupils and ironing out small problems with mothers of children already in the school. Among other things she organized a Mothers' Club which started with a membership of sixteen, meeting every other week in one of the War Homes lounges.

The Club kept going during the early months in spite of great difficulties. Their meeting place was shifted from one lounge to another. Sometimes there were no chairs, no lights, and no heat. The mothers held candles in their hands and sat on tables, huddled in their coats for warmth. They discussed problems of school equipment, laundry, cupboard space, fees, hours, volunteer help, rest periods, health inspection; they planned a Christmas party; and in the spring when they were really under way they gave a card party that brought in $100 for the school treasury. They helped make the change from a play school to a nursery school; they helped to cook lunch when needed; and they made surveys to locate prospective pupils.

The change from play school to nursery school was made in January, 1943. The last main difficulty lay in getting kitchen equipment for the preparation of luncheon. The WPA supervisor secured a refrigerator from a WPA storehouse, and the FPHA undertook to get an electric stove complete with wiring. There was difficulty in getting a priority for the stove and the wire, and it seemed for a time that the nursery school project would have to be postponed. At this juncture Miss Nichols appealed to her friends in the CBI management. They promised the wire and the men to install the stove. With this, and with the WPA supervisor waiting in Seneca to assist in setting up the kitchen, Miss Nichols pressed the FPHA again and they secured a stove. The next week an all-day nursery school was started, running from 8:30 to 3:30 with lunch and rest periods for children aged three to five. At this time the enrollment was about thirty-five.

Early in 1943 money became available for child-care services in war-industry areas through the Lanham Act, just as the WPA child-care program was terminated. The Seneca Child Care Committee set about to request funds under the new legislation. It was necessary for the request to be made in the name of a local authority of some kind, such as the school board or the Village Council. Miss Nichols decided to try to affiliate the nursery school with the school system. She had an eye on the future, and thought that the school board might become interested at least in supporting a kindergarten after the war; and that these chances would be enhanced if the school board had experience with a child-care program. But she found that the school board was preoccupied with the more immediate problems of housing its pupils of school age, and of getting Lanham Act funds for a new school building and for an expanded teaching staff. In her own words, "it was a long, slow, laborious process getting the school board to see the need of a nursery school in Seneca." Eventually, she won over enough of her neighbors and fellow citizens on the board to secure their support for the request for funds.

The telegram came from Washington on March 12, 1943, informing the superintendent of schools that the request was approved. This was the first such grant in Illinois. Then came another difficulty. At the school board meeting that was called to accept the grant, Mr. Henry Harris, the secretary-treasurer of the board, refused to continue with his job because of the extra work involved in the nursery school project. Mr. Myron Swanson, a young businessman, was appointed treasurer of the nursery school fund, and he accepted responsibility for all FWA correspondence in this connection.

The request for funds was made on a threefold basis. It emphasized the lack of play facilities for young children, the need of night-shift fathers for quiet sleep in the daytime, and the growing number of mothers of young children who were accepting employment. This was the first of a series of grants for the nursery school program, which eventually totalled approximately $45,000. Income from fees and other sources came to about $30,000, making a total expenditure from April, 1943, to August, 1945, of approximately $75,000, for programs at War Homes and Victory Court.

The experience at War Homes paved the way for the easy establishment of a nursery school in Victory Court. One room of the administration building was designed at the very beginning for a nursery school. When the enrollment became too large for this room an addition was built to the building and used entirely as a nursery school. A full day program was carried on, for children aged two through five.

The facilities at War Homes were obviously inadequate for a nursery school. The children used the recreation hall, which had to be completely cleared every afternoon for an afternoon and evening recreation program for young people and adults. Consequently, the old construction headquarters, which had been turned into a temporary school until the new elementary school building became available, was reconstructed into a nursery school and opened in April, 1944, as the Little Skipper School. There was a ceremony in which Orville Olmstead, Regional Director of the FPHA, presented the new school building to Frank Johnson, the superintendent of schools, who received the building on behalf of the Child Care Committee. At this time the Victory Court school was named the Jack Tar Nursery. Both schools had a long school day, being open from 6:30 A.M. to 6:30 P.M., so as to accommodate children of working mothers.

Throughout the boom Miss Nichols and the Mothers' Club conducted a continual program of recruiting pupils. The War Homes Mothers' Club raised $40 for color film and had a motion picture made of the school, which was shown to parents' groups in Seneca as well as in the neighboring towns.

There was also a perennial problem of securing well-trained teachers. Miss Nichols searched the Seneca area for them, and she had scouts looking for them in Chicago. As a result of constant effort there was always a group of at least three well-trained people on the staff—a director, and a head teacher for each school. In addition, there were three or four other teachers at each school at the peak of enrollment. These teachers were either Seneca residents with some kindergarten or nursery school experience, or college students who had some special preparation for the work. There was also a cook and a housekeeper for each school.

PROGRAM, ENROLLMENT, AND FEES

During 1943 and 1944 the nursery school program gradually gained the support of people who had at first been lukewarm. The school board was won over; one Board member entered his own child in nursery school, while another member recruited pupils for the school. The superintendent of schools showed increasing interest and visited the school quite often. The CBI management continued to be cordial, and housing management cooperated intelligently through its Project Services Advisor who attended Mothers' Club meetings and nursery school staff meetings.

In July, 1943, the University of Chicago sponsored a conference on "Planning for the Care of Children in Wartime" and forty members of the conference made an all-day trip to Seneca to observe a war-industry community and its provisions for child care. They were met at the train by members of the Mothers' Club who showed them the nursery schools and the housing projects. Then they had lunch at the shipyard cafeteria and were taken on a tour of the yard by CBI officials. This event added prestige to the nursery schools in the eyes of Seneca residents, and thereby increased their acceptance in the community.

The record of average daily attendance at the two nursery schools is shown in Table 18 and in Figure 16. The schools have parallel charts of growth and decline. After an early period of rapid growth, each school settled down to a stable existence, marked by a slump toward the close of each summer and an increase each autumn. This was due to the withdrawal of children in the summer who were approaching school age, to children visiting relatives in the summer, and to the recruiting of new children each autumn.

Enrollment was substantially above average daily attendance, as is always the case with nursery schools. When enrollment reached its peak of 150 in November, 1944, the average daily attendance was 95. However, enrollment figures were not inflated, for a child's name was always taken off the roll if he was absent for a month. Approximately half of the children in the housing projects of appropriate age

TABLE 18

AVERAGE DAILY ATTENDANCE AT THE NURSERY SCHOOLS

Date	Little Skipper	Jack Tar
October, 1942	10	
December, 1942	25	
May, 1943	40	6
August, 1943	35	28
May, 1944	45	35
September, 1944	32	28
November, 1944	51	44
January, 1945	41	30
March, 1945	51	35
May, 1945	30	20
August, 1945	18	Closed
October, 1945	30	
May, 1946	30	* (kindergarten no
November, 1946	25 *	longer included)

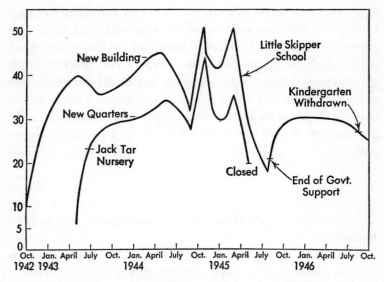

Fig. 16. Attendance at Nursery Schools.

were enrolled at any given time. Over a two-and-a-half-year period, 240 different children were enrolled in Little Skipper School and 226 in Jack Tar Nursery.

Fees were set at $2.50 for a five-day week, for the regular day lasting from 8:30 to 3:30. For the long day, from 6:30 to 6:30, the fee was $3.75 a week. These fees included lunch, fruit juice, and cod liver oil, and breakfast in the case of the long day. The actual cost per meal per child varied from 12 to 14 cents. This low cost was achieved through the use of much free food donated by the government from its "excess" food stores. Menus were provided by the Elizabeth McCormick Memorial Fund of Chicago.

The actual cost of the nursery school program was about $1.50 per child per regular day. In the last year, when operations were most efficient, it was reduced to $1.25 per child per regular day, and $1.80 per child for the long (twelve-hour) day. This did not include any charge for rent, heat, light, or equipment, all of which were furnished by the FPHA. Of this amount one-third was collected from the parents in fees, and two-thirds was paid by the government in the form of grants from the FWA. (The proportion of government support was originally set at 50 per cent, but neither Seneca nor other child-care centers were able to reach a 50 per cent level of local support. Consequently, the government support was raised to about two-thirds of the cost.)

EVALUATION

To evaluate the child-care program it is useful to ask three questions:

What was the quality of the staff and the program, as measured by the usual nursery standards?

To what extent did the child-care program free mothers

for war work and allow fathers to sleep better in crowded homes?

What influence did the child-care program have on the knowledge, attitudes, and practices of people in regard to child rearing?

The quality of staff and program was unusually high—far higher than might have been expected in a community that had no previous nursery school experience and in a period of emergency when trained teachers were scarce. The credit for this belongs mainly to Florence Nichols, who supervised the schools as carefully as a paid supervisor could have done. Miss Nichols also used her connections in the Association for Childhood Education and in the University of Chicago to locate well-trained teachers.

The second aspect of evaluation, the degree to which the program achieved its immediate objectives of freeing women for war work and of improving the sleep of night workers is not so favorable to the program. With no more than a hundred children in average daily attendance at the maximum, it is clear that the number of mothers freed to take war jobs could never have exceeded a few dozen. Probably an equal-sized group of fathers on the night shift benefited from a quieter sleeping period due to the absence of their children. But many fathers of nursery school children were not night-workers.

The parent education carried on by a nursery school is usually considered to be one of its main values. In Seneca this aspect of the program was conducted through the Mothers' Club, which held monthly meetings. About a third of these meetings were distinctly educational in character. There was relatively little contact with fathers.

One significant fact was the small enrollment from trailer homes—homes with many young children. One of the leaders in the program explained this as due to the lower social status of most of the trailer residents. There was other evidence that the child-care program appealed most strongly to improvement-minded women of lower-middle class status. Mrs. S. was an example:

A young woman in her early thirties, with a high-school education, her husband a welder, she became very active in the tenants' organization, in the Methodist church, and in the Mothers' Club. So well liked was she by the other mothers that they gave her a farewell party when the time came for her to leave. She said at the party that no one should be thanking her; she had so much to be thankful for in her experience at Seneca. She felt that she had learned a great deal and grown a great deal. This family moved to Iowa where Mr. S. opened a welding shop in a small city. Very probably Mrs. S. will become a leader in church and parent-teacher association circles in her new home.

Florence Nichols said that most of her support in the child-care program came from thoughtful, hard-working, but not well-educated women. The better-educated group, which may be equated with the upper middle class, were "swept off their feet by the social whirl." They were "all flustered and agog" with the frequent launching parties. Therefore they had no time to assist with the Mothers' Club projects, though they were happy to send their children to the school.

A summary evaluation would place the Seneca child-care program high among wartime nursery programs in terms of what it did for the children. Probably it was one of the most successful in the country. Like most of the other child-care programs in war-industry areas, its value in freeing manpower and making workers more efficient in their jobs was probably of relatively little importance. The child-care project was an improvement in social life that could easily be afforded at a time when government expenditures for social welfare were popular; most government officials and many industrialists thought such a program was a good thing in principle and were quite willing to see it ride through on the war effort.

The real test and perhaps the most critical evaluation of the Seneca program lay in its fate after the boom was over. Most wartime nursery school programs withered away when government support was withdrawn after the war. In small towns like Seneca it was extremely improbable that the war-boom child-care program could survive. Hence the story of what happened in Seneca after the war is an interesting one, and affords another basis for evaluation.

A Postwar Nursery School Program

In the closing months of the boom a number of children were entered in the nursery school from families of Old Seneca residents who were not engaged in war work. These children, together with those of War Homes residents who remained after the boom, made up the nursery school during the summer of 1945.

There seemed to be slight hope of getting further government support for the program since war production had ceased. A representative of FWA came to Seneca in July, 1945, with the intention of closing out the project. She met with the Child Care Committee, and it was in this meeting that Florence Nichols began to find out what impression the nursery school had made upon the community. Father Preston came to the meeting and testified in favor of the program. He said that he had not been a believer in preschool education before the boom, but that his observation of the program in Seneca had converted him. He urged the FWA representative to do what she could to get further federal support for the project, until local support could be organized for it. The FWA representative went away so much impressed that she recommended an emergency grant of a thousand dollars.

This was followed in a few weeks by the action of the school board, which took over support of the kindergarten for five-year-olds. About the same time the newly organized Community Club agreed to give some support to the nursery school.

With financial support fairly well assured, it was only necessary to recruit the children from Old Seneca. But this was no easy task. Mothers who had never seriously thought of letting their children leave the home until time to enter the first grade had to be convinced that a three- or four-year-old could profit from school, and that it was worth fifty cents a day. Miss Nichols gave over her summer vacation to the labor of calling on all the mothers of preschool children. Even then, the project would probably have failed for lack of adequate enrollment had not help come from an unusual source. This was the enrollment of a group of children from the neighboring town of Marseilles. Mrs. Theodore Clark, wife of a Marseilles dentist, was responsible for this development. Wanting a preschool for her own child, and finding none in Marseilles, she decided to make arrangements for transporting her child to Seneca. Then, finding that the school needed pupils, Mrs. Clark recruited ten children from Marseilles. She and the other Marseilles mothers arranged with the driver of the morning bus to pick up the children at 8:30 to carry them to the nursery school, and to pick them up again at 3:30 and bring them home. This transportation cost one dollar per child per week.

With these evidences of community support, the Child Care Committee decided to continue the nursery school without government aid through the year 1945–46. The problem of securing space and equipment was solved through the loan without charge of the Little Skipper School by the Federal Public Housing Authority, which continued to heat and light it. This was fairly easy to arrange, since the Little

Skipper School was under the same roof as the FPHA office in Seneca, and the office was continued in operation because a part of the War Homes project was still in use.

Just as the school was getting under way in September, a seven-year-old in Seneca came down with infantile paralysis, and many mothers decided to keep their young children at home. Consequently, the first month of operation ended with a large deficit.

To supplement the income from fees, the Mothers' Club immediately began to raise money. By the summer of 1946 the Mothers' Club had raised $804. This money came from rummage sales, card parties, bake sales, and such other procedures as the women's ingenuity could devise. At one affair Mrs. Clark donated a pair of nylon stockings for a raffle, just when stockings were most scarce. The nylons brought a total of $25.

The Community Club contributed $144, which was its share of the Community Chest Fund. Mr. Pfeffer, an elderly furniture merchant, gave $100 as a scholarship fund for children whose parents could not pay the fees.

The nursery school operated through the year with an average attendance of about seventeen three- and four-year-olds. The kindergarten, which was also housed in the Little Skipper School, averaged about twelve in attendance. The problem of securing adequate enrollment was the most serious one. For a time, in January, the Mothers' Club was almost ready to admit defeat. But attendance gradually increased and affairs were going smoothly by spring.

When the year was up there was a small balance in the treasury, the Mothers' Club was well organized, and it was decided to go ahead for another year. A summer play school was operated during the mornings under the supervision of one of the mothers. Meanwhile a committee of parents worked on the finances, and another committee, led by

Florence Nichols, called on mothers to recruit children for the school in the fall.

The group working on finances built a refreshment stand at Crotty Park, where baseball games were scheduled through the summer. Led by Mr. Eddie Kein, husband of one of the women in the Mothers' Club, a group of five couples sold soft drinks and sandwiches and netted a profit of $670.

Thus the year 1946–47 started auspiciously. The average attendance of three- and four-year-olds in October was twenty, with four children from Marseilles. By November, attendance was up to twenty-five. The kindergarten, entirely supported by the school board, was moved to the elementary school, where it began with an enrollment of twenty-three. Fees were raised to $3.25 a week for the nursery school. With a budget of about $400 a month, an attendance of thirty children was required to pay expenses. Thirty children were about half of the total number of children aged three and four in Seneca. Hence the nursery school must really be understood and supported in the community if it was to continue to succeed.

Beginning with the autumn of 1947, Mrs. Carl Schaad became the principal teacher, and she continued in this capacity for two years, until her husband, an official with the government War Surplus Corporation, moved away from Seneca. Under Mrs. Schaad the Little Skipper School was moved to the elementary school building, where a rental payment of $15 a month secured the use of two rooms. This move enabled the nursery school to save the cost of a kitchen by using the elementary school cafeteria.

Assistance continued to come from Marseilles, organized now by Mrs. John Hayes, whose husband was an executive of the Bakelite plant in Ottawa. The mother of John Hayes was President of the National Congress of Parents and

Teachers in 1949. Mrs. John Hayes brought five to seven Marseilles children to nursery school daily, and she became vice-president of the Mothers' Club for 1948–49. Her husband spoke on "Being a Father" at a "fathers' night" program of the school.

The big event of the summer of 1948 was the Children's Fair, with pony rides, movies, and refreshments, which drew six hundred people and netted the Mothers' Club $260.

Enrollment was between fifteen and eighteen children during the years 1947 to 1950, which was sufficient to keep the school going with one teacher. The year 1949–50 started with Mrs. Eddie Kein, operator of Seneca's beauty parlor, as president of the Mothers' Club; and Mrs. Baker, a local woman with kindergarten teaching experience, as teacher. Mrs. Baker's approaching motherhood led to the early closing of the school in March, 1950; but the Club carried on with plans for the autumn of 1950. Meanwhile the Club broadened its activities, changing its name to the "Little Skipper League." The League worked to establish a Children's Corner in the Seneca library, donating $100 for children's books, and helping to select a shelf of books for parents.

Thus the child-care program, which started as a war-emergency project, paid for by the government and serving war workers only, was gradually taken up by a village whose people had no previous experience with nursery school or kindergarten. The school board became convinced of the usefulness of a kindergarten and took it over. Young mothers and fathers became convinced of the usefulness of a nursery school. What the neighboring cities of five and ten times the size of Seneca were not ready to do was done in Seneca.

The child-care program, accomplished chiefly by women, was the most successful piece of social pioneering in Seneca.

12

Health, Welfare, and Delinquency

The crowding of people into Seneca created problems in public health and welfare that the village-type institutions were not prepared to meet. Garbage and sewage disposal, water supply, police and fire protection, hospital facilities, nursing service, food care and refrigeration, all required more elaborate and formal arrangements than had been necessary before the boom. In these areas the village of Seneca had to learn institutional ways more befitting to a city. Most of the changes that occurred were brought about through the use of federal government funds and with the advice of federal government officials.

Fire protection, for instance, had been provided to citizens of Seneca by a volunteer system. When fire broke out, a siren was blown and half a dozen men left their jobs and came running to the scene of danger. This system was termed "adequate" in pre-boom days. By June, 1943, however, the village council had voted to employ two full-time firemen at a salary of $150 monthly, the money to be raised through Lanham Act funds. An additional water-pumping engine was also provided through FWA funds.

Prewar Seneca had a municipally owned water supply obtained from a drilled rock well in the center of the village. The well was operated by a 25-horsepower pump with a capacity of 560 gallons per minute. Average daily consumption was 170,000 gallons. By June, 1943, this system had been expanded through federal funds. An additional well was drilled, pumping equipment added, and a new elevated tank was constructed. There was an average of 270,000 gallons of water being consumed daily; and a reserve supply of 200,000 gallons as compared to the 60,000 gallons of a year previous. (The shipyard maintained its own water supplies—a sanitary supply and a fire supply. The sanitary supply came from three drilled wells, and the fire supply by direct pumpage from the Illinois River.) The village water supply was tested weekly by the county sanitary engineer.

The problem of sanitation was a major one. In Old Seneca, sanitary wastes were removed by private systems consisting of approximately 200 septic tanks and 125 privies. At the housing project each unit had some kind of sewage disposal plant. The effluent from the flats at War Homes and from War Homes Trailer Park was discharged into Rat Run, which then meandered through the town and emptied into the Illinois River. Public health officials were fearful of a typhoid epidemic. Finally, a drainage and sewage system was established with a government grant of $187,000. The system was completed about the middle of 1944, in time for the last year of the boom.

An effective limit on population growth in Seneca was set by the town's water supply and its sewage disposal facilities. Water supply became more than adequate with the additional well and pumping equipment, but sewage disposal was a serious problem until the completion of the sewage-drainage system. After this, the population could have increased substantially.

Rat Run should have been dredged, so as to remove the stagnant water that collected in its muddy bottom during summer and fall. It was a disappointment to old Senecans that this was never accomplished.

There was no village ordinance regulating the collection and disposal of garbage and refuse. Private agents collected garbage twice weekly; and refuse was collected once or twice a year by the same agencies. Disposals were made by filling in the low areas surrounding the community. This system went unchanged during the boom. Private agencies collected garbage in the housing projects, and a report early in 1944 said "there is no evidence of nuisance in this connection."

HEALTH SERVICE

Before the boom there were two physicians and one dentist in Seneca. These men made a comfortable living from their practices. The occasional patient who wanted the services of a specialist went to Chicago or elsewhere; the patient who needed hospitalization entered a hospital in a nearby town, usually the Ryburn-King Hospital in Ottawa, thirteen miles away, or the hospital in Morris, ten miles away.

The war took one physician and the dentist into the military service, while another dentist came to town to meet the dental needs of the expanded community. Dr. Coulter, the remaining physician, had to carry on for the most part alone. Even his service was curtailed, for he gave three hours a day to the medical unit of the shipyard. There was a medical staff at the shipyard including two and sometimes three physicians. One of these men lived in War Homes and another lived for a few months in Victory Court. They gave some private service in addition to their industrial practice at the shipyard. Any serious epidemic in Seneca would have created a crisis; but the shipyard doctors would probably have been loaned to the community in such an event.

The United States Public Health Service practically took Seneca under its wing. Dr. Estella Ford Warner, Senior Surgeon, with headquarters in Chicago, supervised the situation, working with a county health organization called the LaSalle County Defense Zone Health Department. This was the regular LaSalle County Health Department armed with federal government backing to meet health problems arising out of war production. Dr. Arlington Ailes, County Health Officer, was the head of the department, and he had an assistant and four nurses on his staff.

To meet the need in Seneca the Public Health Service set up an infirmary in a building constructed at the War Homes project by the Federal Public Housing Authority. The infirmary was staffed by a registered nurse and three nurses' aides. Usually called the Health Center, this building had six bedrooms and twelve beds. There was no operating room or operating equipment; the Center was established primarily for clinical work and first-aid treatment. Patients were sent to the infirmary by the medical staff at the shipyard, and also by the doctors practicing in the community. Single men in the dormitory were sent to the infirmary if they were ill. Also trailer residents were usually put to bed in the infirmary if they became ill, because the trailers were considered too small to house a family with a sick member. Old Seneca residents were admitted if there was room for them.

During July, 1944, a typical summer month, thirty-six patients received bed care at the infirmary. Fourteen of them were men from the dormitories, seven from trailers and housing projects, and fifteen were accident and illness cases from the shipyard and from the village of Seneca. The charge was $2.50 per day, including meals. First-aid service was free.

The Ryburn-King Hospital in Ottawa was expanded in 1943 with the aid of a government grant of $76,000, so as to meet the increased need for regular hospital services in the Seneca area.

The Public Health Service also installed in Seneca a field nurse, Miss Doris Randolph, who proved to be a great asset to the community. In effect, Miss Randolph's job was to show

Seneca how to institutionalize a health program. She set up and kept in motion a program consisting of an immunization drive, school health service, health service for preschool children, Red Cross classes in first aid and home nursing, a health loan closet service, instruction in maternal and infant hygiene, and communicable disease control. In all of this she was nominally the lieutenant of the physicians in Seneca and of the LaSalle County Health Department; but actually her organizing ability and her energy enabled her to take responsibility for many things that a less active person would not have accomplished.

Doris Randolph, public health nurse, was assigned to work in Seneca by the U. S. Public Health Service early in the boom, and she stayed until the end. She was one of the stabilizing influences in times that upset people of lesser emotional balance. She taught Seneca people to regard health as a community concern as well as an individual responsibility. She *institutionalized health* where previously it had been individualized.

Doris was a big girl, slow-spoken, with a wide smile. Physically she gave the impression of strength and stability, an impression which was confirmed upon further acquaintance.

Doris Randolph went to work in a community which before the boom had two doctors, and which multiplied fivefold but lost one of its doctors. The only nurse who was free to visit homes, she often had to act as well as she could in place of a doctor.

She worked with school officials and the County Medical Society on an immunization program first for the schools and then for the entire community. More than five thousand injections and vaccinations were administered through the clinic.

She held Red Cross Home Nursing classes for high school students and for adults that resulted in the issuance of one hundred Home Nursing certificates the first year. These people were then available to take temperatures and give bedside care to their neighbors during a siege of influenza when doctors and nurse could not get around to everybody. People enjoyed working with her and consequently she was able to get volunteers for the several projects that she started.

Doris Randolph instructed expectant mothers and new mothers just home from the hospital in the care of babies. For school children she held a series of child health conferences at the school, dealing with simple health rules and practices.

Thus Seneca adopted an institutional health program that may have prevented serious epidemics. The accomplishments of such a program are hard to evaluate, for no one knows what might have been if the program had not been in operation. For Seneca people, Doris Randolph's warm and busy personality together with her technical skill made questions about the importance of her work irrelevant. Everybody liked her, accepted her, and was ready to learn from her.

All of Seneca was pleased as could be when Doris began going with a handsome Texan who worked at the shipyard. (When the boom was over, they were married and went to Oklahoma to live.)

The fact that Seneca never had a high rate of illness may have been due in part to the immunization program. By June of 1944, 95 per cent of the school children had been immunized against smallpox, diphtheria, and typhoid. The danger of typhoid was real in the early part of the boom, before the new sewer system was installed. During the boom, there were brief epidemics of measles, whooping cough, and chicken pox. There were a few cases of mumps, five cases of scarlet fever, and two of meningitis.

Seneca was fortunate in having no cases of infantile paralysis during the boom. However, Miss Randolph prepared as well as possible for such a contingency. The local Red Cross collected blankets, which they converted into packs for the Kenny treatment. The Health Center kept a supply of convalescent serum. Three cases did develop within a distance of ten miles, but none in Seneca.

Miss Randolph gave a good deal of time to bedside care,

and because of the lack of doctors, she often visited patients before the doctor came, so as to select the most needy cases for the earliest attention. Through a system of visiting the home of each child who was absent from school as long as three days, she was able to catch cases of communicable disease. By her handling of emergencies she probably saved Seneca from serious trouble, as in the following instance.

A family of four, consisting of a man, his wife and two boys, came in during the night in a trailer, looking for war work. The man and the two boys were quite ill when they arrived, and the woman tried to locate a doctor but was unable to do so. The report finally reached the Health Center, and Miss Randolph visited the trailer. She discovered that the three people had scarlet fever. She was immediately afraid of an epidemic. The doctor told her that nothing could be done about quarantining the family because the law made no reference to trailers. Since the infirmary was not crowded, Miss Randolph took all four people in and kept them in isolation for twenty-one days.

The educational program consisted of health classes in the high school, home nursing courses for high school girls and for adult women, all taught by Miss Randolph, and a class in infant care and maternal welfare taught by Dr. Coulter with Miss Randolph's assistance.

The health loan closets included linens, ice caps, trays, utensils, hot-water bottles, etc. Tenant health committees in the various housing projects assumed the responsibility for checking the materials in and out.

The dentist who came to Seneca said he had four times as much business as a dentist normally should have. He worked until nine o'clock in the evenings. Since Sunday was the best time for treating shipyard workers, he worked on Sundays and planned to take Wednesdays off. But soon he had to work Wednesdays, too. He was ready for a vacation when the boom ended.

Welfare Service

Welfare in Old Seneca consisted of occasional relief payments to distressed people by the local County Supervisor, and the activity of charitable and church groups in getting Thanksgiving and Christmas baskets to a few poor families. The Delta Theta Tau, national philanthropic sorority, worked on problems of welfare, and a group of businessmen helped informally in cases of hardship.

In 1942, some twenty families in Old Seneca received assistance from the county. This number fell off to four families in 1943 and one family in 1944—an aged couple who had little left except a house. Of the new families, all came to Seneca to work at high wages, and they had little need of public assistance. Only when a father became ill, or when a man deserted and left his wife and children, was there any need of this sort. At most times there were a half-dozen new Seneca residents on the relief rolls.

There was one tragic welfare case.

The Jones family consisted of the father, about thirty, the mother and six children, the oldest being a girl of thirteen. The children were always dirty. Their mother tried hard, but she could not meet her responsibilities. She seldom used soap when she washed the children, until the Sisters at the parochial school sent home word that they must be bathed well before they came to school.

The father became critically ill, and had to be taken to a hospital in a neighboring city. Soon the money gave out, and Mrs. Jones appealed to the County Supervisor for money for food. She and the children lived for a couple of weeks on this money. One evening Mrs. Jones decided to go and visit her mother who lived in a town fifteen miles away, and to get some help from her mother. She took her baby and left the other children in charge of Patricia, the thirteen-year-old.

Patricia asked the next-door neighbor to call her at 7:15 so that they would not be late for school. She then lit the gas water-heater so that there would be hot water for baths in the morning, closed up the house, and put everyone to bed. When no one responded to their knock in the morning, the neighbors broke through the door. The oldest child was on her hands and knees on the floor, vomiting. The others were unconscious. Four of them died. Their death was blamed on fumes from the water heater.

The children were buried the next day. Father Preston gave them a lot in the Catholic cemetery. Some church ladies of the Altar and Rosary Society dressed them. Four priests assisted Father Preston in the service. There were twenty boys who acted as pallbearers and twenty girls as honorary pallbearers. A collection was taken in Victory Court to help the mother.

CRIME AND DELINQUENCY

Easy money, crowded living conditions, anonymity in a new community, all tended to relax the controls that society exerts on people and to thus encourage delinquency and crime. On the other hand, long working hours, recreational provision for men, women, and children, and the watchfulness of shipyard and housing managements tended to keep down delinquency and crime. The net result was that Seneca had no serious problems in this area. The town was never "wide-open."

The one-man police force was augmented early in the boom by two men, and eventually it was increased to a total of seven men, with a police automobile. The cost of this expansion was paid with money granted by the federal government.

The principal types of immorality were those commonly found in any industrial community. In the order of their seriousness, as viewed by the people of Seneca, there were drinking, theft and vandalism, sexual immorality, and gambling. There were no murders and there was remarkably little fighting.

Drinking. For many shipyard workers and for quite a few of their wives the favorite place to spend their leisure time was in the taverns. This led to some neglect of children, and there were frequent stories about babies crying in their buggies outside the taverns, children locked in trailers by their parents who went out to spend the evening, and children allowed to run loose on the streets while their parents sat in the taverns.

Whatever its effect upon the children, drinking does not seem to have resulted in much disorderly conduct. The justice of the peace turned over to the village council a total of $260 in fines for three months in 1944. Probably the bulk of these fines were of the five- and ten-dollar variety, assessed for disorderly behavior. This would mean an average of less than one case a day.

One notable exception to the general peacefulness of the town occurred in October, 1943, when "the famous street fight" took place. A drunken man was creating a disturbance on the street, and the policeman attempted to arrest him. The man fought the policeman, and in the struggle that followed, the policeman's pistol was discharged, seriously wounding two bystanders. This was the only dramatic disturbance reported during the entire boom.

Theft and vandalism. Such theft as took place was burglary rather than robbery. There were no holdups. One peculiar theft was the gradual loss of dishes and silverware from the basement of the Lutheran church. It was discovered that a group of boys were stealing these articles and selling them to residents of the War Homes.

Another piece of thievery, which bordered on vandalism,

was the pillaging of victory gardens that had been planted by residents of Victory Court in 1943. Until the middle of August most of the garden produce was looted. Finally a group of fifteen Victory Court children were taken before the police for questioning, and several of them admitted guilt. The looting stopped after this.

Vandalism was more of a problem in Seneca than theft. There was a good deal of deliberate window-breaking at the housing projects. This was climaxed one night in January, 1944, at Victory Court where six windows were broken in the service building and two quarts of paint were thrown on walls and sidewalks. This was blamed on boys, though the culprits were not caught. A group of four elementary school boys were caught one night after they had broken a number of windows in the high school.

More serious, three boys aged twelve, ten, and nine placed wood and other obstructions on the Rock Island tracks one day, and did minor damage to the Des Moines Rocket when it came along at seventy-five miles an hour.

There was no evidence that newcomers were any more active than oldtimers in these acts.

A frightening set of episodes occurred at War Homes in the winter of 1943–44, when windows were broken in a number of apartments at night, where women were staying alone while their husbands were at work. It was found that some of the single men from the War Homes dormitories were throwing rocks at the windows. When the raids continued for some time, the CBI sent over some of the Coast Guard police. While nobody was caught, the affair soon quieted down.

Sexual immorality. There was very little open sexual immorality. CBI officials were on the lookout for it, and twice they called in FBI men to close houses where prostitution was being started.

The principal complaint was that some of the girls of the community were associating too freely with shipyard workers. Several over-age girls in the elementary school were said to be running around with older men. For example, two fourteen-year-olds were said to be visiting two men in the War Homes dormitory. Another case that attracted the attention of teachers was that of an eighth-grade girl who lived in the country, but came to school with a relative who worked in the shipyard. She did not go home until 10 P.M., when another member of her family finished his work and drove her home. She had no place to stay from 3:30 until 10 P.M., and she often hung around the bowling alley.

Gambling. Gambling in Seneca seems to have remained on an amateur level except for the slot machines and the handbooks. There was one anti-gambling crusade, a one-man campaign by Policeman Killilea in the spring of 1944. He entered several taverns, and asked the barkeepers to close because they were running gambling dives. At the Barge Inn, the barkeeper told the policeman to mind his own business and get out. Mr. Killilea struck the bartender, who filed a complaint for assault and battery against him. The Ottawa judge put Mr. Killilea on $500 bond, and restored him to work, after a hundred Seneca citizens had signed a petition backing Mr. Killilea. Upon the policeman's charges, however, the owner of the Barge Inn pleaded guilty to operating a "bookie joint" and was fined $100. He also pleaded not guilty to the charge of operating slot machines, but was found guilty and fined $50.

Playland was closed for two or three days after this, and it reopened minus pinball machines. Slot machines also disappeared for a time from other taverns and restaurants. The weekly bingo parties at War Homes and Victory Court were discontinued, because of the gambling element involved. The activities of the "Men's Poker Room" in the War Homes were also stopped.

It was generally said in the town that the mayor, the chief of police, and several members of the village council were not back of Mr. Killilea in his one-man anti-gambling drive. In a few months the gambling machines were back in full operation, the weekly bingo games were back in War Homes and Victory Court, and the men were playing poker again.

Juvenile delinquency. In order to keep the children off the strees at night a 9 o'clock curfew was established for boys and girls under eighteen. Quite a number of children were in the position of ten-year-old Bennie Atkins from Texas, who lived in a trailer with his father, mother, and older brother. The father came home in the afternoon from work and had supper with his family. Then the mother went to her job as a welder on the night shift. Bennie walked downtown with his father, as far as the tavern where his father spent his evenings; then he hung around town until about ten minutes to nine, when he scuttled for home. Bennie was somewhat afraid to go home alone. He said he would be happy when he could go back to Texas. He said, "I don't like it here. There are lots of people who are not good people. Sometimes I'm afraid of people. People move in and out of Trailer Camp, and you never know who is around."

Mrs. D. told about her next-door neighbors in Victory Court. The father and mother both worked in the shipyards and both frequented the taverns on their free evenings. The fifteen-year-old daughter, a very pleasant and attractive girl, had most of the care of the two younger children. This girl once disappeared for a week, in the company of a boy. Mrs. D. said, "Yes, she is a good girl at heart, if only she had something to look forward to in life."

Mrs. H. was calling at the homes of Victory Court tenants one evening to ask for gifts to the Red Cross when she came to an apartment where the shades were drawn. Hearing voices and laughter, she knocked. The knock was answered by a young girl, hair piled high on her head, clothed in a towel which she held around her, sarong fashion. "Oh, I don't live here," said the girl, and one of four men sitting around a table with bottles and glasses came to the door. "What do you want?" he asked rudely. "Lady, I don't care about the Red Cross," and he shut the door.

While the cases of obvious immorality were few, they occasioned a good deal of talk, and the CBI management kept watch on them. In August, 1944, the management called a conference on juvenile delinquency, with representatives from the community, the county government, government projects, and shipyard management. About half of those present felt that measures should be taken against delinquency; the remainder were not inclined to take the matter so seriously. One of the ministers proposed the establishment of a Commission on Juvenile Welfare, with a policewoman, or a retired juvenile officer from the Chicago police force to be employed. The superintendent of schools reported that he had money in his budget for a visiting teacher, who could probably help to prevent juvenile delinquency. It was finally agreed that funds should be requested for a person to work as a police representative, in addition to the visiting teacher. At this meeting several people suggested that a part of the trouble was due to mothers working at the shipyard and neglecting their children. A representative of the shipyard reported that they had released a dozen mothers in the past few months when it had become clear that their children were being neglected.

In the end, nobody was brought in to work on the problem of juvenile delinquency. A visiting teacher could not be found, and the closing of the shipyard forestalled further efforts to do anything.

EVALUATION

Problems of health, welfare, and delinquency were dealt with adequately, through a combination of federal government funds; health officials; and cooperation among the leaders of the local community, CBI, and housing management. Crime was kept in check, and health was good. Traditional attitudes about crime, welfare services, and health services were respected. There were no conflicts of policy involved; no strange health services or police practices for people to adjust to; and there was plenty of government money to pay for the services needed.

13.

Government

As a result of the boom, government in Seneca passed rapidly from the hands of a village council and a county board of supervisors into a complicated set of relationships between local officials, federal government officials, and CBI and United States Navy officials. Before the boom Seneca's government was largely a community and county matter, with a small amount of assistance from state agencies and almost no contact with federal agencies. During the boom most of Seneca's governmental decisions were made in federal agencies outside of Seneca, and local government became an instrument for carrying these decisions into effect. The power of initiative was largely withdrawn from the local community.

At the same time the government took on functions that would ordinarily have been performed by private agencies. The national government provided Seneca and many other war-industry areas with housing, employment service, health service, and public utilities. Thus there was a twofold aggrandizement of the national government—it participated in the local government of communities like Seneca and it took over functions it would not have touched in peacetime.

In this unprecedented situation, the following questions may be asked:

1. What new governmental agencies entered into the Seneca situation?

2. How did local governmental institutions adjust to the new conditions?
3. What conflicts and problems of cooperation occurred between the various governmental authorities?

LOCAL, COUNTY, AND STATE GOVERNMENT

Before the boom, Seneca had a mayor, a village council, a village clerk, volunteer firemen, a town night watchman (policeman), a lay health officer, and a health committee. With the exception of the village clerk and the policeman, these officials were not paid for their services.

The village had no debt and the assessed valuation for the year 1942 was $478,813 based on 33 per cent of the real value. The total tax rate was about the average for villages of comparable size in central Illinois.

The local tax rate did not increase materially as a result of the war boom. Most of the increased cost of public services and the cost of public improvements were financed by payments received from the federal government. Although the tax rate remained the same, a greater number of people paid taxes. Newcomers, although they did not pay real property taxes, were required to pay local personal property assessments. The Federal Public Housing Authority, since it was not taxable by local taxing bodies, paid a sum of money "in lieu of taxes," which amounted to what its tax bill would have been if its property had been assessed in the usual way.

Although a considerable part in Seneca's pre-boom government had been taken by county officials, including the county superintendent of schools, the sheriff, the highway department, and the health and welfare departments, the county government was largely by-passed during the boom by local and national government agencies in Seneca. One exception (and this was a temporary one) was the LaSalle County

Housing Authority, which was at first given responsibility for the construction and management of the public housing projects. The conflict between federal and county officials over housing, to be reported in more detail below, ended with the elimination of the county authority from the Seneca situation. The one county agency that was active in meeting the needs of the boom in Seneca was the health department, which supervised the federally financed health program.

The state government before the boom had little direct contact with Seneca, except in the administration of relief through the WPA program. In the early months of the boom the WPA program in Seneca was extended under state auspices to include recreation as well as the previously established library. With the ending of the WPA program in 1943 the state government ceased to figure directly in the administration of affairs in Seneca.

THE FEDERAL GOVERNMENT STEPS IN

Before the boom, local government had no direct contact with federal government. But the series of emergency needs that arose in Seneca demanded and secured direct action by federal government agencies. There arose a series of joint projects by federal and local government agencies. These were financed by the federal government under the Lanham Act (Community Facilities Act). The principal federal government agencies and their activities in Seneca were as follows:

War Manpower Commisison—Studied the availability of labor in the Seneca area and advised other agencies on how many workers would have to be brought in from a greater-than-commuting distance.

National Housing Agency—Determined the amount of federal housing to be provided.

Federal Public Housing Authority—Supervised the construction and management of public housing projects, and later actually managed the projects.

Federal Works Agency—Determined the need for public buildings and public services, and recommended grants accordingly.

U. S. Public Health Service—Established and administered an infirmary and a health service, in cooperation with the County Health Department.

Office of Civilian Defense—Organized a War Services Committee of the Civilian Defense Council. This Committee broke up into several smaller committees, which worked under various local auspices.

Office of Community War Services—(Earlier called the Office of Defense Health and Welfare Services.) The functions of this office were to coordinate the efforts of various federal agencies in war-production areas, and to advise local agencies in these areas. Operating under the Federal Security Agency, the Regional Office had on its staff experts in recreation and social protection (venereal disease control). In addition, field representatives of the U. S. Office of Education and the U. S. Public Health Service were in close touch with the office. The FWA often called on the office for advice on the grants to be recommended for educational and recreational services.[1]

Other federal agencies that were involved directly in the production of ships but not directly in the local government of Seneca were: The United States Navy, the War Production Board, Selective Service, the Office of Price Administration (gasoline and tire rationing to shipyard workers), the Office

---

[1] The work of the Chicago Regional Office of the OCWS has been described by Arthur Hillman in "A Federal Agency's Relation to Community Planning," *Social Forces*, XXV (December, 1946).

of Defense Transportation, and the Food Distribution Administration.

Expenditures of federal funds. Table 19 shows how federal government funds were expended in Seneca for purposes other than the direct cost of constructing ships.

TABLE 19

FEDERAL GOVERNMENT GRANTS FOR PUBLIC SERVICES IN SENECA

Project Number	Description	Cost	
	War Public Works Projects		
11–231, 238, 316	Construction and equipment of schools	$216,726	
11–235	Waterworks	49,548	
11–236	Fire-fighting equipment	5,500	
11–258	Sewers	187,000	
	Total		$ 458,774
	War Public Services Projects		
11–M–28, 94, 135	Elementary school operation Sept., 1942–July, 1945	$75,620	
11–M–29, 95, 134	High school operation Sept., 1942–July, 1945	89,057	
11–M–50	Child-care services March, 1943–July, 1945	45,474	
11–M–66	Recreation services July, 1943–July, 1945	31,722	
11–M–31	Police and fire services Nov., 1942–July, 1945	31,092	
	Total		272,965
	Federal Public Housing Projects		
Land and construction cost of housing units in Seneca (Excludes initial cost of trailers)		$5,945,000	
Operating expenses, June, 1942–July, 1945		884,348	
Payments in lieu of taxes to local taxing bodies		76,734	
		6,906,082	
Income on housing projects		1,284,119	
Net Cost			5,621,963
Total cost of public projects in Seneca			$6,353,702

FEDERAL-LOCAL RELATIONS

Seneca people had actual contact most often with representatives of the FPHA, the OCWS, and the FWA. With the first two agencies the local authorities shared in the administration of federally supported services and projects. In some cases the actual responsibility for administration lay with the local agency, and in other cases with the federal agency, but in all cases a close working agreement was necessary.

The general policy behind federal-local relationships was that the local community had full responsibility for all problems related to the war-production emergency, but was free to call upon federal agencies and federal funds when local facilities were inadequate. Supplementing this policy was that of certain federal agencies to keep their eyes on war-production areas and to discover needs before the local community was aware of them. Thus the federal government was to a limited extent the instigator of action in the local community. This appears to have been true in Seneca in connection with the community recreation program. On the other hand, local initiative was predominant in the educational and the child-care programs. In particular, the child-care program was promoted by local people who stimulated the interest of federal representatives.

The federal government took the initiative in providing for the following needs: an employment census in the LaSalle County area, the construction of public housing projects, the construction of a health center, the expansion of the local water supply, the selection of a health staff.

The federal government left responsibility for the conduct of these services and projects in local hands, wherever possible, but federal authority was never so removed as to prevent its stepping in and redirecting an activity that was not going to its satisfaction.

How the Various Agencies Worked Together

Any agency, local or federal, public or private, implements its policies only through the particular persons who represent it. Thus, to assess cooperation or lack of cooperation between agencies means to examine the relationships between individuals. The boom in Seneca brought together persons of varied interests and backgrounds who now had to work together, and to get work done under emergency conditions. The persons who represented various governmental agencies fell into several groups, each group with its own goals and its own characteristic modes of work. How these goals and methods of work failed to fit together becomes obvious in the following paragraphs:

The U. S. Navy personnel had as their goal getting ships built in the shortest possible time. Their characteristic mode of working was that of giving and following orders within a rigid hierarchy. They expected efficiency, and made few allowances for mitigating circumstances when a job was not done.

The CBI management, while not a governmental agency, must be included in this list, since they played an important role in most of the decisions that had to be made. As will become clearer in the description of events that follows, CBI played a role equivalent to that of a government agency in many instances. Their goal was to get ships built efficiently and economically, and to have a plentiful supply of contented workers and of materials for work. Their characteristic mode of working was to plan the use of men and materials with efficiency and economy. It must be noted that they were forced to adapt their mode of working to a situation in which speed of output was given priority over economy and efficiency, and in which they had to rely upon government agencies for their manpower and material supplies.

The village officials of Seneca had as their goals preserving the stability of their social institutions, protecting the interests of the oldtimers among the population, and directing new projects in such ways as to promote their long-run usefulness to the village. They were accustomed to working at slow tempo, with plenty of time for decisions, and to avoiding decisions that could be put off until events had settled the issue. They now had to work under emergency conditions with people who were in a hurry, and who were accustomed to making quick decisions.

The goal of federal government officials was to get their part of the Seneca project done fast and well; and at the same time to elevate the prestige of their own particular government agency. Their characteristic mode of operation was to work within their own agencies in accordance with a formal procedure, and to avoid contact with other government agencies. In the Seneca situation they were now forced to a maximum of cooperation with other agencies.

Social service personnel in government agencies saw their goal to be that of improving the quality of human life in the area. In the Seneca situation they were prepared to work for social change, and to try experiments that would have to proceed more slowly in normal times. This group was accustomed to using discussion methods in such a way as to get a maximum of general agreement among the people affected, before taking decisive action. It should be noted that as things worked out, discussion methods were subordinated to the need to make emergency decisions and to that of getting rapid production.

On the whole, the relations between the members of the various groups remained on a formal level. They worked together under duress, and did not come to understand one another. Every person had to change his characteristic mode of working, at least to some extent. Having the common patriotic goal of increasing the war effort, these persons made compromises—but only at the cost of much inner conflict.

To a neutral observer there seemed to be a great deal of frustration involved in the work of most of these people, with consequent hostility that at times could not be suppressed. At such times there was a good deal of name-calling, and sometimes a general resort to making a scapegoat of one or another agency.

These observations are illustrated in the following account of a meeting called by the Office of Community War Services in Chicago, on February 26, 1944, to discuss an impending housing shortage in Seneca. The report is taken partly from an account written by one of the authors, who was present at the meeting, and partly from the official summary prepared by OCWS.

The meeting was arranged to exchange information, and to consider community problems in the Seneca area resulting from the stepped-up shipbuilding program. There were forty people present at the meeting, representing all the groups that have been described in the preceding paragraphs, including village officials from Seneca and from Ottawa (the latter community housed about as many of the workers as did Seneca), and labor union officials.

The meeting began with a statement by a Navy representative that a total of 12,000 workers was needed; that 1,100 workers had been added in the past five weeks, and 2,700 more must be put to work in the next sixty days. The LST ships had an overriding priority; they were a "must," as European invasion plans were heading up into action. The ships were needed in the next few months, not next year. The CBI Company was now three ships behind schedule.

A War Manpower Commission representative reported that a telegram had been received from Washington asking them to make every effort to bring the number of workers up to the required 12,000 within sixty days. All possible local workers had been recruited from the area (a radius of 35 miles around Seneca); the balance must be provided by in-migration. The housing situation was such that workers could not be recruited until additional housing was available to them. Data were presented to prove that no vacant housing existed, and that there were no more employable workers in the area.

A representative of the Federal Public Housing Authority reported that plans had been made for 400 additional units, some in Seneca and some in Ottawa. These would be ready within 60 days. But no further housing had been programmed, such as would be needed if there was to be an in-migration of the size estimated by the Manpower Commission. He suggested, however, that the National Housing Agency had information from Washington to the effect that some of the Seneca contracts might be transferred to a Pennsylvania shipyard where there were 1,300 vacant houses.

At this point the highest ranking Navy officer rose and informed the group that the Navy was not going to transfer contracts to the Pennsylvania yard, which was already working to capacity; that all present contracts would remain at Seneca and would be increased; that this was the most urgent war job in the whole United States; and that new housing was absolutely necessary. He also said that this was not a limited six months' program but a two- or three-year undertaking.

A spokesman for CBI said they estimated their need for housing to be twelve hundred units, including 300 trailers. They had requested these additional units, and nothing had been done about it. He wanted to know who was holding up this program.

A representative of the National Housing Agency said that his agency had not been able to program additional housing because the WMC had not certified the additional in-migration of workers. On the basis of the information obtained at this meeting, however, NHA would be in a position to program additional housing.

Representatives of health service, transportation, schools, recreation, child care, and general community services then reported how their services would be affected by increased population in Seneca and Ottawa.

The OCWS representative who was chairman of the meeting then summarized the understandings at which the conference had arrived; some 800 additional housing units should be programmed and brought in without delay; local community facilities were to be expanded as needed, with the assistance of FWA and the cooperation of local authorities; and developments were to be reported to OCWS in order that the work of all could be properly coordinated.

This account of the meeting follows in general the official summary, which of course was a rearranged and logical organization of the actual sequence of events. However, the authors' record of the meeting shows a good deal of conflict and irritation to have been present, which does not appear in the official minutes.

It appeared that when CBI first recognized that it would need 4,000 additional workers, it estimated that it would need 800 housing units. It wrote a letter to the NHA requesting this number of new housing units. Later, when the WMC was notified by CBI of the proposed housing expansion, the WMC did not report the expected population figures, but requested the NHA to construct 400 housing units. The NHA did not grant either request; instead it asked the CBI to report to the WMC just how many new workers they expected to employ. Then the NHA requested from the WMC a report on what in-migration was expected. Once this procedure was followed, said NHA, it would then estimate the number of housing units needed and approve a program for the FPHA to follow. The difficulty was that both CBI and WMC had assumed the function of NHA, which was that of estimating the need for new housing on the basis of information about in-migration to be supplied by WMC; WMC's information to be based, in turn, upon the need for new workers estimated by CBI and the Navy.

When the CBI spokesman reported that the newspapers had carried an announcement of a program for adding a thousand more housing units in the Seneca area, the NHA spokesman retorted that this story had never been authorized by the NHA; that it had been released to the papers by the CBI when there had actually been no government approval of such new housing. (Actually, the principal news release in January, 1944, was credited by the newspapers to the U. S. Navy.)

As these points came out in the discussion, there was a good deal of arguing and bickering. Housing officials were the butt of the attack. The various agencies seemed to be trying to get themselves established in the "Federal Peck Order," and it was clear that the housing agencies were at the bottom. It was something of a circular order, however, for the NHA representative was a man of considerable spirit. When a CBI vice-president said he thought the housing people were holding up the whole program, and he wanted to know just whom he would have to see about it, the NHA representative replied, "I am the man to see."

The CBI man stood up and said, "Then, I suppose we'll have to make love to you." The NHA man replied, "You don't have to make love to anybody. All you have to do is to give the essential information to the right agency."

Incidents occurred at this meeting that illustrated the concern of local government officials over the maintenance of the *status quo*. For example, a representative from the Illinois State Department of Public Welfare expressed interest in the possibility of placing Negro workers in the shipyard. At this point the mayor of Ottawa asked for the floor and told of his city's restrictions on the number of Negroes allowed to live in Ottawa. He said he didn't think the people would be willing to accept Negroes immediately. He thought that the federal agencies should consider the traditions of these small cities and should protect them against invasion by large Negro populations.

The Director of Personnel of the shipyard responded, "I have hired 19,000 different workers at Seneca. I have talked to about forty colored people and have hired thirty-eight. Not one of the thirty-eight has completed a day's work at the shipyards. We have shown no discrimination; but they have decided not to work here." A WMC representative reported that there were no Negroes available locally, and therefore the housing of Negroes was not a problem.

While this conference resulted in a set of agreements on the need for additional public housing that were immediately put into operation, it illustrates some of the difficulties of cooperation among the various groups involved in the Seneca situation.

ADMINISTRATION OF PUBLIC HOUSING

The outstanding example of failure of cooperation between local and federal agencies was that of the administration of the public housing projects. Since this situation illustrates so many of the complexities of inter-agency adjustment, it will be described in some detail:

The responsibility for the construction, maintenance, and operation of the public housing projects in Seneca shifted uncertainly for the first nine months of the boom between the Federal Public Housing Authority and the LaSalle County Housing Authority.

The LaSalle County Housing Authority (LCHA) was established in 1939 by the county board of supervisors. It consisted of five men who were interested in LaSalle County politics, real estate, and the construction business. Beyond conducting surveys to discover substandard housing, the LCHA had done very little until the coming of the boom gave it a real job. Membership of the Authority was then changed by dropping two of the old members and adding two Seneca men, Frank Johnson, superintendent of schools, and Andrew Diebold, county supervisor from Seneca.

Since there was a local public housing authority in existence, the FPHA followed its usual policy of working through the local group. The LCHA was given contracts for the development and management of the Seneca projects. "Development" consisted of preparation of the sites and construction of the buildings. "Management" consisted of operation of the project and maintenance of the property.

The LCHA named as executive director, Fred Bretz, one of the county supervisors, who lived in a small village not far from Seneca. Bretz was nominally in charge of all the work at Seneca, and all project staff members were under his supervision. Actually, the Chicago regional office of FPHA kept close supervision of the situation, and interviewed and employed the major staff members. Bretz had little choice in the matter of hiring or firing his principal subordinates.

The FPHA felt it had a great deal at stake in Seneca. Not only was there a government investment of several million dollars, but also Seneca was one of the critical war-production centers of the Midwest. Housing had to be satisfactory. To leave the administration of such a large and complicated project in the hands of an untried county authority and an inexperienced executive director might be foolhardy. Not a week passed, therefore, without one or more people from the Chicago office going down to Seneca to help the project staff. Private telephone lines connected the Seneca office with the Chicago office.

The first six months. The FPHA at first selected a general housing manager for Seneca who, though nominally under Bretz, actually was not chosen by him. Reports from all sides indicated that this man was incompetent. He resigned in October, 1942, after less than three months.

Again the Chicago regional FPHA office selected a general housing manager, this time a woman who had been a supervisor of housekeepers in a Chicago hotel. She was not successful in gaining the respect and cooperation of her staff or of the tenants, and she was discharged in February, 1943. It was said by others on the staff that she "did not know how to get along with people."

Meanwhile Bretz had appointed a Seneca man as assistant housing manager, who had been working in this capacity since September, 1942. In February, 1943, he, too, was discharged at the request of the FPHA on the ground that he lacked experience in housing management.

This period was one of uncertainty and friction between the FPHA and LCHA. The division of authority and responsibility between the two agencies was not clear.

Another major source of difficulty in the first six months was friction between shipyard management and housing management over the authority of each group in the allocation of housing space. CBI was responsible for certifying to housing management that a given individual was employed by CBI, and that he was doing important work that qualified him for assignment to a place to live in the housing project. Housing management claimed that CBI went far beyond this, and interfered in the management of the projects.

One complaint during the early months had to do with the size of the "backlog" of living space that CBI insisted on keeping for key people who might need to be employed, such as superintendents and foremen. While the working force was expanding rapidly, and while housing space was at a premium, there was constant friction over some nineteen dwelling units in War Homes that CBI insisted on keeping open for emergencies. Housing management claimed they could not make a strong case for new housing construction as long as the existing units were not 100 per cent occupied.

The shipyard management claimed that housing was their chief problem, although in truth they were taking much more responsibility and assuming more authority over housing than was legally theirs. A sign at the main gate of the shipyard told about War Homes and said that inquiries should be made at the personnel office in the yard. The personnel staff of shipyard management was always busy with housing. One day in the spring of 1943 one of the authors came into the office of the CBI Director of Personnel at 3 P.M. The Director said, "I've been here since 7 A.M. and I've done nothing but housing." While the visitor was present there were frequent interruptions, all having to do with housing problems. The

Director made assignments as to the size of dwelling unit, and explained a floor-plan diagram in detail to a secretary.

Because of what seemed to them to be incompetence on the part of housing management, and because of their solicitude for the welfare of employees, shipyard management felt called upon to assist in many problems of maintenance as well as management of the housing projects. To get materials for maintenance, CBI priorities had to be used because housing management could not get priorities. When the central heating plants in War Homes failed during the first cold spell, shipyard management took over the situation, secured stoves, and repaired the damage done to frozen water pipes.

Even some employees of housing management thought that the authority and the controls lay in the hands of shipyard management. For example, one woman clerk in the management office of Seneca War Homes told a visitor from Washington, "The houses are built by FPHA but the CBI Company controls it, don't they?"

All these factors caused the prestige of housing management to decline, and the tenants took to operating through plant officials instead of working out their problems with housing management.

Perhaps shipyard management would have assumed less responsibility for housing if housing management had been competent at the start. Certainly shipyard management receded somewhat into the background of housing affairs later on when housing management became effective. On the other hand, there were examples even toward the end of the boom when CBI took initiative that housing management felt should have been theirs. For example, shipyard management sent an investigator into the housing projects to investigate rumors of sexual immorality; and then called a meeting on juvenile delinquency, inviting representatives from the community and from Chicago, as well as from housing and shipyard management. Housing management felt that the whole thing was exaggerated and were angry because they had not been consulted before the meeting was called.

The complaints of housing management about shipyard management were of two kinds. The first was that shipyard management took more authority than was rightfully theirs, and by controlling certification for housing, which was a bottleneck, prevented housing management from doing its job of filling the dwellings in an orderly and efficient manner. For instance, a housing management official with two stenographers sat in her office with nothing to do for several weeks early in 1943, when Victory Court was being completed, because CBI would not certify people for Victory Court. CBI delayed because Victory Court was not yet ready, but housing management claimed they could have made the assignments in a more satisfactory manner if they had been able to use the several weeks before the Victory Court houses were ready.

The second type of complaint was that shipyard management managed to cast the blame for all inadequacies of housing on housing management, but took credit to themselves for all satisfactory aspects of housing. Housing management thought it was being made a scapegoat. There were charges, for instance, that CBI became dissatisfied with certain workers and asked housing management to move them out, rather than taking the responsibility of discharging them.

There was a third and higher source of authority in the situation, the United States Navy. The naval officer in charge was inclined to say "a plague on both your houses." He said that housing management was incompetent in the early months, and that shipyard management had to take over housing as well as build ships. However, he thought the CBI Company was not handling its workers very well. He said that shipyard management asked housing management to put some people out of their houses so as to be relieved of the disagreeable task of firing them. He assured a representative of FPHA that when housing management became really efficient, he would order shipyard management to drop its housing management efforts. He said, "If they continue to run housing, or try to run housing after you people are really running it, you let me know and I'll tell them to get out of there."

The second six months. At this point the FPHA decided to put the responsibility of management more fully in Bretz's hands. Instead of Bretz's having a general housing manager who was in effect coordinate with him and who could deal directly with FPHA, Bretz himself was made General Housing Manager in March, 1943, with an increase of salary to $400 a month. FPHA held a joint meeting of housing and shipyard management staffs to explain the change, and to assure everybody that things would go better.

Matters went smoothly at first. Cordial relations existed between Bretz and the Chicago office. With improving spring weather, the tenants had fewer troubles. Victory Court was being opened up, thus relieving the pressure for housing. Tenants' organizations were developing in the two housing areas. Victory gardens were planted. A new life was beginning for everybody.

But after about a month difficulties began to appear. Management problems were not being handled to the satisfaction of FPHA. The regular reports did not come promptly from Bretz. He was not following the regulations in dealing with people who wanted to move from one unit to another in the housing projects. Other departures from management regulations occurred.

Representatives of the Chicago office came to Seneca to meet with the staff and clear up the problems. Bretz became disturbed and defensive, and began to criticize the FPHA quite openly. During the month of May matters worsened. In the eyes of the FPHA, Bretz was ascribing all the difficulties of the situation to faults of the FPHA, and was avoiding his own responsibility. When tenants complained about one thing or another, Bretz was believed to be saying that his hands were tied by the Chicago office of FPHA.

Bretz felt that the people in the Chicago office did not understand how to deal with the kind of tenants who lived in the Seneca projects. He said to one of the authors,

"Those FPHA people don't know anything about anything except low-cost housing in cities. They don't understand the situation out here. They think they can take their time about everything. In a place like Jane Addams housing in Chicago they can talk an hour with the applicant, visit his home to see that he has good habits, and then tell him that he may have a place in the housing project in about a month. Out here they are dealing with different kinds of people. These people come in a car, loaded down with all of their children and all of their goods. They want service and they can pay for it. They're hard-boiled. You can't close the office at five p.m. and quit thinking about your job until the next morning. Why, we had a freeze-up in December when a lot of pipes froze and the tenants began to complain. They did something right away, too. About seven men came over from the CBI with torches and began to thaw out the pipes. Pretty soon we had things in working order again. The Chicago people bawled us out. They said, 'You should have explained to the tenants what the trouble was and asked them to be patient until we could send people out to fix things up.' But when it's zero in the apartment and their children are cold, you can't reason with them."

Finally the Chicago officials of FPHA came to the conclusion that Bretz was not capable of administering the project, and they determined to present their case to the LCHA, which was responsible for Bretz's employment, and to request his resignation. This was done in June.

The LCHA voted to support Bretz. "If Fred goes, we go," they said.

The FPHA then terminated its contract with LCHA for the management of the housing projects, but left the LCHA to continue the development contract for Victory Court to its conclusion, a month or two later. The LCHA protested, and sent resolutions to the Investigating Committee of the U. S. Senate headed by Senator Truman of Missouri, to the United States Senators from Illinois, and to the Congressman from the local district. The protest apparently had no effect on events in Seneca.

Local sentiment, both in Seneca and in the housing projects, was largely in Bretz's favor. One of the members of LCHA, who had earlier told one of the authors that he thought Bretz was not a good enough man for the job, nevertheless sided with Bretz at this time and blamed the difficulties mainly on poor planning and poor administration in the FPHA. When the Regional Director of FPHA came to meet with LCHA and discuss the complaints against Bretz, he was met by a delegation of businessmen from Old Seneca, by representatives of CBI management, and by a delegation from the Tenants' Councils of the housing projects, all three groups protesting against Bretz's removal.

Despite local disapproval, the FPHA stuck by its decision. It managed the housing projects directly, without further dealings with LCHA. Herbert Brim was sent in as General Housing Manager to replace Bretz; and from this time on, the difficulties with tenants subsided and there were no major management troubles. When Riverview Homes was constructed later, FPHA handled it directly.

The immediate objective of FPHA was achieved; to get a management that could operate the housing projects efficiently. At the same time the opportunity was lost to build a local housing authority that might set an example to the state in the field of public housing.

In retrospect it seems obvious that a friendly spirit of co-operation implemented by actual coordination of effort between CBI and housing management, and between LCHA and FPHA, would have improved the housing situation tre-mendously. Yet this never did come about. During the last two years of the boom there was an uneasy truce, for exam-ple, between CBI management and housing management. While both groups lived close together in a small community, not a single case was observed of friendly visiting or card-playing or convivial drinking between members of the two groups.

INTER-AGENCY RELATIONS

Social distance was preserved to a similar degree among the representatives of other governmental agencies. So few were the exceptions that they stand out notably. Several Old Seneca people who had considerable influence in village af-fairs became friendly with shipyard executives. But these friendships were isolated warm spots in the glacial climate that surrounded most of the official relationships in Seneca.

The "Federal Peck Order" to which reference has been made was undoubtedly a reality, though the order shifted somewhat from time to time. While the authors made no at-tempt to get objective data on this matter, they would rank the various federal agencies as follows in their ability to com-mand deference from other federal agencies and from non-governmental people:

United States Navy
United States Public Health Service
War Production Board

Federal Works Agency

War Manpower Commission

The Social Service Agencies—Housing, Education, Child Welfare, Social Protection (Venereal Disease Control).

The United States Navy actually was the final authority on matters in Seneca. All other federal agencies yielded to it. The Navy had the last word on the number to be employed in the shipyard, the amount of public housing to be constructed, and even some essential details of administration of government projects, such as the question of who should be given priority in getting space in the housing projects. The Navy had a broad veto power. For example, as has already been described in the chapter on "Recreation," after FWA approval had been given for the construction of a Community Building in Seneca, in late 1944, the Navy quietly killed the project in Washington.

The authors were impressed by the difficulties of mutual understanding and cooperation, and they wondered whether the situation might have been peculiar to Seneca as compared with other boom towns. While they could not make comparisons of each group in Seneca with similar groups at other places, they were able to get a small amount of comparative information on the CBI as against other industrial corporations, and on the U. S. Navy in Seneca as compared with Army and Navy officers in charge at other war-production establishments.

A letter was sent, in May, 1946, to nine people who had worked in various government agencies during the war and had all been actively involved in the various projects at Seneca and at other war-production centers. Some of the people were still in government service, while others had left it. The significant paragraph in this letter was the following:

(1) How did the Chicago Bridge and Iron Company compare with other companies in the amount of attention it gave to problems of morale and the welfare of its employees?

(2) How did the CBI compare with other companies in the smoothness and cordiality of its relations with your agency?

(3) How did the Navy compare with the Army in these same respects in the projects with which you have had experience?

Replies were received from seven of these people. They were unanimous in their favorable rating of the CBI and also of the U. S. Navy officials. They had found the CBI more interested and more intelligent in its interest in the welfare of its employees than most other corporations they had dealt with in similar situations. They had a high regard for the Navy officials at Seneca.

From this small bit of evidence it would appear that the situation at Seneca was certainly no worse, and probably better, than the average in its potentialities for mutual cooperation and understanding.

The war boom in Seneca created strange bedfellows who seem to have remained strange to the end. Probably all of the principal persons who were thrown together so incongruously by the boom were very happy at the boom's end to get back among their own kind again, and thus to avoid the irritations of working on a common project with people of different basic interests and ways of life.

PART IV

PERSPECTIVES

14.

Aftermath—Seneca in 1950

In Seneca, ships were built costing the American taxpayers two hundred million dollars. Ninety million dollars were paid out in wages and salaries. Steel weighing 330,000 tons was put together and sent down to the sea in ships destined to be sunk or scrapped within a few dozen months. Twenty-seven thousand different people worked in the shipyard at one time or another. Twelve thousand different people came to Seneca and lived and worked, and went away again. A thousand new children appeared on the scene, and two new school buildings were constructed for them. Two new churches were built and one church was renovated.

These and many other things happened in Seneca in the space of less than three years. What marks did they leave on Seneca's people and Seneca's institutions?

THE BOOM WAS TEMPORARY

If Seneca had been a town on the Pacific Coast, its attitude toward the boom would have been radically different from what it was. The oldtimers would have expected the boom to be permanent. They would have risked their capital to expand business. They would have clamored for public works of permanent value. Newcomers would have watched for opportunities to invest money and to secure firm places for themselves in the expanding economic and social structure.

This happened on the Pacific Coast in towns and cities of all sizes. Federal housing projects were built for long-term use. New schools were built for permanence. Private building of houses continued all through the war. The war workers who came for high wages stayed for whatever the future might bring. Veterans of the war came from all over the country to California as soon as they were discharged.

But Seneca's boom was only temporary, and nobody really expected it to be otherwise. A few hopeful people in Seneca nursed their hopes into rumors that some industrial corporation would move in and make the boom permanent. "The CBI has been asked to manufacture spare parts for boats and ships" was one rumor. "The Army may establish a rest home in the housing project." "Two men from the Ford Motor Company were in town yesterday looking over the situation. They might establish an assembly plant in Seneca."

Finally in October came word that the U. S. Navy had asked Congress to declare its Seneca plant to be surplus property. By this time nobody expected that the shipyard would be used again. It was a mild surprise to learn in December, 1945, that a government warehouse for surplus material and equipment was to be established at the shipyard, the work to be done by the Potomac Engineering Corporation, which would employ a hundred or more men. Thus, by the end of 1945, the boom was definitely a thing of the past, except for the last lingering puff provided by the warehouse.

The streamlined Rocket train quit stopping in Seneca some time in May, and in August the morning train from Chicago changed back to its old habit of stopping only to drop off passengers. The evening train going to Chicago slowed down, and if the engineer saw nobody on the platform he opened the throttle and rolled on, glad to make up lost time. Most of the new business establishments closed, and the oldtimers who were in business took long vacations in the summer and fall of 1945. In November, 1945, there were ten store buildings vacant on Main Street.

First the Riverview Homes were folded up and carried away on trucks to relieve the housing shortage in midwestern cities. Then the trailers were hauled off to college campuses for the use of veterans returning to their education. Then Victory Court houses were torn down, and finally War Homes began to disintegrate under the crowbars of a dismantling crew. Only sixty-seven apartments were left, to be used by war veterans who wanted housing and who were willing to live in Seneca and commute to work in surrounding towns. The Administration Building, the Recreation Building, and the Little Skipper Nursery School were also left standing.

Schools opened in September, 1945, with only about thirty more students than had been there in June of 1942. The Boy Scouts dropped back to one troop.

The People's Attitudes

Probably no one in Seneca felt entirely glad or entirely sad during the summer of 1945, when the boom was on its way out.

Mr. Harris said, "The war boom's been a good thing for the town, yes. Anybody ain't made money these last three years, it's his own fault." But he was glad to go off to California for a long vacation.

Mr. Barsi said, "Yes, the boom's been a good thing for business, of course. But we'll get along without it; we did before. We've got to work hard, that's all."

Mr. Marshall said, "Am I glad to get a rest? You said it!

I like to have a fishing trip every summer; that's the only vacation I ever take. I've missed my fishing for three years now. I go up into northern Wisconsin."

Mrs. Zimmerman, in the library, said, "Oh, I can't bear all these goodbye's. I'm so blue all the time. And the Seneca folks who grumbled most at first are all sorry now."

Mrs. Wheeling complained, "Well, it's getting awfully lonely here! I had the nicest men for roomers; and I always gave them a piece of pie when I baked—things like that. They were so nice it was a pleasure. But now they're gone."

Mrs. Sheedy said, "Oh, I'm sorry to see my roomers go, especially these last two. I got to know them and liked them so well, they were as nice to me as any friends I ever had. Now what'll I do? I'm afraid I'll have to get a job."

Miss Meagher, who worked in Clark's garage, said, "It's going to be as hard to get used to being without them as it was to get used to being with them, I guess. But it'll be nice to be going to each other's houses again in the evening, playing cards and such."

Mrs. Maurus said, "We'll have our safe, quiet town back again soon. I always said I wouldn't be afraid to go alone anywhere in Seneca, at any time of day or night; but of course it hasn't been safe the last three years."

Mr. Thomas Killilea, one of the new policemen, said, "Yes, I'm still policing, 'til July first. Then I suppose the town will go back to its one policeman or maybe two. Well, we've had our fun; now we can go back to the farm. We got along before, and we can again."

New Life in Seneca

The statement had often been heard in Seneca during the boom, a statement usually attributed to Father Preston, that "Seneca needs three things—a community building, the

dredging of Rat Run, and a toilet at the Rock Island Depot."
Rat Run never was dredged; the community building was
authorized but never built. The Rock Island Depot, however, was renovated and a toilet was installed in the spring
just before the boom ended. Perhaps this story epitomizes
the differences between what Seneca hoped for and what
Seneca actually got out of the boom.

Still, Senecans had seen and felt a life in their town that
could not leave them entirely unchanged. They were bound
to do some new things: as Reverend Mr. Telfer explained it,
"Seneca became important during the war. Now the people
want to keep it on the map."

Dr. Coulter was more positive. "Well," he said, "we've
had a great time here. This town has certainly profited.
We're doing things we never could have thought of, if we
hadn't had the shipyard. We've got sewers, better streets, a
bank, a new school building. And we've all got new ideas."

The first sign of the new life was the founding of the
Community Club. Although it was a successor to the old
Commercial Club, the Community Club was meant to be
wider in its appeal. Instead of being limited to businessmen,
it was open to everybody at a fee of a dollar a family. The
Club started off with a community chicken dinner at the
elementary school cafeteria, and everybody was given all the
chicken he could eat, a favorable auspice during the meat
shortage of the summer of 1945.

Two big projects of the Community Club were the organizing of a bank and the securing of the War Homes Recreation
Building for community use. Success in these projects led to
others, such as road improvements to make it easier for
farmers to get to Seneca, and the clearing and lighting of the
Crotty Park ball field. A committee of the Community Club
was put in charge of the Recreation Building, which was
loaned to the people of Seneca by the FPHA. The west wing

of the building was turned over to the American Legion for use as a clubroom.

The new bank, named the Community State Bank, was established in 1945, after 250 shares of stock had been sold to local people at $140 per share. The directors were: Jesse G. Baker, Dr. W. E. Coulter, Tim Crowley, Armour Danielson, Simon Jackson, M. P. Koch, Bernard Pfeffer, Jesse A. Sand, and Vern A. Wheeler. The bank was opened on December 1, 1945, with Elmer P. Maier, lifelong resident of Seneca, as cashier; and Miss Meagher as assistant cashier.

Business improved slightly after the emptiness of the first months following the boom. The Seneca Grill, after changing hands several times, and after Johnson's Restaurant closed due to the death of Mr. Johnson, appeared to have achieved stability. The Grill was serving about two hundred meals a day in 1950. Sampson's Royal Blue Grocery Store closed temporarily; but reopened when young Mr. Sampson had finished building several small houses on the land he had bought next to his store at the south end of town.

The motion picture theater, after closing temporarily, reopened with a daily showing. A new four-lane bowling alley was put into the location formerly occupied by the Brown Derby Tavern; and the tavern moved next door. An upholsterer moved his shop from Morris to Seneca, because he could rent working space more easily in Seneca.

In November, 1946, seven of thirty-seven store buildings on Main Street were vacant. In June, 1949, only five buildings were unoccupied.

The new elementary school building remained in use, and was purchased from the federal government for $15,000. The kindergarten class of the nursery school was taken over by the school board, and made a part of the school system. This gave Seneca the distinction of having one of the few public

kindergartens in northern Illinois. The nursery school continued to operate entirely with local support.

The old elementary school building was torn down in 1949,
and in its place, at a cost of $250,000, was erected an addition
to the high school. A bond issue for this building was approved by the voters by a ten to one majority, with 75 per
cent of the voters voting. Some of the outlying rural territory
voted to join the Seneca high school district, thus enlarging
the area served by the high school to 100 square miles and
2,500 population.

The Assembly of God and the Holiness Methodist churches
had their new buildings; and the Methodist church had a
new interior. The Lutheran church had a new parsonage;
however, it united once more with the Lutheran church at
Stavanger under a single pastor.

The library continued to operate with a budget larger
than in the pre-boom period, with 4,000 usable books and
400 active cardholders in 1949. Tax support was increased
in 1949 from .062 to .104 cents on the dollar. For the year
ending April, 1949, the circulation was 5,699. The library
was forced to move from its quarters in the bank building
as the bank business expanded; and the library board purchased the building of the Bungalow Beauty Shop, which
was across the street from War Homes. This building was
moved to a vacant lot on Main Street, the land being donated
by the Nichols and Westcott estates. In the campaign to
raise money for the new building, Dr. Coulter wrote to the
Chicago Bridge and Iron Company, thinking they might
give a twenty-five or fifty dollar contribution. He received
a letter in return with a check for $2,000. By May, 1950,
when the new library was opened, the fund had reached
$4,500.

The American Legion Post, with the addition of veterans

of World War II, took on new life. A Lions' Club was established in Seneca in 1949, sponsored by the Ottawa Lions' Club. Leading professional and businessmen were joined in the new Club by several prominent farmers.

The sewer system, which had been constructed by the federal government at a cost of $176,000, was purchased by the village for approximately $10,000.

The police force in 1950 consisted of two men, the man on daytime duty also hauling mail and express from the railway station.

In the five years after the end of the war, thirty small houses had been built or were under construction, increasing the number of houses in Seneca by 10 per cent. Old houses were painted and improved, and the town had an air of neatness and newness that it had not possessed for fifty years.

Not more than five or six shipyard families remained in Seneca; but another forty families moved into town during the years after the war. Most of them were young people looking for a place in which to settle down.

Thus, Seneca got perhaps a little more than the average of the material prosperity of the years immediately following World War II. The sleepy, down-at-the-heel village of 1940 gave way to an enterprising, spic-and-span town in 1950.

15.

Evaluation

To evaluate Seneca's adjustment to the war boom, one may ask how well the various institutions and services met the demands that were made upon them—how well did they compare with similar institutions and services in a stable community?

As one approach to this kind of evaluation, a number of judges rated the performance of certain institutions and services in Seneca. There were five judges—four residents of Seneca and the senior author. Three of the Seneca judges were oldtimers, one a businessman, one a professional man, and the other a woman of a leading family. The fourth Seneca rater was an official of the housing management.

The judges were asked to think over their experiences in Seneca, and then to rate each of the institutions and services listed in Table 20 at approximate six-month intervals from 1942 to 1945. Their ratings were to be A (adequate), P (passable, but not satisfactory), or I (definitely inadequate). The consensus of the five judges is shown in Table 20. Agreement was best on Commercial Facilities, Schools, Nursery Schools, Recreation; and poorest on Police and Medical Service.

In this table, Schools, Nursery Schools, Medical Service, and Police Protection have the best records; while Recreation and Sewage Disposal have the poorest records.

In the introductory chapter of this book, it was predicted that the success of any given institution or service in Seneca in meeting the demands of the war boom would depend upon four factors:

1. Physical and economic facilities.
2. Institutional experience—the extent to which Seneca had institutions already well established, which needed only to be expanded.
3. Leadership.
4. The attitudes of people toward such changes as might be involved in meeting the boom situation.

It is now possible to examine the major institutions and services in the light of these predictions.

TABLE 20

ADEQUACY OF COMMUNITY INSTITUTIONS AND SERVICES IN SENECA

A—Adequate
P—Passable, but not satisfactory
I—Definitely inadequate, a continued source of discomfort or a danger to morale and health.

Facilities or Services	1942 Sept.	1943 May	1944 Jan.	1944 May	1944 Nov	1945 May
Commercial Facilities	I	P	P	P	P	A
Housing	I	I	A	P	A	A
Schools	I	I	P	I	A	A
Nursery Schools	I	P	A	A	A	A
Recreation	I	I	P	P	P	P
Medical Service	I	P	P	A	A	A
Police	P	P	P	P	A	A
Transportation	I	P	P	P	P	P
Sewage Disposal	I	I	I	I	A	A

Schools. The record of the schools was good, in spite of a need for threefold expansion. All four factors enumerated above were present to a favorable degree. Seneca had adequate institutional experience with schools, and needed simply to expand them along their old lines. Leadership was good. Public opinion supported the necessary expansion of facilities. Government money was available as needed for new buildings and new teachers.

Medical service. Medical services also had a good record. In this area there was an institution ready—the County Health Department—under competent leadership. The local medical practitioner was a good man. The public health nurse who was brought in was exceptionally good. The attitudes of people were favorable toward the infirmary and the services it gave. Government money was available to build the infirmary and to staff it with well-trained personnel.

Housing. Housing was the crucial service that had to be provided without delay; and it was bound to be the focus of some degree of dissatisfaction. Although ample government funds were available, the time was too short to get adequate housing in the first months of the boom. Coupled with this delay was the relative ineffectiveness of the housing management during the early months. Institutional experience with large-scale public housing was lacking in the Seneca area; and people's attitudes toward public housing were generally negative. Many people thought of it as "socialistic," while others thought of it as paternalistic. Even the relatively low rentals did little to improve people's attitudes. Eventually the housing situation became reasonably satisfactory, as physical facilities caught up with demand, and as leadership on the part of housing management improved.

Commercial facilities. Business facilities were never comfortably adequate. Stores were crowded; sales personnel were poorly trained. The obvious source of difficulty here was the general shortage of food and other consumer goods, combined with the relatively small capital expansion to support a fourfold to fivefold increase of business. It is interesting to speculate on the probable outcome of a government-financed merchandizing project. Had the government built a large market, hired a manager and salespeople, and sold goods at cost, such a move probably would have roused a storm of disapproval. Public attitudes supported the "free enterprise" solution of the problem.

Recreation. The Community Recreation Program did not succeed, due to the absence of three of the four basic factors. The one factor that was present was money for equipment and staff. But leadership was ineffective until the very end; there was no institutional experience with community recreation in Seneca; and the attitudes of people were, at best, lukewarm toward public-supported recreation. Thus the recreation program operated under a severe handicap. Where school expansion was accepted as obviously desirable, a public recreation program was regarded by many people as unnecessary. Furthermore, some of the recreation leaders were regarded with suspicion by some parents, because of their toleration of gambling, and their use of profane language in the presence of children. Finally, a Recreation Commission had to be created and had to discover effective ways of operating so as to win public confidence. This required time.

Consequently, the recreation program made little or no impression on Seneca life. When the boom was over the young men, with time on their hands again, mowed the weeds in Crotty Park and began playing baseball, just as they had done before the war.

Nursery Schools. The Nursery schools' success was as brilliant as the recreation program's failure was dismal. Why was this? Principally because of the leadership factor. Florence Nichols provided the leadership, and government funds provided teachers and nursery school facilities. Public opinion, at first lukewarm, was won over by Florence Nichols and the organization she built up. Her parents group was able, with her continuing aid, to carry on the nursery school into the postwar era.

Police, and sewage disposal. Police service and sewage disposals became adequate when government money became available for them.

Transportation. Transportation was never more than passable, due to restrictions on gasoline and the shortage of motor cars.

Churches. Although the churches are not included in the table of ratings, they, too, illustrate the principle that adjustment depends on the four factors described. Institutional experience was present; public opinion was favorable to church work and church expansion; money was not difficult to obtain. Leadership was the principal factor in the performance of the churches. How this factor could overcome lack of physical facilities was illustrated by the Assembly of God church, which built a new building in the space of a few months under able leadership. The Catholic church had strong aggressive leadership; but the Methodist church suffered from lack of continuity in its leadership. With three pastors in three years, this church met its opportunities and responsibilities less well than the other churches.

LACK OF COORDINATION

While the Seneca enterprise succeeded well enough to get ships built on time, to keep workers on the job, and to get children educated, it fell short of complete success, partly because of lack of coordination at the local level. People representing local institutions, state and national governments, and industry, were such a diverse lot in their goals and methods of work that they did not enjoy working together. It was partly this reason that lay, for example, behind the failure to attack aggressively the problem of juvenile delinquency. Only if this problem had become more serious would the various groups have cooperated on it, and probably then only at the instigation of the Chicago office of OCWS. This government agency did act as coordinator when necessary, but it stepped in from outside, so to speak, and only upon occasion. An active local coordinating agency, such as might have been expected, never developed in Seneca.

There was an unsuccessful attempt at coordination at the local level. In the spring of 1943, the Office of Civilian Defense for Illinois sent a field man to organize a Defense Council in Seneca. He called a meeting that was attended by local leaders, shipyard management, and housing management; and this meeting organized a council. The Council in turn organized the Seneca War Services Committee, with sub-committees for recreation and child care. Later, the sub-committee on recreation became the nucleus of the Seneca Recreation Commission, named by the mayor; and the child-care committee became responsible for the nursery schools. But the central body withered away.

Possibly one individual should have been named as coordinator and made responsible for promoting joint action. This was tried in a somewhat similar situation—Charlestown, Indiana.[1] Such an official might have bullied or cajoled the various groups into more joint action; but it seems likely that he would have run into difficulties caused by the underlying differences of goals and characteristic methods of working that ran beneath the surface in Seneca.

The conclusion seems inescapable that coordination through the OCWS in Chicago was about all that could be expected in Seneca, unless emergencies had arisen to make the issue more pressing.

[1] Oliver P. Field and John E. Stoner, "The Charlestown Coordinator," *Public Administration Review*, Vol. 3, No. 1 (Winter, 1943), 42–50.

James E. Zachary, "When a Defense Boom Hits a Defenseless Village," *American City* (October, 1941).

Conclusions

On the whole the judgment must be made that Seneca was very little changed by the war boom except for temporary material improvements. Possibly the people of Seneca developed some attitudes of civic optimism and enterprise that they would not otherwise have shown, with the result that the village became more "progressive."

But the people of Seneca did not change their attitudes about public housing or public recreation. They did not learn to respect the expert community planner, without whom community development of major proportions can hardly take place.

Seneca did the war job well enough to deserve its Army-Navy award for excellence. Emergencies were met with reasonable speed, through the action of government agencies or of CBI management. The village of Seneca played a passive, willing role; but it emerged from the boom relatively unchanged, with the familiar basic characteristics of a midwestern rural town.

Appendix A
The LST

The LST was 327 feet long, 50 feet wide, and displaced 5,500 tons. Actual weight of hull and machinery and other equipment was about 2,200 tons. There was a broad central space for carrying tanks, with hinged doors at the bow, and an enclosed ramp to be lowered for landing operations. The ship was powered with twin Diesel engines.

In practice the LST was used for many other purposes than carrying tanks. Its long clear hold, 30 feet wide, 200 feet long, and two decks in height, could be packed with tanks, men, ammunition, planes, hospital beds, or any other cargo. It would move in water, and land on beaches where no other large ships could go. Because of its shallow draft it was seldom struck by torpedoes.

The average cost per ship was in the neighborhood of two million dollars. About half of this was accounted for by material and equipment furnished by the government. The approximate amount paid by the government to the CBI Company is shown in Table 21. The government paid for constructing and equipping the shipyard, at a total cost of approximately six million dollars.

TABLE 21

APPROXIMATE AVERAGE COST PER SHIP
(Exclusive of government-furnished equipment and material)

Cost of raw materials and machinery other than government-furnished items	$ 381,000
Cost of fabrication at Chicago, Birmingham, and Greenville Plants	78,000
Construction cost at Seneca shipyard	585,000
Total per ship, excluding government-furnished items	$1,044,000

TABLE 22

JOB CLASSIFICATIONS OF SHIPYARD WORKERS
(Based on an average of employment records of June, 1943, and July, 1944)

Classification	Per Cent
Supervisory	10.5
Engineering	2.3
Medical	0.2
Clerical	7.0
Machinists	8.0
Welders	13.0
Electricians	7.5
Pipefitters	10.0
Fitters	3.9
Erectors	1.5
Crane Operators and Oilers	0.8
Chippers	2.0
Burners	2.4
Sheet Metal Workers	5.0
Insulators	1.3
Carpenters	2.5
Painters	5.2
Outfitters	4.6
Warehouse	2.3
Guards and Firemen	1.5
Yard Maintenance	0.3
Launching Crews-men	1.0
Unloading	1.0
Laborers	6.0

TABLE 23

TYPES OF HOUSING IN FPHA PROJECTS IN SENECA

	Units	Single Rooms	0 Bedroom Units	1 Bedroom Units	2 Bedroom Units	3 Bedroom Units	Regular Trailer	Expansible Trailer
Seneca War Homes........	478	......	229	219	17	13	......	......
War Homes Dormitory........	300	300	......	......	......	......	......	......
Victory Court....	485	......	106	304	75	......	......	......
Riverview Homes........	380	......	......	38	202	140	......	......
War Homes Trailer Park...	225	......	......	......	......	......	200	25
Victory Court Trailer Park...	125	......	......	......	......	......	100	25
Total.........	1,993	300	335	561	294	153	300	50

TABLE 24

OCCUPANCY OF FPHA PROJECTS IN SENECA

	War Homes	Dormitories	War Homes Trailer Park	Victory Court	Victory Court Trailer Park	Riverview Homes	Total
1943							
January	443	298	209				950
April	450	298	199	114			1,061
July	446	273	213	317			1,249
October	448	283	176	433			1,340
1944							
January	460	299	210	448			1,417
April	470	297	222	474	23		1,486
July	467	291	193	472	91	32	1,546
October	473	297	137	410	39	215	1,571
1945							
January	470	295	127	398	—	315	1,605
April	422	247	94	312	—	305	1,380
July	88	5	—	36	—	64	193

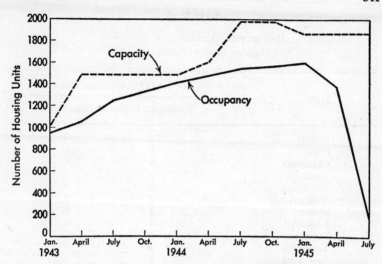

Fig. 17. Capacity and Occupancy of Public Housing
in Seneca.

TABLE 25

RENTAL RATES FOR SENECA PUBLIC HOUSING IN 1943

Unit Size	Description	Monthly Rate
War Homes Apartments		
0 Bedroom	Furnished	$30.50
1 Bedroom	Furnished	34.75
2 Bedroom	Furnished	41.25
Victory Court		
0 Bedroom	Unfurnished	24.50
0 Bedroom	Furnished	26.50
1 Bedroom	Unfurnished	27.50
1 Bedroom	Furnished	30.00
2 Bedroom	Unfurnished	30.50
2 Bedroom	Furnished	34.00
War Homes Trailer Park		
Regular	Furnished	26.00
Expansible	Furnished	31.00
Dormitory		
Bedroom	Furnished	20.00

TABLE 26

WHERE THE NEWCOMERS CAME FROM
(Housing Projects Residents Only)

State	Per Cent of Total Family Heads	
	November, 1943	August, 1944
Illinois	72	68
Iowa	4	4
Oklahoma	4	4
Texas	3	3
Wisconsin	3	4
Missouri	2	2
Indiana	1	2
Kentucky	1	2
Lousiana	1	2
Tennessee	1	1
New York	1	.5
Arkansas	—	1
Minnesota	—	1
California	—	.5
Kansas	—	.5
Michigan	—	.5
Mississippi	—	.5
Ohio	—	.5
Miscellaneous (25 states)	7 (20 states)	3

TABLE 27

WHERE THE NEWCOMERS CAME FROM, DISTANCE IN MILES
(Housing Projects Residents Only—November, 1943)

Miles	Per Cent of Total
0–49	12
50–99	34
100–149	11
150–199	8
200–299	10
300–499	8
500–999	9
1000–1499	6
1500 and over	2

TABLE 28

WHERE THE NEWCOMERS CAME FROM—REGIONS
(Housing Projects Residents Only)

Region	November, 1943					
	Victory Court	War Homes	Dormitories	Trailer Park	Nov., 1943 Total	August, 1944 Total
Illinois	69%	67%	83%	74%	72%	69%
South	17	19	6	11	14	17
Plains	9	5	3	8	6	4
North Central	3	6	7	6	6	6
Others	2	3	1	1	2	5

TABLE 29

AGE OF FAMILY HEADS
(Housing Projects Residents Only)

Age	November, 1943			Total	August, 1944 Total
	Victory Court	War Homes and Dormitories	Trailer Park		
15–19	0%	3%	4%	2%	2%
20–24	10	8	12	9	9
25–29	23	17	21	20	17
30–34	25	19	22	21	21
35–39	21	13	15	16	16
40–44	10	9	8	9	9
45–49	5	11	8	9	9
50–54	4	9	6	7	7
55–59	2	6	2	4	6
60 and over	0	5	2	3	4
Mean age	34.6 years	38.4	34.5	36.7	37.0

TABLE 30

FAMILY STRUCTURE IN THE HOUSING PROJECTS
(November, 1943, and August, 1944)

	War Homes		Victory Court		Trailer Park		Victory Court Trailer Park	River-view
	1943	1944	1943	1944	1943	1944	1944	1944
Project Population.........	1260	1247	1499	1574	603	690	261	182
No. of Families..	446	448	427	468	187	215	76	48
Average Family Size..........	2.6	2.8	3.5	3.4	3.2	3.2	3.4	3.8
Family Size Range........	1–8	2–7	1–8	2–8	1–8	2–8	2–8	2–5
Children under 18...........	309	345	634	620	225	262	105	86
Average Number of Children per Family.......	0.7	0.8	1.5	1.3	1.2	1.2	1.4	1.8

Appendix B
Food-Buying Habits in Seneca

Records of food buying and food habits were obtained from 175 families during the period from February through May, 1944. From these records it is possible to construct a picture of the typical food habits of American workers in 1944 and to answer questions such as the following:

Did these people, with increased purchasing power, improve their diets?

Did people from cities buy and use food differently from people who came from rural places?

Did people of different socioeconomic levels buy and use food differently?

METHODS OF THE STUDY

The interviewing was done by Dr. Minna Denton, a home economist. She talked with the housekeeper, usually the wife and mother of the family, for thirty minutes to an hour and a half, and filled out a questionnaire dealing with: family composition; times and character of meals; difficulties due to food rationing; quantities of various foods, such as milk, butter, eggs, meat, fruit, vegetables; home food production;

* This material is drawn from a manuscript entitled "Food Buying Habits in a War Boom Town" in the files of the Committee on Human Development, The University of Chicago. Participating in this study were: Professors Margaret H. Brookes and Lydia J. Roberts of the Department of Home Economics, and research workers Helen Brecht, Minna C. Denton, and Dorothy M. Greey.

changes since coming to Seneca; amount of money spent now and formerly for food.

It was planned to include one-eighth of the families in the study, the sample to be chosen by taking every eighth dwelling unit. But the attempt to follow this plan proved unsuccessful mainly for two reasons: men on the night shift were usually asleep during the day, and their wives had no place to talk with the interviewer without disturbing them; women who worked at the shipyard were seldom at home. Accordingly, the interviewer went from one home to another, knocking at doors to find a woman sufficiently at leisure to answer questions.

TABLE 31

RESIDENCE OF THOSE INTERVIEWED IN THE FOOD-BUYING STUDY

Location	Number of families present in May, 1944	Number of families interviewed
War Homes Apartments	464	82
War Homes Trailers	224	15
Victory Court Apartments	480	48
Victory Court Trailers	125	17
Private Trailer Camps	115	10
Village of Seneca	350	3
Total	1,758	175

A special attempt was made to get full representation from the 700 and 800 blocks of War Homes apartments, which contained a high proportion of stable and higher-paid men. Records were secured from 24, or 75 per cent, of the houses in these two blocks. The result of the sampling process is shown in Table 31. The sample cannot be said with certainty to represent the entire population. Probably it represents fairly well the families in which the wife gave all of her time to housekeeping—that is, the larger and the more stable families. Southern states, with 26 per cent of the sample, were slightly overrepresented. The distribution of the sample with respect to occupational status was not far different from that of the total group of shipyard employees.

Results of the study will be reported under three heads: Food Expenditures, Adequacy of Diet, and Consumption of Specific Foods.

FOOD EXPENDITURES

For comparison of food expenditures it was necessary to take account of the variation of family size, age and sex of family members. Accordingly, a consumption unit was defined as follows:

One adult man at moderately hard work	1.4 consumption units
One adult woman at house work	1.0
Adolescent boy, 13 to 20 years old	1.4
Adolescent girl, 13 to 20 years old	1.0
Child, 10 through 12 years old	1.0
Child, 7 through 9 years old	0.8
Child, 4 through 6 years old	0.6
Child, 1 through 3 years old	0.5
Infant under 1 year	0.3

The average food cost per consumption unit in the sample was $5.35 per consumption unit per week, compared with $3.66 before coming to Seneca. Families from rural communities tended to have lower costs, both before and after arrival in Seneca. Before arrival, the rural families were able to produce some of their own food and thus to reduce food costs. But they apparently also had more frugal spending habits, which persisted after they came to Seneca. Nevertheless, the families with lowest pre-Seneca food costs, most of them from rural places, more than doubled their food expenditures after coming to Seneca; while families with the highest pre-Seneca food costs did not increase these costs much in Seneca.

The United States Bureau of Labor Statistics reported an increase in the Food Price Index in Chicago of 14 per cent between April, 1942, and April, 1944. This compares with an increase of average food cost of 46 per cent for the shipyard employees after coming to Seneca. Thus there must have been other factors at work in the Seneca situation as well as the general increase in food price level. These other factors probably included: decrease in amount of home food production after moving to Seneca, local food prices slightly higher than food prices in larger cities, possible differences between methods of collecting data in Seneca and the Bureau of Labor Statistics study.

Adequacy of Diet

In order to study the quality of diet in Seneca, a rating scale was worked out for the consumption of milk, eggs, oranges, and meat. Each of the four items was scored on a scale of 3, thus permitting a maximum score of 12. A diet was said to be *satisfactory* if all four ratings scored 3, for a total of 12. If one or more ratings scored 2, total score 11, 10, 9, the diet was said to be *marginal*. But if a diet was scored 11 due to a score of 2 for eggs or meat, which are to a large degree interchangeable, that diet was said to be *intermediate*. Diets were said to be *unsatisfactory* if one or more ratings scored 1, where the total score might be from 10 down to 4. The lowest score actually found was 7.

The rating scale was as follows:

1. *Rating for Milk Used per Person per Week*

    Satisfactory   Score 3   1 pint or more per adult per day or at least 3½ quarts per week

                                                3 to 4 cups per child per day making 5¼ to 7 quarts per child per week

    Marginal   Score 2   1 cup per adult per day

                                                  1¾ quarts per adult per week

                                                  2 cups per child per day

                                                  4½ quarts per child per week

    Unsatisfactory   Score 1   less than marginal quantities

2. *Ratings for Eggs Used per Person per Week*

    Satisfactory   Score 3   4 or more eggs per person per week

    Marginal   Score 2   2–3 eggs per person per week

    Unsatisfactory   Score 1   less than marginal

3. *Ratings for Oranges Used per Person per Week*

    Satisfactory   Score 3   6 times or more per person per week

    Marginal   Score 2   4 or 5 times per person per week

    Unsatisfactory   Score 1   3, 2, 1, or no times per week

4. *Ratings for Times Meat Used per Person per Week*

    Satisfactory   Score 3   Used at least once daily; 7 times per person per week

    Marginal   Score 2   Used occasionally

    Unsatisfactory   Score 1   Used seldom

The records were complete enough to permit scoring 100 families. Of these, 28 per cent had satisfactory diets, 9 per cent were intermediate, 32 per cent marginal, and 31 per cent unsatisfactory.

When the diets scoring 11 and 12 are distributed according to the size of former place of residence, such diets were enjoyed by 74 per cent of the former metropolitan dwellers, 61 per cent of former town dwellers, and 58 per cent of former rural families.

In order to find out whether these families were eating a more adequate diet than they were formerly, it was necessary to devise another rating scale so that the adequacy of the former diet could be rated. If the current consumption of meat, milk, eggs, and oranges was the same as the former consumption of each commodity, each type of food was scored a 2 which would give a total of 8 if current and former diet patterns were the same. If the current consumption was better than the former diet each commodity received a rating of 3 which would give a maximum score of 12 if the consumption of all four commodities was greater now. If the current consumption was not as adequate as the former diet each commodity received a rating of 1, which would give a maximum rating of 4 if the consumption of all four commodities was not as great as formerly.

It was possible to obtain data on 50 families complete enough on former consumption to permit this comparison. Of these families, 60 per cent had improved their diet, and 24 per cent had the same level of diet as formerly. Although the sample is small, this comparison gives some basis for the statement that Seneca war workers improved their diets over the pre-boom level.

Of those families that improved their diets, 87 per cent were spending more money than formerly for food. Of those whose diets were less adequate, 75 per cent were spending more money than formerly.

Adequacy of diet was compared with income level. There was a tendency for families in the higher income brackets to have more adequate diets. Of the executive group, 83 per cent scored 11 or 12, 56 per cent of the skilled group, and 43 per cent of the unskilled group.

When families were compared on the basis of size, it was found that the families with fewer children had a higher proportion of adequate diets. Combining families with scores of 11 and 12, such diets were found in 72 per cent of two-adult-no-children families, 84 per cent of two-adult-one-child families, 34 per cent of two-adult-two-child, and 42 per cent of two-adult-three-or-more-child families.

The question of changes in the quantity of food consumed, without regard to its quality, was answered by comparing the food intake before and after coming to Seneca for five foods—meat, milk, eggs, oranges, and butter. Data were obtained from 93 families. The unskilled group were eating slightly less than formerly, while the skilled and executive families were eating slightly more than they had in pre-Seneca days, but the differences between the three groups were very slight in this respect.

CONSUMPTION OF SPECIFIC FOODS

The per capita consumption of eggs for 121 families composed of 389 persons was 8.4 eggs per week or 437 eggs per year. The United States Department of Agriculture gives the per capita egg consumption for 1944 in the U.S.A. as 337 eggs. There are several factors that might be responsible for this high consumption of eggs: eggs might have been used to replace rationed meat; it was the spring of the year and eggs are more plentiful at that time; eggs are a quick and easy type of food to prepare and so frequently were used. The schedules show that there was an unusually high egg consumption for breakfast. The war workers were working hard and they needed large breakfasts. This very factor influences the validity of all the average figures on egg consumption. In some families the male war worker consumed far above his "per capita" average.

To test whether there were any statistically reliable differences between the number of eggs consumed by different size families and by families from different types of communities, a statistical analysis (analysis of variance) was made. This analysis showed no reliable differences.

Meat Consumption. Sixty-five per cent of the families reported having meat at least once a day. Forty-five per cent had meat usually twice a day. Fifty per cent reported no change in meat consumption from pre-Seneca days, while 42 per cent reported an increase. Seventy-two per cent of the families reported that the meat ration was adequate. Another indication of the feeling that the ration was adequate is to be found in the fact that the workers in 83 per cent of the families took a homemade lunch to work with them, while only 11 per cent bought their lunches at the shipyard cafeteria. If many had felt a shortage of meat, more would have bought lunch at the cafeteria, where they could get meat without ration coupons. Sixty-nine per cent of the workers carried meat in their lunch from home every day, and practically all the rest had meat for lunch "usually" or "often."

Family composition and type of community origin did not seem to influence the consumption of meat in Seneca.

Milk Consumption. Seneca families consumed an average of 0.72 quart of milk per capita per day, or 263 quarts per year, which is 5 per cent above the average for the nation in 1944, as reported by the U.S. Department of Agriculture. Fifty per cent of the families were above the suggested standard of the National Research Council of one quart of milk per day per child and one pint per day per adult; while another 13 per cent were at the standard level. Sixty-two per cent of the families were consuming the same amount of milk as formerly, and 20 per cent were consuming more milk than formerly. The highest per cent of families with increased milk consumption was in the groups with the most children.

Orange Consumption. Data for orange consumption in 107 families showed the average to be 6 oranges per week. This is probably higher than the national average, though exact data on national consumption are given in pounds, rather than unit oranges. Fifty-four per cent of the families were consuming more oranges than formerly, and another 40 per cent were eating the same amount as formerly. There was no reliable difference in orange consumption between families of various sizes or different types of previous residence.

Butter and Margarine Consumption. The per capita butter consumption for 111 families was 0.33 pound per person per week, or the equivalent of 10 tablespoons per person per day. Twenty-five per cent were eating more butter than formerly, and 59 per cent were using the same amount as formerly. Families with larger numbers of children had smaller per capita butter consumption.

For margarine consumption there are data on only 39 families, which indicates that margarine was not an effective substitute for butter in Seneca. The per capita average, 0.33 pound per person per week, was the same as the average butter consumption.

Consumption of Bread, Beans, and Potatoes. The average bread consumption for 112 families was 0.33 pound per person per day. Families of metropolitan origin ate slightly less than families of town or rural origin. Forty-one per cent of the families were consuming more bread than formerly, and 58 per cent were eating the same amount as formerly. The increase was probably largely due to the fact that workers and children were carrying lunches, usually including sandwiches, probably more than they did in pre-Seneca days.

Fifty per cent of the former rural families were using more bread than formerly, as compared with 34 per cent of the town families and 35 per cent of the metropolitan families.

It was possible only to compare current with former consumption of dry beans. The quantities did not change much for any type of family. The same facts were found for canned baked beans.

Of 145 families for whom data were available, 17 per cent had potatoes twice a day, 72 per cent once a day, 10 per cent three to four times per week, and 1 per cent seldom. Large families and families of rural origin tended to eat potatoes more frequently than other families.

Conclusions

The conclusion is that most Seneca workers made use of wartime wages to improve their diets, both in quality and quantity. Like working-class people generally during World War II, these people managed to get a better diet than they had in prewar times, in spite of the restrictions of food rationing on their consumption of meat, fats, sugar, and canned goods. Still, the people of higher occupational level secured an optimum diet in larger proportions.

People of different socioeconomic levels and from cities, towns, and rural places showed relatively slight differences in consumption of specific foods while they lived in Seneca, though these differences cumulated to give the people of higher socioeconomic status slightly better diets.

Index